Local Communities
and the
Israeli Polity

SUNY Series in Israeli Studies
Russell Stone, Editor

Local Communities and the Israeli Polity

■ *Conflict of Values and Interests*

edited by
Efraim Ben-Zadok

State University of New York Press

Published by
State University of New York Press, Albany

© 1993 State University of New York

For information, address the State University of New York Press,
State University Plaza, Albany, NY 12246

Production by Bernadine Dawes
Marketing by Nancy Farrell

Library of Congress Cataloging-in-Publication Data

Local communities and the Israeli polity : conflict of values and
    interests / edited by Efraim Ben-Zadok.
        p. cm.—(SUNY series in Israeli studies)
    Includes index.
    ISBN 0-7914-1561-9 ISBN 0-7914-1562-7 (pbk.)
    1. Israel—Politics and government. 2. Pressure groups—Israel.
3. Community power—Israel. 4. Central-local government relations-
-Israel. 5. West Bank—Politics and government. I. Ben-Zadok,
Efraim. II. Series.
JQ1825.P359L63   1993
306.2'095694—dc20   92-40893
                                                                CIP

1 2 3 4 5 6 7 8 9 10

To My Father,
Eliyahu

CONTENTS

LIST OF TABLES
AND FIGURES

TABLES

FIGURES

PREFACE

The chapters in this book shed light on a new trend which is likely to change social relations and the distribution of power in Israel in the years to come. Since the early 1970s, local communities and regions began to demand their share of power from the central government and gained importance in the politics of the country. Their struggle for autonomy contributed to the decentralization of the relations between them and the center. This is an important development in light of the nature of the Israeli political system. The system is still highly centralized, burdened since its inception by national-level tasks in defense, economy, and immigrant absorption, with relatively little attention to local and regional issues.

A trend of decentralization in the relations between the Israeli center and its local communities was described in my earlier study on the impact of national characteristics (e.g., cultural, social, and political) on local citizen participation. That study conceived the embryonic ideas for this book. The ideas matured and expanded into another study, with Giora Goldberg, on the relations between the Israeli center and two sectors of local communities: the development towns and Gush Emunim religious settlements on the West Bank. The study of the two sectors prepared the ground for their advanced analysis in this book, where one chapter is devoted to each sector. Six other sectors, each a chapter contributed by an Israeli or American scholar, completed the plan for the book.

Each chapter in the book describes the social and economic conflicts of one major sector of local communities with Israeli society and the central government. The attempt of each sector to promote its values and interests, and the political process around it, is the focus of the chapter. The sectors are West Bank and Gaza Strip Arabs (chapter 2) and Israeli Arabs (chapter 3); development towns (chapter 4) and re-

newal neighborhoods (chapter 5), largely populated by relatively poor
Oriental Jews; ultra-Orthodox religious neighborhoods in the urban
centers (chapter 6) and Gush Emunim religious settlements on the
West Bank (chapter 7); and kibbutzim and moshavim (chapter 8), the
agricultural settlements of Labor Zionism which had been at odds
with the right-wing Likud government. The book concludes with the
city of Jerusalem (chapter 9), a city where all ethnic, religious, and
social-class groups intersect, and which thus represents a microcosm
of Israel's social and political tensions.

ACKNOWLEDGMENTS

I am especially grateful to two colleagues. Each of them, throughout the years, encouraged and advised me on the preliminary idea, content, and feasibility of this project. The following is only the highlight of their contribution. Giora Goldberg from Bar-Ilan University collaborated with me on the preliminary conceptualization of the tense relations between sectors of local communities and the Israeli political center. At the same time, he patiently reintroduced me to Israeli political science after my long tenure in the United States. Gershon Shafir, now a sociologist at the University of California, San Diego, broadened my theoretical understanding on the comparative value of this project in the Israeli and international contexts. At the same time, he helped me to clarify my own thoughts.

I am thankful to my editors at the State University of New York Press: Russell Stone, Rosalie Robertson, and Bernadine Dawes. Without their cooperation the manuscript would not have been transformed into this book. I am grateful to the three anonymous referees of the manuscript for their thorough review. I am also indebted to all the contributors to the book for their patience and responsiveness to my long-distance communications, much of it between Israel and the United States. Without their cooperation the project would have been far more difficult to accomplish.

I owe warm gratitude to Klarit Ziegler, the librarian of the Central Bureau of Statistics, who provided valuable assistance when I collected the statistical data in Jerusalem. I also thank Susan Gelman from Florida Atlantic University where the manuscript was completed. She assisted me diligently and methodically with all the technical aspects of the final version.

I conclude with acknowledgments to my wife and my father. Throughout the years, Wendy was a constant source of encouragement for the manuscript and a persistent commentator on all its parts. Her support was crucial to its completion. The countless talks with my father, Eliyahu, in my adolescence, nourished my first idea of Israel as a more socially diversified society than I had believed it to be. The talks were cut off a few years later when he died much too young. But the idea has lived on. I dedicate its mature version, this book, to him.

Efraim Ben-Zadok

Introduction:
1 ■ National and Spatial Divisions in Israel

Efraim Ben-Zadok

In the *The Origins of the Israeli Polity*, Horowitz and Lissak (1978) describe the Yishuv, the pre-independence Jewish community in Palestine, as a minority within a wider political system, yet with its own central political institutions that enjoyed a large degree of authority resembling that of a sovereign state. At the end of the British rule and the establishment of the state of Israel in 1948, power was transferred from these institutions to the formal government and was consolidated there. A highly centralized unitary political system quickly emerged. The system emphasized the strengthening of the state authority and statism for itself as prominent national values (Weiss 1979). Shortly after independence, the Israeli system was already recognized as the most centralized and governmentally controlled system among all Western-type democratic states (Akzin and Dror 1966), and basically remained as such until today. Sharkansky (1987, 10) indicates that the most prominent elements of the Israeli system are the size and dominance of the government and its quasi-governmental extensions, which seem to be the largest in all the democratic states.

It is not unusual for scholars to focus on the salient characteristics of their own society. Thus, Israeli social scientists have been preoccupied with studying their national politics and their powerful center, and have also devoted some attention to local politics and policy. Completely neglected, however, has been the study of the regional level, as well as the impact of both the local and regional tiers on national politics. Despite the relative weakness of the local and regional tiers, the lack of attention paid by Israeli social scientists to these two levels and to their relations with the national tier, is still notable. To cite only one example, the heavily studied area of Israeli elections is covered with research on all national (Knesset) elections, yet only a

1

handful of studies deal with local elections or the regional implications of elections.

It is this emphasis on the national level in the literature, followed by the relative lack of attention to the local and regional levels, that is covered in the first section of this introductory chapter to the volume. The contribution of the volume as a whole is described in the second section. In short, the contribution is that the volume represents a systematic effort to analyze the role and the growing importance of local communities and regions in Israeli society and politics. All levels—national, local, and regional—are then integrated in the third section which provides the theoretical framework for the volume. After defining the local/regional unit of analysis for each of the eight subsequent chapters of this volume, each chapter is reviewed in the fourth section with an emphasis on the conflict of the unit in question with the national level. Conclusions and policy guidelines are then drawn in the final two sections.

THE LITERATURE: NATIONAL CENTER, REGION, AND LOCAL COMMUNITY IN ISRAEL

The weakness of the local and regional tiers in Israel is reflected in the limited role of the bodies that govern the two levels. Local governments in Israel are dependent on the central government with relatively little discretion in their affairs. They are under the jurisdiction of the Ministry of the Interior. The ministry is also in charge of the state's intermediate regional level: six districts with minor operational functions. The main function of local governments, service delivery (especially education and health), is closely controlled and monitored by a few national ministries. These ministries, primarily Interior and Finance, determine the budget allocation from the capital to local governments. Local governments, thus, must constantly search for access to penetrate and influence these ministries and their bureaucrats. They must bargain and apply political leverage to obtain their budgets from the central government. What remains under their jurisdiction is local tax collection (especially property tax) and special local endowment funds. A very successful example of the latter is analyzed in chapter 9 on Jerusalem.

A powerful national tier complemented the weakness of the local and regional levels in Israel. This tier and its politics have been studied extensively through four major social science theories. These theories are the structural-functional (e.g., Parsons 1951), pluralist (e.g., Dahl 1961), elite (e.g., Hunter 1953; Mills 1956), and dependency (e.g., Hechter 1975). Common to all four theories, in the Israeli context, is that they have been applied almost exclusively on the national level. The distinction among them, however, is that the functional and pluralist approaches focused on national-level social groups which shaped the policies of the Israeli social-political center; the elite and dependency approaches concentrated on the social-political center itself.

National-level social groups in Israel are primarily ethnic, class, religious, and interest groups. The functional approach views such groups as contributing individually, based on value consensus among them, to the stability of the social system as a whole (e.g., Horowitz and Lissak 1978). The autonomous groups make compromises, build coalitions and, as a result, a loosely unified consensual-democratic political center is formed. A much less stable center, with no value consensus among groups, and constantly changing power distributions according to the different issue-areas, is portrayed by the pluralist approach. In this approach, the groups cooperate and make compromises at least in a single issue-area. In other policy areas they operate separately. In a well-known study by Smooha (1978) the reference is primarily to Israel's major ethnic groups—obviously, national-level forces. But even a recent book by Yishai (1987), which follows the American tradition of interest groups analysis in the pluralist approach, focuses on Israeli groups that operate on the national level. The vast majority of these interest groups have close relations with the parties, direct or indirect lobbying in the Knesset as well as parliamentary "watchdogs" for their interests, and direct access to the executive branch. Most of the groups consistently express their particularistic interests in national-collective terms.

While the functional and the pluralist approaches claim the Israeli social-political center to be a by-product of national-level forces, applications of the elite (e.g., Shapiro 1978) and dependency (e.g., Swirski 1981) approaches view this center as an independent entity, a strong leader representing the dominant class of a basically stratified society. The elite and dependency approaches reject the functionalist view of the Israeli social system as consensual and stability-oriented. They rather emphasize its stratified class structure, its conflictual and change-oriented nature. Proponents of the elite and dependency approaches also blame Israeli scholars for their unwillingness (or perhaps inability) to criticize the egalitarian and pluralist assumptions of their own society, which was founded on socialist-Zionist ideology (Shapiro 1985, 8). Elite theorists view Israel as governed from the center by a relatively small group that controlled the political and economic spheres through the dominant Labor party, at least until 1977 when the right-wing Likud party rose to power. Dependency theorists argue that the Israeli center is controlled by Ashkenazim, Jews primarily of European and American origin, who are in the upper level of the occupational ladder. According to dependency theorists, this dominant class established an ethnic division of labor that ensures the placement of lower-priced providers of cheap labor power, Oriental Jews from the Islamic countries of North Africa and the Middle East, at the bottom of the ladder (Bernstein and Swirski 1982).

Implicit or explicit in all four theories (functional, pluralist, elite, and dependency), in the Israeli context, is the utilization of Shils's concepts of "center and periphery." The concepts were applied to both the Yishuv and State periods (e.g., Galnoor 1982, 112–40; Horowitz and Lissak 1985, 40–42; Horowitz and Lissak 1989). Shils's concept of the "center" includes both values and activities supported by society. It is a general "central zone" defined in terms of dominant societal values. It is also "a structure of activities, of roles and persons, within the network of institutions" (Shils 1975, 3). Accordingly, the social-political center is part of the general "central zone" of values and the main meeting point of the activities. National-level groups are part of the activities which affect the "central zone," the value system. The "periphery," in comparison to the "center," is less attached and committed to the dominant value system. It also has less control over political resources and institutions. To enhance political integration, the "center" must penetrate the more problematic groups in the dependent "periphery," mobilize them, and obtain their support. The Israeli center, according to Galnoor (1982, 131–40), had to penetrate seven such target groups until the mid-1960s. Three of them—Israeli Arabs, Oriental Jews, and ultra-Orthodox Jews—are the focus of chapters 3, 4, 5, and 6 in this volume.

Shils's broad abstract concepts had no specific spatial definitions. Yet when applied, they frequently focused on specific territorial locations and boundaries. This was especially the case in studies about centers and peripheries in Western European countries during the 1960s and 1970s (e.g., Gottmann 1980; Rokkan and Urwin 1982). Two important concepts in these studies were "regionalism" and "ethnoregionalism," which indicated group protest against the center and a demand for regional autonomy. Again, Israeli literature on the interaction between regional concentrations of local communities and national-level politics is minimal. Indeed, the political manifestations of "regionalism" and ethnic upsurgence were analyzed only in two studies: one about the development towns (Gradus 1983 and 1984) and the other about the Jewish settlements on the West Bank (Goldberg and Ben-Zadok 1983). By emphasizing spatial-political explanations, these studies go beyond Israeli research on regional inequality which concentrated on socioeconomic indicators (e.g., Shachar and Lipshitz 1981). These initial studies must be developed more systematically. Such efforts are being made in this volume: in chapter 4 on the development towns, in chapter 7 on the Jewish settlements on the West Bank, and in other chapters covering other regions.

While only a few studies dealt with the regional level, a growing number of studies on local community politics in Israel appeared in the 1970s (e.g., Cohen 1974). Some of them explained the relationship between individual local communities and national politics, mainly through the mediation of the political parties (e.g., Deshen 1970; Aronoff 1974). One important study observed that in the 1970s Israeli society was transforming from a national ideologically based politics into territorially based politics (Elazar 1975). The study viewed this distinction between national and local politics as a sign of voter maturity. The distinction was indeed formalized in a 1976 local elections law passed by the Knesset. Accordingly, the mayor, who used to be elected by the local council on the base of its party list, is now elected as an individual directly by the voters. The council is elected separately and, still, through proportional representation of the parties.

The new emphasis on local issues was followed by increasing demands for local autonomy and new forms of citizen participation such as local voluntary associations, environmental groups, and local planning committees (Ben-Zadok 1986). The trend was documented in studies of citizen participation. Many of them focused on Project Renewal which is described in chapter 5 here. The project introduced strong elements and unique forms of citizen participation and local decision-making (Churchman 1987; Alterman 1988; Liron and Spiro 1988). Again, however, these forms of citizen participation, whether in individual communities or their aggregate, were not related to national politics in the literature.

CONTRIBUTION: THE LOCAL-REGIONAL FOCUS AND ITS NATIONAL CONTEXT

The contribution of this volume to the theories and concepts mentioned in the previous section is that they can all benefit by incorporating ideas from the volume about the role of local communities and regions in Israeli society and politics; something that these theories and concepts failed to do in the past. Such an effort to link local and regional forces to the larger Israeli system may facilitate better understanding of the system and, possibly, its reinterpretation. A brief review of these theories and concepts illustrates this point. The functional and pluralist approaches will clearly benefit if they breakdown their homogeneous national-level units of analysis into spatial properties. Interesting differences will then emerge, for example, between Oriental Jews—one national-level ethnic group—in the development towns and the renewal neighborhoods as discussed in chapters 4 and 5. Such diversity of spatial properties means that compromise and stability in the Israeli system as a whole is also achieved as a result of trade-offs among local and regional values and interests (functional). In addition, while such trade-offs may contribute to consensus in one or more issue-areas, the overall increase in bargainers, due to the local and regional interest groups, portrays a more diversified and perhaps even less stable system than previously assumed (pluralist). The contribution of the volume to the elite and dependency theories is in the identification of local communities and regions as representing the ruling or subordinated class, and by explaining why local and regional inequalities are important to understand conflict and change in Israeli society.

Turning to Shils's concepts of "center and periphery," this volume helps to define the values and political resources of spatial units. The local and regional values and interests of these units are then related to those of the "periphery" or the "center." Patterns of agreement and incompatibility are identified. Further, the specific concepts of "regionalism" and "ethnoregionalism" are elaborated here, that is, trends of regional autonomy in Israel. As for community politics and citizen participation concepts, not only is the localistic context emphasized in this volume, but a more important contribution is the discussion of aggregates of local communities and local participation activities as well as their impact on national politics.

As mentioned earlier, the overall contribution of the volume is in its systematic effort to analyze the role of local communities and regions in Israeli society and politics. This analysis is based on the concept of "spatial sector,"[1] that is, the dual membership of the population in the spatial sector itself (all the population) and in one social group (the overwhelming majority of the population). The membership in the spatial sector is the local- and regional-level component of the concept. The membership in the social group is the national-level component of the concept. The contribution of the concept to the literature is in the intersection of the two memberships of the same population. Previous studies mainly covered only one of the two.

Gush Emunim new settlements on the West Bank, for example, are the spatial sector discussed in chapter 7. All the settlers of the Gush reside in local communities on the West Bank. This is the local- and regional-level component of the concept. The overwhelming majority of the settlers are religious Jews. This is the national-level component. The Druze communities in northern Israel, for example, although comprised of a much larger population than that of the Gush settlements on the West Bank,[2] are merely a spatial unit. They do not qualify as a spatial sector because their population has no membership in a clearly identified national-level social group.

In the following section, the national-level component of the concept of "spatial sector" is briefly discussed and the local- and regional-level of the concept is elaborated. The concept itself, which integrates all levels, is further analyzed.

A THEORETICAL FRAMEWORK: NATIONAL CLEAVAGES AND SPATIAL SECTORS

As indicated before, national-level social groups such as ethnic, class, religious, and interest groups shape the policies of the Israeli social-political center. These groups are clearly more vocal and successful in their claims from the system than local and regional groups. The interactions, tensions, and conflicts among these groups were conceptualized in Israeli social science as the four well-known national "cleavages": Arab-Jewish, ethnic-class, religious-secular, and left-right.[3] These cleavages are the most salient feature of Israeli society and politics. Membership in one of the social groups that each of them represents, intersects with one or two of the spatial sectors discussed in this volume (see table 1.1).

As presented in this volume, a spatial sector refers to numerous local communities contained in one or two regions of the country, or dispersed nationwide. In one special case the sector is one city, albeit a central city (Jerusalem). The pattern of dispersion of each of the spatial sectors, the type of settlement of its communities, as well as a list of the eight sectors themselves, are presented in table 1.1. In addition, figure 1.1 presents a map of the sectors and their patterns of dispersion.

The population of each sector, its percentage of the total population and of the Jewish population, and its number of settlements, all appear in table 1.2. An important methodological limitation avoids an accurate estimate of the relative weight of the combined population of the eight sectors in the total population of Israel. That is, the populations of some sectors intersect (overlap) with each other (see table 1.2, footnote a).

A quick glance at table 1.2 reveals the salient "demographic power" of the combined population of all the sectors versus the total population of Israel. Moreover, the nationwide dispersion, rather than regional concentration, of five of the eight sectors tends to increase their social and political clout. This nationwide dispersion distinguishes these sectors from their counterparts in studies of "regionalism" and "ethnoregionalism." This distinction is required due to Israel's small size.[4] Because the country is so small, sectors spread nationwide are still "sufficiently concentrated" so that they can obtain significant social and political clout.

The social and political clout of each spatial sector is strengthened through the common demographic, social, economic, and political characteristics that cut across its numerous local communities.[5] Moreover, each of the two Arab and the two Oriental sectors is clearly of a lower socioeconomic status and represents a "periphery" in Shils's terms. Thus, altogether these sectors and the others pose major problems for the future of Israeli society and politics. Their relationship with the society is described below.

Table 1.3 shows three major components around which a spatial sector conducts its interaction within Israeli society: the other party in the interaction, the subject of the interaction, and the sector's mode of operation for the interaction. To begin, a spatial sector—Gush Emunim will serve as an example—might interact with four major parties. First, the sector interacts with the general Israeli polity, that is, the larger society and its central government. The term "larger society" covers all social groups including the sector's own social group or all other religious Jews in the case of Gush Emunim. Second, the sector interacts with the general Israeli polity, the larger society and central government, excluding its own social group (which it represents). Spe-

Table 1.1. Spatial Sectors in Israel: Social Group, Dispersion, and Type of Settlement

PART. CLEAVAGE			
Chapter. Spatial Sector[a]	Social Group	Dispersion	Type of Settlement
I. ARAB-JEWISH			
2. West Bank and Gaza Strip Arabs	Arabs	Regional	Rural[b]/Town/City
3. Israeli Arabs	Arabs	Nationwide	Rural/Town/City
II. ETHNIC-CLASS[c]			
4. Development Towns	Oriental Jews	Nationwide	Town
5. Renewal Neighborhoods	Oriental Jews	Nationwide	Neighborhood
III. RELIGIOUS-SECULAR			
6. Urban Neighborhoods	Religious Jews	Nationwide	Neighborhood
7. Gush Emunim Settlements	Religious Jews	Regional	Rural
IV. LEFT-RIGHT			
8. Kibbutzim and Moshavim	Left[d]	Nationwide	Rural
V. MULTICLEAVAGE[e]			
9. Jerusalem	Arabs Oriental Jews Religious Jews	One City	Neighborhood— City[f]

a. Each part of the book, from I to IV, represents one cleavage. Each chapter of the book, from 2 to 9 (1 is this introduction), represents one spatial sector.
b. "Rural" in this table represents mainly small size, nonurban life-style, and agricultural activity. It may also include other economic activities such as industry and services.
c. Represents Oriental Jews versus Ashkenazim.
d. A broadly defined social group based on the ideology of Labor Zionism.
e. The three cleavages are the Arab-Jewish, ethnic-class, the religious-secular (see above). They are all within one city—Jerusalem. Jerusalem, as the subject of Chapter 9, serves as a special case study in the book.
f. Largely homogeneous neighborhoods populated by Arabs, Oriental Jews, or religious Jews are common in Jerusalem. The city as a whole is a "spatial sector."

cifically, Gush Emunim, representing religious Jews, interacts with secular Jews. The term "larger society" here refers to the opposing social group, for the interaction is within the context of the national cleavage. This is the main interaction covered in the volume. That is,

Figure 1.1
General Map of Spatial Sectors in Israel

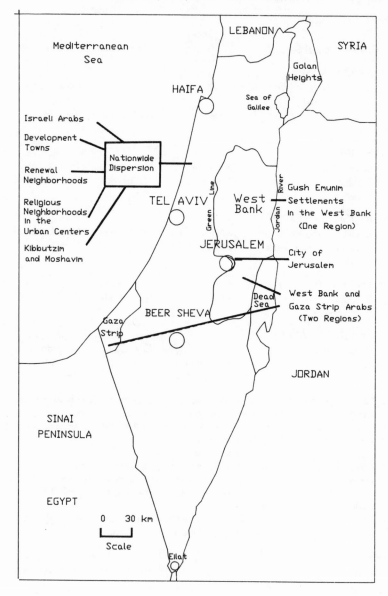

Table 1.2. Spatial Sectors in Israel: Population (1987) and Number of Settlements

Spatial Sector	Population[a]	Percentage of Total Population[a]	Percentage of Jewish Population[a]	Number of Settlements (estimate)
ARABS				
West Bank and Gaza Strip	1,383,200	24	—	460
Israeli Arabs	793,600	14	—	158
ORIENTAL JEWS				
Development Towns	756,520	13	21	33
Renewal Neighborhoods	700,000	12	19	90
RELIGIOUS JEWS				
Urban Neighborhoods	722,580	12	20[c]	—
Gush Emunim Settlements	10,672	0.2	0.3	39
THE LEFT				
Kibbutzim and Moshavim	284,100	5	8	715
THE CITY				
Jerusalem	482,700[b]	8	13	1
Total—Sectors[a]	n.a.	n.a.	n.a.	n.a.
Total—Israel	5,789,700	5,789,700[d]	3,612,900[d]	n.a.

Sources: Central Bureau of Statistics 1988a; various chapters in this book.

a. In this category, the population or its percentage is calculated independently for each sector regardless of its partial intersection (overlap), in some cases, with other sectors. The Total—Sectors category is therefore marked as n.a. No accurate data are available on these intersections. Cases of intersection include the Development Towns with Renewal Neighborhoods/Urban Neighborhoods; Renewal Neighborhoods also intersect with Urban Neighborhoods/Jerusalem; Jerusalem also intersects with Urban Neighborhoods and Israeli Arabs.

b. Including East Jerusalem.

c. The ultra-Orthodox alone are roughly 8 percent of the population (of Jews and Israeli Arabs).

d. The base figure for calculating the percentages.

Table 1.3. Interaction of a Spatial Sector: Other Party, Subject, and Mode of Operation

Other Party
1. General Israeli polity, i.e., larger society and central government
2. General Israeli polity except own social group
3. A sub-group of own social group
4. Another spatial sector

Subject
1. Values
2. Interests

Mode of Operation
1. National-level (emphasis on social group and cleavage)
2. Local- and regional-level (emphasis on sector)
3. Mix of national-level and local- and regional-level

the term "larger society" usually refers to the opposing social group. Depending on the content, the term sometimes refers to the first party as above. The third possible party for the interaction with the sector is another spatial or nonspatial subgroup of the sector's own social group. In the Gush Emunim case, that party might be any other Jewish religious element. The fourth party might be another spatial sector of a distinct social group. In the Gush Emunim case, that party might be religious urban neighborhoods, development towns, or West Bank and Gaza Strip Arabs. Interactions with the third and fourth party are also covered in the volume, (and are specifically indicated in the index), yet interaction with the second party is the central subject.

The interaction between a spatial sector and the other party is frequently tense, particularly when occurring in the context of the national cleavage. The interaction evolves around two subjects: values and interests (table 1.3). Each subject represents one type of conflict. The two types, though not mutually exclusive in practice, can be distinguished analytically. The first type, "conflict of values," is around broad normative issues, primarily ideological, political, social, cultural, and life-style issues. The second type, "conflict of interests," is around specific policies, primarily economic, budget, and land policies. Because these policies are frequently centralized through the Israeli government, this conflict is usually between a spatial sector and the central government (which is also controlled by an opposing social group). Both types of conflict, values and interests, are an important part of the political process.

The conflicts of values and interests between a spatial sector and the larger society and central government sometimes overlap with the conflicts between Shils's "periphery and center." This is largely the case of the first four sectors in table 1.1. In other cases, such an analogy is misleading. The values or interests of a certain sector can be a part of the "periphery" or the "center." This mixture characterizes the rest of the cases in table 1.1. These sectors, though not dominant, might have a significant influence on the values and interests of the larger society and the central government. This is due to sociohistorical reasons or to Israel's parliamentary and coalition government system. As minorities, however, they still have to struggle for their positions, and frequently through the political process.

In the political process, a spatial sector might employ three modes of operation for protecting and advancing its values and interests (table 1.3). Each mode is a unique strategy which carries its own terminology. The first mode is exclusively around the sector's national-level social group and cleavage with no acknowledgment of the spatial sector. This mode is also frequently used by Israeli political parties. Israeli parties are highly centralized on the national-level, dominated by national leaders and issues, and touch upon every segment of Israeli society. The second mode of operation of the sector is exclusively within the terms of the local and regional level. In other words, the emphasis is on the sector itself. The third mode is a mix of the national-level and local- and regional-level. That is, the social group and the cleavage are explicitly employed to help the sector.

THE CHAPTERS: VALUES, INTERESTS, AND POLITICS

The conflicts of values and interests of each spatial sector with the larger Israeli society and the central government, in the context of the national cleavage, is the main subject of the chapters in this book. Each cleavage constitutes one part and each sector is one chapter in the book (see table 1.1). Part I, the Arab-Jewish cleavage, covers West Bank and Gaza Strip Arabs (chapter 2) and Israeli Arabs (chapter 3). These are two sectors with all-Arab population in a Jewish state. Part II, the ethnic-class cleavage, describes the development towns (chapter 4) and renewal neighborhoods (chapter 5). These are two spatial sectors largely populated by relatively poor Oriental Jews that are in a tense relationship with the middle-class Ashkenazim who dominate the national value and economic systems despite their slight numerical disadvantage. Part III, the religious-secular cleavage, deals with religious neighborhoods in the urban centers (chapter 6)[6] and Gush Emunim new settlements in the West Bank (chapter 7). These are two orthodox sectors that are in conflict with the secular majority in Israel. Part IV, the left-right cleavage, focuses on kibbutzim and moshavim (chapter 8). These rural cooperative settlements, the ideological center of Labor Zionism in the past, are at odds with the new trends in the Israeli society and the ruling right-wing government. Finally, part IV analyzes Jerusalem (chapter 9) in the context of the three national cleavages that divide the city. The city as a whole serves as a special case study of a spatial sector with memberships in a number of social groups, yet still distinct vis-à-vis the larger Israeli society and the central government. Jerusalem exemplifies a degree of complexity and potential tension with no parallel in other Israeli local communities. It thus serves as an interesting concluding chapter for the book.

The chapters of the book are reviewed below in the order mentioned above. The review of each chapter, or spatial sector, begins with highlighting the conflicts of values between the sector and the larger Israeli society. It continues with the conflict of interests, primarily with the central government. Some demographic and social characteristics of the Israeli society as a whole, relevant to this conflict, appear in table 1.4. The table may provide a general comparison between the society and the specific sector reviewed. The review then continues with the politics of the sector. Observations on politics are also made throughout the discussion of the conflicts. Results of Knesset and local elections in Israel appear in table 1.5. The table also provides a more general comparison between the society and the specific sector reviewed.[7]

The book opens with the Arab-Jewish cleavage which is presented in two chapters: on the West Bank and Gaza Strip Arabs written by Donna Robinson Divine, and on Israeli Arabs by Majid Al-Haj. The conflicts of these two spatial sectors with the larger Jewish society reflect the century-old struggle between two national movements, each with distinct cultural, religious, and ideological identities. The ultimate challenge to the fundamental tenet of Zionist ideology, the Jewish society's moral right to exist in its own state, comes from the Palestinians in the West Bank and Gaza Strip. Divine shows how two decades of passive hostility and instrumental cooperation with the Israeli occupation culminated in the civil disobedience and violent riots of the Intifada which began in December 1987. Coupled with elements of Islamic fundamentalism, the Intifada stressed again the

Table 1.4. Demographic and Social Characteristics of Israel, 1970, 1980, and 1989

Demographic/ Social Characteristic	1970	1980	1989
Population (Percent Jewish)[a]	3,022,100 (85.4)	3,921,700 (83.7)	4,559,600 (81.5)
West Bank and Gaza Strip (Arabs)	985,600[b]	1,163,300	1,413,900
Percentage of Population in Coastal District (Haifa, Central, and Tel Aviv)	62.7	60.1	57.6
Percentage of Population in Urban Localities	88.6[c]	89.6[d]	89.8
Density per km^2	154.8[c]	191.8	208.7
Number of Settlements	884	1,031	1,159
Number of Local Governments	192	210	230
Percentage Employed in Industry	24.3	23.7	21.6
Percentage Employed in Services	31.7	35.8	36.9
Percentage Employed in Professional or Administrative Occupations (Jews)[e]	43.0[f]	—	51.6
Percentage of Unemployed Adults	3.8	4.8	8.9
Median Years of Schooling	8.8	10.7	11.6
Percentage with One Private Car (Jews)	15.4	35.6	42.9[g]
Percentage of Households with Less than One Person per Room (Jews)	18.2	31.3	42.4

Sources: Central Bureau of Statistics 1976, 1988a, 1989, 1990.
a. Excluding the West Bank and Gaza Strip.
b. This figure is for 1967.
c. This figure is for 1972.
d. This figure is for 1983.
e. Professional—scientific, academic, professional, and technical workers. Administrative—administrators, managers, and clerical workers.
f. This figure is for 1975.
g. This figure is for 1987.

Table 1.5. Results of Knesset and Local (Council) Elections in Israel (Percentage of Valid Votes for 1977, 1978, 1983, 1984, and 1988)

	Political Bloc[a]					Voting
	Labor	Likud	Religious	Local	Other	Turnout
Knesset						
1977	24.6	35.3	13.9	—	26.5	79.2
1984	37.1	33.1	12.6	—	17.0	78.9
1988	32.5	31.1	14.6	—	21.7	79.7
Local[b]						
1978	34.9	26.3	16.5	17.6	4.7	57.3
1983	36.9	23.5	19.5	16.5	3.6	58.0

Sources: Central Bureau of Statistics 1988a, 1988b; Goldberg 1987.

a. The most effective way to understand Israel's diversified multiparty system is to classify the many parties and lists into major political blocs. Accordingly, the "Labor" bloc includes Mapai, later Labor party or Alignment, and Mapam, a junior partner. The "Likud" bloc includes Gahal (Herut and the Liberal party), later Likud. Each of the two blocs might also include another one or two minor parties, depending on the election year. The components of the "religious" bloc are the National Religious Party (NRP), Agudat Israel and, depending on the election year, Tami, Shas, and smaller parties. "Other" includes numerous small parties and lists that are clearly left of Labor, right of Likud, and at the center. "Local" indicates genuine local lists with no affiliation, formal or informal, to any of the parties classified under the blocs above.

b. The results by "political bloc" include Jewish and Jewish-Arab mixed communities; communities with exclusively Arab population are not included. However, all communities are included in "Voting Turnout." The formal results of the 1989 local elections are not published yet by the Central Bureau of Statistics. The results published in the daily news papers (e.g., Yedioth Ahronoth, 1 March 1989) showed a significant increase in votes for the Likud and religious blocs, and a significant decrease for Labor. The voting turnout was extremely low—48%.

threat of secular life, introduced mainly through the Jewish society, to the two Arab regions that are still experiencing much ambivalence towards modernization. Modernization, followed with much reliance on education as a channel for mobility, with no parallel economic development, resulted in social turmoil for a society based on family and kin relations.

Divine argues that economic growth, a rising standard of living, and access to modern goods and services, provided temporary stability in the past but no economic security and occupational mobility in the long-run. The static economy of the Intifada and the rising unemployment further weakened the low socioeconomic status and forced the return to simple self-sufficient local and regional economies with less reliance on manufactured goods. The Intifada increased the gaps between the economic interests of the Jewish center and the two Arab regions. Struggle for the scarce resources of water, land, and agriculture also continued. Yet the economy of the regions is still highly dependent on the center.

The conflict is heightened due to the strategic-security function of the West Bank and Gaza Strip to the state. In the geography of a small country like Israel, the two regions are peripheral. But their proximity to the densed metropolitan areas of Jerusalem, Tel Aviv, and Haifa is a major threat to Israel's national security.

To a large extent, according to Divine, the Intifada was the result of the basic contradictions in policies and the lack of consensus among the government agencies in charge of the two occupied regions. Nonetheless, it did not foster a united policy among the military administration in the regions, the civil administration, and the different ministries of the government. At the same time, the Intifada created new opportunities for the Palestinians. They began to rely more and more on local economic resources. It also opened new channels of political behavior for people with no citizenship and equal rights. The young Palestinian generation and its leaders became more politically aware and clashed directly with the Jewish center. The ultimate demand of the two peripheral regions, for self-determination and home rule, became more vocal and effective.

Unlike their counterparts in the occupied regions, Israeli Arabs enjoy the formal rights of their citizenship and cooperate, at least instrumentally, with the larger Jewish society. The latter, however, considers them as a "hostile minority" and a threat to national security, which the Arabs view as an excuse for the discriminatory policies against them. In his chapter, Al-Haj notes the growing national consciousness among Israeli Arabs since the 1970s and the rise of Islamic fundamentalism in the 1980s. Interestingly, these trends are intertwined with the realistic desire to link their future more firmly to the state. They remained excluded, however, from the modern nation-state building process. Moreover, they are still ambivalent towards the modern Western values which are dominant in the Jewish society; despite their significant level of individual modernization reflected in their rising level of education and standard of living.

The ethnic stratification of the Israeli society placed clear limits on the lower socioeconomic status of the Arab minority. The class gaps between Arabs and Jews have remained. The attempts of the Arabs to reduce the gaps concentrated on their local-level interests.

They requested from the central government higher budget allocations for local services and education as well as for local planning and
construction.

Israeli Arabs focused on local-level interests because they had
little share in the values of the Jewish majority and in the national
power structure. With no other choices, politics became locally oriented. The conflict with the Jewish center around local interests characterized all the strategies of political mobilization employed by Israeli
Arabs in order to penetrate the Israeli power structure and to bargain
over resources. Three such strategies are conceptualized by Al-Haj.
The first, parliamentary politics, delivered minor returns. The second,
local politics, became a central activity and a very important means
for political mobilization. The third strategy, mobilization through
extraparliamentary national organizations, is gradually gaining importance. This strategy relies on the expertise of Arab professionals
and is focused on social services, education, local planning, construction, and industrialization.

For the time being, according to Al-Haj, the attempts of Israeli
Arabs for greater integration and equality have failed to meet their expectations and needs. They have only five Knesset members and one
of sixty senior government positions. The national Jewish center is
practically closed to them. Their communities remained segregated
from the Jewish society. Most of their political energy is now geared
towards their community-level needs. However, because they are still
dependent on the Jewish center, they will continue their national-level
parliamentary activity. They will also continue to search for overall
political solutions, including some arrangement for autonomy within
the state.

The ethnic-class cleavage is discussed in two chapters: on the development towns written by Efraim Ben-Zadok, and on the neighborhoods of Project Renewal by Hana Ofek. Both authors note the
difficult transition of the Oriental immigrants from the traditional Islamic societies of North Africa and the Middle East to Israel, a new
society dominated by the relatively modern Western values of European Jews. The traditional family, community, religious, and cultural
patterns of the immigrants were repressed to build a homogeneous national culture based on secular modern values. The Western-oriented
"melting pot" ideology resulted in a limited integration process. But
since the early 1970s, cultural pluralism was accepted as less threatening to the political system. Oriental ethnicity and pride has surfaced
and became more pronounced. Opening up to more cultural pluralism

and to the Middle Eastern patterns of the region, the Ashkenazim became more tolerant of the Middle East culture of the region represented by Orientals. The latter continued to adopt Western patterns. The mutual cultural infusions, concludes Ben-Zadok, will probably reduce the conflict of values in the future.

Nevertheless, the development towns and renewal neighborhoods are still relatively isolated and homogeneous communities experiencing "negative selection" of population and with limited opportunities for class and cultural exchange. The integration ideology of the establishment lagged behind in its implementation. This point is especially ironic for the development towns, which were planned as a part of the pioneering building of a new society. In the renewal neighborhoods, the residents' perception of the gaps between them and their middle-class neighbors and on the favorable treatment of Soviet immigrants may provoke waves of protest.

The conflict around class and economic interests, however, may intensify in the future according to both authors. Despite the progress, socioeconomic disparities have remained between each of the two spatial sectors and the larger Israeli society. The development towns and renewal neighborhoods are mainly populated by lower- and working-class Oriental Jews; Ashkenazim tend to be middle-class. The disparities are in the very indices that constitute the concept of "class" in the two chapters, that is, education, income employment, housing, and standard of living. Disparities in these indices were already observed in the 1950s when the ethnic-class division was formed. Currently, Orientals still rank lower on these indices and hold blue-collar, service, and small-business jobs. Ashkenazim still control Israel's public and private sectors and hold key positions in the parties, academia, and the arts.

Much of the class gaps originate in the local economic problems that the development towns and renewal neighborhoods are still experiencing. The class gaps will not be closed without community- and neighborhood-based comprehensive policies to solve the continuous problems of lagging industrial growth, unemployment, the budget deficit, and inadequate housing. Such policies are largely funded by the central government in Israel. The two sectors are dependent on the government and must bargain for their economic interests.

The ethnic-class gaps described above became the center of the electoral debate in the 1970s. Feelings of injustice and discrimination were eventually infused into the political process. Consequently, the Labor bloc suffered a sharp decline in votes, while the Likud, in turn, enjoyed a significant rise in the two sectors. In the development towns this process involved a dramatic "ouster of the old guards." The older immigrant leadership was replaced by younger and educated leaders, products of the Israeli school system, who quickly climbed through the open-mobility ranks of the right-wing party. The results were striking: in 1990, fourteen Knesset members and three ministers of the right-wing cabinet were residents of the development towns. Clearly, the periphery of the past is becoming a major political center of the present. Moreover, cooperating as one forum across party lines, the towns' representatives are aggressively promoting the local and regional economic interests of their communities through the legislative process. Grassroots support and demands to respond to community needs also increased significantly the vote for local lists in the towns. Similarly, such trends of local autonomy were expressed in a clear rise in resident participation in planning and policymaking in the renewal neighborhoods. As part of the decentralization plan of Project Renewal, the residents contributed directly to design policies that effectively reduced the socioeconomic disparities between their neighborhoods and the larger society. The interests of the neighborhoods are represented by a few Knesset members.

The religious-secular cleavage is reviewed in two chapters: the ultra-Orthodox neighborhoods in the urban centers written by Yosseph Shilhav, and Gush Emunim settlements in the West Bank by Giora Goldberg. In contrast to the larger Israeli society, the ultra-Orthodox subculture blatantly rejects modern values and life-styles as well as the technology, such as television, that transmits their messages. At the same time, the ultra-Orthodox exploit all value-neutral components of modernity such as computers. Shilhav opens by explaining this point, which may seem contradictory to a secular person, yet it is ideologically consistent to a religious one. A similar logic is expressed in the relations of the ultra-Orthodox with the Zionist ideology and its Jewish state. While the ultra-Orthodox clearly reject these as a secular intervention in their spiritual messianic world, they exploit every means to pursue their interests within the very system which they disqualify.

In accordance with this dual behavior, they have less interest in the acute national issues of defense, security, or foreign affairs. But they maintain functional and instrumental relations with the state to ensure budgets for the school, social, welfare, and religious needs of their local communities. In these state-funded self-segregated homogeneous communities, they strictly preserve their faith and life-style.

But as demonstrated by Shilhav, scarcity of land and housing due to their fast-growing population propel the ultra-Orthodox toward direct confrontation with their secular neighbors. The conflicts, sometimes violent, usually erupt around the preservation of their religious laws and life-style.

The key question is how such a fundamentalist counter-culture, which clearly disassociated itself from the larger society, gained so much legitimacy from the state. The answer has both social and political dimensions. To begin, as mentioned earlier (note 6), although the ultra-Orthodox represent the deepest level of the religious-secular cleavage, they still constitute less than one-half of the population of the larger sector of religious urban neighborhoods, which is more moderate as a whole. The neighborhoods of this sector have always enjoyed the right to preserve their culture and life-style. The secular Israeli public, nonobservant yet with a traditional attitude towards religion, basically accepted peaceful terms of existence with its religious neighbors. Furthermore, the secular public, as reflected in Shilhav's essay, grants wide legitimacy to religious institutions, laws, practices, and symbols. This social environment helped the Israeli political system establish a blurred legislative status quo of state-synagogue relations, leaving basic constitutional questions unresolved.

The "gray" constitutional areas were facilitated due to the special leverage of the religious parties in Israeli politics. Whether there was a left- or right-wing regime, the small religious parties were always the vital element required to form the parliamentary majority upon which the secular-controlled coalition governments were built. Because they always joined the coalition governments as such key partners, these small parties had much bargaining power, which enabled them to receive disproportionally large slices of government budgets. The financial sponsorship of the state moderated the conflict of interests with the religious sector. Yet, as Shilhav points out, the thirteen ultra-Orthodox Knesset members elected in 1988 are liaisons to the surrounding world and primarily serve as safeguards for the interests of their community. Eighteen Knesset members represent the religious sector as a whole. The sector controls important ministries such as Interior and Religious Affairs.

It is from the national-religious camp of this larger sector, religious urban neighborhoods, that Gush Emunim ("Bloc of the Faithful") emerged in the early 1970s. Following their parents, and in contrast to the ultra-Orthodox, the young members of the Gush support the Zionist ideology and its secular state while adding to it a new normative religious significance. They resent, however, the routine political bargaining style of the national-religious camp on both ideological principles and services to their neighborhoods. Clear and loud in the 1970s as a broad social movement and much softer during the 1980s as a limited regional interest group, argues Goldberg, the fundamental Judaism ideology of the Gush called for a new direction for the national-religious camp as well as for Israeli society as a whole. Accordingly, the essence of Judaism is spiritual, messianic, and incompatible with the materialistic and consumption habits of a modern Western society. This ideology is inseparable from a physical Jewish presence, which is to be fulfilled by settling the land of Israel. The target region for the new pioneers of Zionism, the Gush settlers, is the spiritual core of biblical Israel—the mountains of Judea and Samaria or the West Bank.

But the tones of values have been moderated. Goldberg explains that the ideology of national-level reform has been transformed into a policy-oriented regional-level platform. As a regional interest group of the 1980s, the Gush pragmatically concentrated on the land and financial needs of its West Bank settlements. With the drop in central government's funding since 1984, the settlement arm of the Gush (Amana) promoted the infrastructure and service needs of the communities. It thus overshadowed the normative principles of the political arm. The Gush is still successful in mobilizing financial support through the central government. However, being almost totally dependent on it, and with communities that suffer major economic difficulties, the Gush developed a regional-interest strategy to struggle on its budget's allocation from the government. In light of its declining budget and increased alienation from the Israeli public, the Gush will continue to strengthen its regional characteristics.

Despite its consistent attempt to maintain a dialogue with the secular public, and even to integrate nonideological lower-priced-housing-motivated members into its communities, the Gush's West Bank settlement has remained extremely small in size and isolated, and for the most part socially homogeneous and middle-class. Having said that, the Gush still attracts an enormous amount of public debate. Much of the political debate is due to its uncompromising territorial position on the West Bank, which has a measure of support in almost every secular party in Israel, if not for spiritual then for security reasons. The academic debate is no less intriguing. In the intense and centralized party system of Israel, this small extraparliamentary group has been quite successful in advancing its particularistic ideology.

Nonetheless, as Goldberg concludes, if the Gush is manipulated by the establishment more than vice versa, then it will culminate as another case of "the region against the center," a case where the regional organization form has become an interest group rather than a political party. The three Gush Knesset members, indeed, represent three different right-wing and religious parties.

In principle, there is a similarity in the transformation of the new religious pioneers of the Gush "from social movement to regional interest group," and the transformation of their old counterparts, the pioneers of the left, "from ideological symbol to interest group" as observed by Neal Sherman in his chapter on kibbutzim and moshavim, which represents the left-right cleavage. The nature of the cooperative settlement sector and its conflict with the larger society and the central government, however, are completely different. The kibbutzim and moshavim that spearheaded the nation-building ideology of Labor Zionism since the beginning of the century are losing much of their prestige in light of the individualistic and materialistic trends that prevail in Israeli society. The collective and egalitarian values of the rural-agricultural sector, which in the past enjoyed much support in the cities as well, are losing their appeal to the new widespread consumption and class norms. The sector itself became more industrialized and service-oriented. Its fulfillment of a national mission through security-oriented settlement in the hinterland is no more an acute priority.

The eroding support for the values of Labor Zionism reflects not only ideological and cultural changes. Much of it is a protest against the politics of the parties that represent these values, the parties of the Labor bloc which ruled until 1977, when the Likud rose to power. Less than a decade later, according to Sherman, the long-established ground rules governing the relations of the kibbutzim and moshavim with the state were cast in doubt. The liberal economic policies of the Likud, and the decline in government support for the cooperative settlement sector in general and for its agricultural activities in particular, all led this sector into an acute economic and organizational crisis. The current symptoms of the unresolved crisis are heavy debts, lack of financing, and, in the moshavim, which were hurt most severely, the collapse of the purchasing organizations and economic cooperation among the members.

The changes forced the cooperative settlement sector into a new position. Losing its political clout, the sector began to increasingly operate as an interest group that is bargaining with the central government for immediate needs, rather than reminding the government of its national contribution and expecting the appropriate compensation. Because national and settlement interests are not necessarily considered identical anymore, it speaks like any other sector. Its closed and socially homogeneous communities are sometimes criticized, by the right, for having lost touch with the national mission. Yet hundreds of communities that are spread nationwide, especially the kibbutzim, are still functioning as a united sector under their regional and national organizations. Moreover, although the kibbutzim and moshavim are no more a major source for leadership recruitment, and their traditional overrepresentation in the Knesset is in decline, the number of their delegates after the 1988 elections, eleven (five of them Labor), still exceeds proportionately the small size of their population.

The final chapter on Jerusalem by Ira Sharkansky serves as a special case study. It treats the city as a whole as a distinct spatial sector vis-à-vis the larger Israeli society and the central government. It also demonstrates the tensions embodied in the national cleavages in the context of one local community populated by people who vary sharply in their ethnicity, class, and religious traits.

Jerusalem is a spatial sector with special values. The capital is unique as the universal-historical crossroad of cultures, religions, and politics. The "Holy City," with its special atmosphere and physical appearance, has a strong emotional appeal to Jews, Muslims, and Christians. City and government officials appreciate and use Jerusalem's international status. They do not adopt it literally or formally, however, because they prefer the city to remain united under Jewish rule. Most Israelis probably appreciate these distinct characteristics. At the same time, they do not identify with the values and life-styles of many residents of the city, namely, the Arabs and ultra-Orthodox Jews.

With respect to interests, Sharkansky formulates a thesis based on two different elements. On one hand, Jerusalem depends on the central government and is dominated by central financial policies like other Israeli cities. As the nation's historical capital it may enjoy better budget allocations than other cities along with more intervention of national officials in local affairs. On the other hand, the city's distinctive national and international status as well as the financial and political entrepreneurship of the mayor facilitate a solid mix of public and private resources which enables a fairly independent policy of urban development.

Because Jerusalem is under the centralized governmental system of Israel and, at the same time, enjoys much discretion in raising private funds, its budget politics is fairly complex. It is a process which blurs the boundaries among the different public and private sources of funding.

The chapter on Jerusalem also covers the three cleavages within the city: Arab-Jewish, ethnic-class, and religious-secular. Jerusalem is well known as a city of highly homogeneous neighborhoods. Neighborhoods largely populated by Arabs, Oriental Jews, or religious Jews can be easily identified. They are frequently the sources of the social and economic tensions described in the previous chapters.

The Arabs of East Jerusalem, over one-quarter of the population, refuse the offer of Israeli citizenship. They continue to travel to Jordan on Jordanian passports and to use Jordanian currency. They are concerned about the massive building of Jewish neighborhoods around their communities. At the same time, they have been integrated into the urban economy since the 1967 war, a process which was retarded by the Intifada. The neighborhoods of Oriental Jews, over one-half of the city's population, which in the early 1970s supplied Israel's most militant lower-class protest groups, the "Black Panthers" and "Ohalim," calmed down in the 1980s, due in part to Project Renewal, which increased their power of local decision-making. But their tensions with both the central government and city hall bureaucracies, and with the new wave of Soviet immigrants, were not eliminated. Strong emotions about religious values and life-styles, intertwined with scarcity of land and housing, also make Jerusalem the most visible national arena for both political and physical confrontations between ultra-Orthodox and secular Jews. Sharkansky discusses the 1989 local elections, when a coalition of secular parties joined successfully to help Mayor Kollek's party hold back the ultra-Orthodox. Kollek's party, interestingly, has its roots in the left. But the mayor, who began his tenure in 1966, always ran on a compromising "catch-all" left-right platform. It has proved to be not only a winning electoral strategy, but also as the most effective one for urban development in a city with citywide heterogeneity along with neighborhood-level homogeneity.

CONCLUSIONS: AREAS OF CONFLICT

The three common themes that run through the review of the chapters above—values, interests, and politics—are crucial to understand the interaction between each of the eight spatial sectors and the general Israeli polity. The tense and conflictual nature of the interaction creates much social and political pressure on the general Israeli polity, namely, the larger society and the central government. Suggestions on how to relieve the pressure and reduce the conflicts between a specific sector and the polity are presented by the authors in their respective chapters.

This section deals with the interaction between two or more sectors combined and the Israeli polity. Two such interactions are possible. First, between two or more sectors combined and the polity when the sectors share many values and interests, namely, a coalition. Examples of this are the two Arab, Oriental, or religious sectors; each pair might form a coalition based on a membership in the same social group. Second, an interaction between all sectors combined and the polity. In this interaction, whether or not all sectors have certain common values and interests, or even if they are split among themselves (e.g., the development towns versus Gush Emunim or the development towns versus the kibbutzim and moshavim on central budget allocations for economic development), their total combined disagreement with the larger society and the central government creates much pressure on the latter two. This social and political pressure is also a by-product of the large population of the eight sectors and the nationwide dispersion of five of them.

This section identifies the common values and interests, of two or more sectors, that are incompatible with those of the general Israeli polity. In other words, it focuses on policy areas that are problematic for a number of sectors. The section begins with problematic policy areas from the discussion of values and proceeds to interests while politics is integrated into both. Policy guidelines for conflict management and reduction in these areas are proposed in the next section.

The two Arab and the two Oriental sectors expressed ambivalence towards modern Western values. The two religious sectors expressed strong rejection of such secular values. The two Arab and the two religious sectors also supported fundamentalist ideas. The two Arab sectors and the sector of religious urban neighborhoods did not accept the idea of the state of Israel as a Jewish nation-state. This attitude clearly distinguished these three sectors from the two Oriental sectors, Gush Emunim, and the kibbutzim and moshavim, who fully endorsed the Jewish state. Moreover, because their disagreement with the Jewish state is coupled with an ambivalence or rejection of the modern Western values prevalent in the society, the two Arab sectors and the religious neighborhoods are constantly threatening the stability of the Israeli government and society. For these three sectors, membership in the Arab or religious social group is far more meaningful than their partial membership in the state.

The last observation is somewhat more complex with respect to the sector of religious urban neighborhoods. The sector was represented by close to one-half of its population: ultra-Orthodox Jews. The sector held eighteen seats in the Knesset before the 1992 elections; thirteen of them were occupied by the ultra-Orthodox. The National Religious Party, which represents the rest of the sector, held twelve Knesset seats in 1977. The weakening of the national-religious camp and the growing influence of the ultra-Orthodox within the sector explain its retreat from both Zionist and moderate modern orthodoxy values. This trend, apparent at present, might become strong and crucial in the future. Consequently, the religious-secular cleavage might become more volatile. For the ultra-Orthodox Jew, a national and secular Jewish identity is invalid. But while this boundary is so sharply drawn, the cleavage can still be moderated because the ultra-Orthodox are also pragmatic and use the political system effectively. No less important, the secular public shares with them some traditional religious values which serve as integrative mechanisms.

The ultra-Orthodox, the West Bank and Gaza Strip Arabs, and Israeli Arabs were not penetrated by the Western-oriented nation-building ideology of Zionism. For all other sectors, except the kibbutzim and moshavim, the penetration was only partial. The ideology of a homogeneous secular culture as socially integrating, and a strong state as nationally uniting, failed to liberate the masses of Jews and Arabs from the traditional and institutional constraints of their ethnicity, class, or religion. These social differences, which remained subtle for more than two decades of independence, surfaced vocally in the early 1970s when cultural pluralism became more prevalent. When the repressed values eventually emerged, they were frequently reinforced by counter-culture or fundamentalist elements, some of which were imported from abroad. Much of the protest was in local/regional units. The territorial context only increased the normative distance and strain between these sectors and the Israeli polity.

Some students of Israeli political culture may further argue that closing the gaps between the sectors and the Israeli polity is an extremely difficult, if not impossible, task. Both Liebman (1989) and Sprinzak (1986) show that most Israelis share a communitarian concept of the state. Israelis feel that the state should pursue its interests

according to its members; it is not an impersonal entity which can le-
gitimately pursue interests of its own. Accordingly, their first commitment is to serve the interests of their community or reference group.
Moreover, Yuchtman-Ya'ar and Peres (1991, 24) show that in 1990
Israelis trusted local government agencies, which directly served their
community or group, more (53%) than they trusted the Knesset
(48%), the government (46%), the Histadrut (40%), or the political
parties (32%).

Closing the gaps between the two Arab and the two Oriental sectors and the rest of the Israeli society is especially difficult due to their
location in the lower socioeconomic stratum of society. The class gaps
increased the distance between these sectors and the society. The four
sectors experienced major economic and financial problems. It was
evident in their scarce resources, lagging industry, unemployment,
budget deficit, and inadequate housing. In all four sectors, these difficulties, and the class gaps, no less than their cultural and ideological
values, have nourished the emergence of young, educated, and professional leaders as well as elements of civic localism and citizen participation. Two other sectors, albeit middle-class, that suffered from
budget cuts and troubled economies were Gush Emunim and the kibbutzim and moshavim. Their cultural and ideological national-level
mission was therefore relegated to a lower priority and they both
transformed their main role to that of an interest group bargaining
with the central government for its acute economic needs.

Some of the class gaps and economic problems are the result of
the basic conditions of Israel's political economy. Israel is a small and
relatively isolated country with scarce natural resources, relying
heavily on foreign trade and financing, and with an unusual high expenditure on military and defense. The state has certain ground rules
for economic and redistributive welfare policies towards the Arab sectors as well as towards the politically weaker or stronger Jewish
sectors. A recent study (Kraus and Hodge 1990) further argues
that while there is no intrinsic discrimination built into the Israeli
economy, ethnic attachment is the base for economic rewards. The
main explanation (which can be challenged) is that Oriental Jews
are streamed into vocational high schools while Ashkenazim finish
regular high schools. The social control of the latter is thus secured
through educational credentials.

Having said that, the social and economic disparities between the
four lower-stratum sectors and the rest of the society, and the troubled

economies of almost all the sectors in this book, must raise some questions about the efficiency of the centralized economic and administrative system of the state. In an article entitled "Israel's Economy in the Post-Begin Era," Plessner (1990, 306) concluded that Begin's government (1977–83) was too weak to uproot decades of economic mismanagement by all Israeli governments including itself. Consequently, the economic problems exploded after Begin's resignation. In an article entitled "The Overloaded State," Sharkansky (1989) describes the Israeli government as almost totally dominating the economy, and its bureaucracy as probably the most powerful in all of the democracies. Accordingly, some of the negative characteristics of this system are poor management of public enterprises and social services, and many centrally defined rules that are evaded in the interests of a flexible administration. It all implies that the centralized system must rewrite its guidelines for economic and administrative policies.

Moving towards changes in the centralized system is imperative in light of the relations between the local communities in this book and the larger Israeli society. Although they are intimately cooperating among themselves within their respective sectors, most of these communities are relatively closed and isolated from the larger society and enjoy a high degree of social homogeneity. Further, some of their attempts to break beyond their boundaries are through blatant hostility towards their neighbors. This was shown in the struggle over land of the Palestinians, the ultra-Orthodox, and Gush Emunim. The territory, in summary, is far more fragmented than previously assumed; and the calls for local self-determination are becoming increasingly vociferous. The highly centralized system cannot function effectively in such an environment.

POLICY GUIDELINES: CONFLICT MANAGEMENT IN A DEMOCRATIC ENVIRONMENT

Future policy directions for the sectors appear in the chapters. In this final section, broad policy guidelines are recommended rather than specific solutions prescribed for each sector. The guidelines for conflict management and reduction cover the problematic policy areas previously identified. While the sequence and the analytical distinction between values and interests are maintained, each guideline, if implemented, obviously carried both normative and economic impacts.

The underlined premise of the recommendation below is that the Israeli polity must develop policy guidelines which provide all the eight spatial sectors with a significant level of discretion over their social, cultural, economic, and political life. The polity must recognize the growing pluralism in modern, traditional, secular, religious, individual, and collective values. It must come to grips with the changing times of the last two decades and respond to the sectors, who all demand an acknowledgment and reward for their different values.

The new tasks are not easy in light of the past. The Israeli polity did not undergo the gradual evolution of a modern democracy state-building which involved centuries of centralized government and secular liberal policies. Instead, the young state experienced a fast process of government centralization which was instrumental in implementing national goals. It dictated an ideology of a homogeneous culture and strong national unity to masses of immigrants.

At present, however, local and regional units in Israel demand much more discretionary power. For three sectors, the guidelines below may apply only within different autonomous home-rule arrangements which will greatly minimize the role of the state. These are the two Arab sectors and religious urban neighborhoods. The three sectors are self-determined by their values which, for them, far exceed those of the state. They provide the most severe challenge to the continuity of the state. An explicit recognition of their political autonomy, culture, and life-style is imperative in order to keep their identification with the state. The recommendation for home rule for two sectors should be further clarified. For the Palestinians in the West Bank and Gaza Strip, a state of their own is one possible solution. Such a solution is extensively covered in the literature (e.g., Heller and Nusseibeh 1991). For the religious urban neighborhoods, a home-rule arrangement is inevitable if the power of the ultra-Orthodox within the sector continues to increase.

To ensure that all sectors participate as equals in the state, procedural and distributive justice policies must be fully developed. This is an enormous task to execute in Israel, a polity built on a political culture with three conflicting legitimacy principles. These are a Jewish nation-state, a secular liberal democracy, and a "security state." The inherent contradictions among the three principles impose a heavy burden on the judicial system. It must constantly rule in the "gray" areas between the principles on issues of citizenship, civil rights, and state-synagogue relations. In the absence of a state constitution, all these issues are subjected to the political status quo.

Procedural justice policies will benefit every sector. For the non-citizen Palestinians, for example, it means a clarification of their civic status. For Israeli Arabs, formally equal citizens, it means a clarification of their civil rights as full-fledged citizens. At present, because they do not serve in the army they are deprived of the welfare and educational benefits provided to veterans and they have no access to most public sector positions. For religious and secular Jews, procedural justice policies mean clarification of the blurred religious-secular package of laws which governs their personal lives.

Additional distributive justice policies are required to decrease the socioeconomic gaps between the four lower- and working-class sectors and the rest of the Israeli society. For the two Arab and two Oriental sectors, the development of equal opportunity policies in education, health, housing, social services, and employment is imperative. Such policies should be delivered on the base of an equal partnership between central and local governments. This is to assure that the social and economic preferences of the local residents will be incorporated into these policies. In education, for example, it means not only high quality schools but also recognition for the traditional culture heritage of certain ethnic groups. In employment, it means not only more access to jobs but also vocational counseling and training for these jobs.

The development of distributive policies becomes more acute in light of the dramatic increase in Jewish immigration from the Soviet Union in the early 1990s and, as a result, the rising unemployment, which reached 11.5 percent in the first quarter of 1992. This new reality may elevate the tension between the Soviet immigrants and the four relatively poor sectors. If a clear spatial concentration of Soviet Jews is formed in the future, it might emerge as a new spatial sector, with all the implications involved.

The final conclusion on the conflict of interests is that the highly centralized system must reform its economic and administrative policies. This could be done by granting significant discretionary powers to local communities in their relations with the central government. Specifically, the required mechanism to manage and reduce this conflict is decentralization, primarily of the budgetary relations between central and local governments. That is, to decrease the heavy reliance of local governments on central budgets, to increase their ability to develop their own self-sufficient financial resources, and to allow them more freedom to allocate their budgets according to local and regional (rather than national) needs and priorities. One mechanism to facilitate central-local decentralization policies is through the empowerment of regional government bodies. That is, authority and power has to transfer from the center to the intermediate regional level which directly controls local communities.

At present, the communities of each sector, via their local governments, pressure the central government to redistribute national resources according to their own priorities. The sectors also compete among themselves. The fierce competition and bargaining is also due to the weakening political parties that no longer serve as effective mediators between central and local governments. Israeli parties are losing their tremendous past influence over the political process. They are also losing their image and status in the eyes of the public (Goldberg 1992, 17). The state bureaucracy, which is beginning to replace the parties (Galnoor 1982, 368–70), and is becoming more professional, cannot negotiate effectively with all the different groups. With weak regional government bodies, central-local bargaining and competition among local governments thus become more severe. To sum up, the central government cannot respond effectively to the growing specialized demands of local communities and regions; to the social and economic disparities among them which must be addressed; or to local conflicts between Arabs and Jews, Orientals and Ashkenazim, and religious and secular people, so evident in the case of Jerusalem.

Indeed, the government is slowly moving towards decentralization; specifically, in central-local budgetary relations (Ben-Zadok 1986, 33). Project Renewal here is an example of local-level empowerment and increasing resident participation in planning their neighborhoods. Jerusalem is an example of much local discretion in raising private funds. In other areas, local governments were the first to introduce political and administrative reforms. The 1976 local elections law calling for personal elections of mayors is a prime example.

These are all good examples of decentralization policies. Yet the Israeli government is not willing to relinquish its centralized power so quickly. When it does, it frequently backs down for reasons such as the efficiency of a centralized economy-of-scale in a small country or national security threats. Eventually, decentralization policies are short-lived unless they are complemented by long-range structural reforms in the political system.

The most widely discussed reform aiming to revitalize the Israeli political system is that of the national electoral system. A reform in the Knesset elections has been debated since the establishment of the state. It became a salient issue in light of the parliamentary deadlock between the two leading parties after the 1984 and 1988 Knesset elections and the dismantling of their National Unity Government in 1990. Still, proposals for national electoral reform are moving very slowly in the political channels and have many opponents. One of them for example, Dror (1989, 88–96), argues that a reform based on individual candidates (rather than party lists) and districts is a drastic change, inappropriate for a small country like Israel, and carries grave consequences. He contends that it will further destabilize and reduce the flexibility of the already troubled Israeli political system.

There are a number of proposals for electoral reform (e.g., Elazar 1988). Their main goals, listed below, should be seriously considered for adoption. All the proposals aim to minimize the number of the parties represented in the Knesset,[8] to reduce the inflated power of the small parties which are crucial to the stability of the coalition-government, and to break the tie between Labor and Likud. More important to the subject matter here, all these advantages over the present proportional representation system will be provided through a new system based not only on party lists, but also on individual candidates and districts. Consequently, the representation of local communities and regions in the Knesset, as well as of their values and interests, will increase significantly. The decentralization of power will deemphasize the prominency of national objectives and will respond to the "growing regional consciousness" in Israel (Gradus and Eini 1985, 15–16). Finally, it will empower Israeli voters, to an unprecedentedly high degree, to decide the fate of individual political candidates.

The recent emergence of young, educated, and professional leaders in some of the sectors described in this book will be reinforced as a result of an electoral reform. The Likud, the preferred choice of the poor Jewish periphery (the development towns and renewal neighborhoods), was the first to open its mobility channels to grassroots local leaders who climbed to important national positions. The move is spreading to other parties. The enhancement of such trends through electoral reform will further empower the representatives from the deprived sectors towards the negotiation of their values and interests with the central government. They will then be able to obtain more support to solve the economic and financial problems of their sectors and thus to enhance the social and economic progress of their communities.

Notes

1. For a brief preliminary discussion, see Ben-Zadok (1990).
2. The Druze population was 80,300 in 1989. The Gush population was 10,672 in 1987.
3. The classic cleavage model was formulated by Lipset and Rokkan (1967) for party cleavages in West Europe. For a more recent elaboration of cleavages in West European countries, see Knutsen (1989). For discussion of Israeli cleavages, see, for example, Galnoor (1982, 48–64) and Smooha (1988).
4. The size of the country is 28,000 km^2 with 6,042,900 people (1989) including the West Bank and Gaza Strip. Excluding the two regions, Israel is about the size of New Jersey, 21,946 km^2 (or 8,302 sq. mi.), with a population of 4,559,600 (1989).
5. The term "sector" is used due to these characteristics and also to distinguish the "sector" from the larger social group of which it is only one part (e.g., Gush Emunim—religious Jews).
6. Chapter 6 analyzes the ultra-Orthodox neighborhoods, whose population constitutes close to one-half of the spatial sector of religious neighborhoods in the urban centers. While not in full agreement with the rest of the Orthodox community, the ultra-Orthodox element represents the deepest level of the religious-secular cleavage in Israel. It thus serves here to explain not only the maximum potency of this conflict, but also as an interpretation of the implications of the conflict between the general Orthodox community (all religious neighborhoods) and the secular society. It should be noted that the development of an accurate spatial definition for all religious neighborhoods is the most difficult methodological task in comparison to all the other spatial sectors. The focus on the ultra-Orthodox concentrations provided a far more accurate spatial definition.
7. Before proceeding, it might be helpful to alert the reader to several key terms that are frequently used in this review. Key terms to be noted for conflicts of values are: rejection or acceptance of the state, rights of justice or equality, Zionism, Labor Zionism, fundamentalism, materialistic, collective, modern, and traditional. Key terms for conflicts of interests include: industry, agriculture, housing, employment or unemployment, services, class, socioeconomic status, income, occupation, educational level, and standard of living. Key terms used for politics are: power, parties, voting, coalition government, dependency on the center, legislation, Knesset members, leadership, local autonomy, and citizen participation.
8. Indeed, in March 1992 the Knesset increased the votes needed to guarantee at least one of its seats from 1 to 1.5 percent.

References

Akzin, Benjamin, and Yehezkel Dror. 1966. *Israel: High Pressure Planning.* Syracuse, N.Y.: Syracuse University Press.

Alterman, Rachelle. 1988. "Implementing Decentralization for Neighborhood Regeneration: Factors Promoting or Inhibiting Success." *Journal of the American Planning Association,* Vol. 54, No. 4:454–69.

Aronoff, Myron J. 1974. *Frontier Town: The Politics of Community Building in Israel.* Manchester: Manchester University Press.

Ben-Zadok, Efraim. 1986. "The Impact of National Characteristics on Local Citizen Participation: A Developmental Research Framework Applied to Israel." *Contemporary Jewry,* Vol. 7 (Annual): 19–42.

———. 1990. "Clusters of Communities in Israel: Conflict with Society, Development at Home." *Community Development Journal,* Vol. 25, No. 2:122–30.

Bernstein, Deborah, and Shlomo Swirski. 1982. "The Rapid Economic Development of Israel and the Emergence of the Ethnic Division of Labour." *British Journal of Sociology,* Vol. 33, No. 1:64–85.

Central Bureau of Statistics. 1976. *Statistical Abstract of Israel, 1976.* No. 27. Jerusalem: Central Bureau of Statistics.

———. 1988a. *Statistical Abstract of Israel, 1988.* No. 39. Jerusalem: Central Bureau of Statistics.

———. 1988b. *Monthly Bulletin of Statistics* Vol. 39, No. 12 (December 1988). Jerusalem: Central Bureau of Statistics. (Hebrew)

———. 1989. *Local Authorities in Israel, 1986/87 Physical Data.* Special series no. 841. Jerusalem: Central Bureau of Statistics. (Hebrew)

———. 1990. *Statistical Abstract of Israel, 1990.* No. 41. Jerusalem: Central Bureau of Statistics.

Churchman, Arza. 1987. "Issues in Resident Participation—Lessons from the Israeli Experience." *Policy Studies Journal,* Vol. 16, No. 2:290–99.

Cohen, Erik. 1974. "The Power Structure of Israeli Development Towns." In *Comparative Community Politics,* ed. T. Clark, 179–201. New York: John Wiley and Sons.

Dahl, Robert A. 1961. *Who Governs?* New Haven: Yale University Press.

Deshen, Shlomo A. 1970. *Immigrant Voters in Israel: Parties and Congregations in Local Elections Campaign.* Manchester: Manchester University Press.

Dror, Yehezkel. 1989. *Memorandum for the Israeli Prime Minister: II. To Build a State.* Jerusalem: Academon. (Hebrew)

Elazar, Daniel. 1975. "The Local Elections: Sharpening the Trend toward Territorial Democracy." In *The Elections in Israel, 1973,* ed. A. Arian, 219–37. Jerusalem: Jerusalem Academic Press.

———. 1988. "How to Achieve Electoral Reform for Israel." *Moment,* June, 30–35.

Galnoor, Itzhak. 1982. *Steering the Polity: Communication and Politics in Israel.* Beverly Hills: Sage Publications.

Goldberg, Giora. 1987. "Local Elections." In *Local Government in Israel,* ed., D. Elazar and C. Kalchaim, 89–110. Jerusalem: Jerusalem Center for Public Affairs. (Hebrew)

———. 1992. *Political Parties in Israel—From Mass Parties to Electoral Parties.* Tel Aviv: Ramot Publishing. (Hebrew)

———, and Efraim Ben-Zadok. 1983. "Regionalism and Territorial Cleavage in Formation: Jewish Settlement in the Administered Territories." *State, Government, and International Relations,* Vol. 2, (Spring): 69–94. (Hebrew)

Gottmann, J., ed. 1980. *Center and Periphery: Spatial Variation in Politics.* Beverly Hills: Sage Publications.

Gradus, Yehuda. 1983. "The Role of Politics in Regional Inequality: The Israeli Case." *Annals of the Association of American Geographers,* Vol. 73, No. 3:388–403.

———. 1984. "The Emergence of Regionalism in a Centralized System: The Case of Israel." *Environment and Planning D,* Vol. 2:87–100.

———, and Menachem Eini. 1985. "Regional Representation in the Knesset in a Proportional Representative Voting System." *City and Region,* Vol. 4, No. 4:5–21. (Hebrew)

Hechter, M. 1975. *Internal Colonialism.* London: Routledge and Kegan Paul.

Heller, Mark A., and Sari Nusseibeh. 1991. *No Trumpets, No Drums: A Two-State Settlement of the Israeli-Palestinian Conflict.* New York: Hill and Wang.

Horowitz, Dan, and Moshe Lissak. 1978. *The Origins of the Israeli Polity.* Chicago: University of Chicago Press.

———. 1985. "Authority without Sovereignty: The Case of the National Center of the Jewish Community in Palestine." In *Politics and Society in Israel,* Vol. III, ed. E. Krausz, 19–42. New Brunswick: Transaction Books.

———. 1989. *Trouble in Utopia: The Overburdened Polity of Israel.* Albany: State University of New York Press.

Hunter, Floyd. 1953. *Community Power Structure.* Chapel Hill: University of North Carolina Press.

Knutsen, Oddbjorn. 1989. "Cleavage Dimensions in Ten West European Countries: A Comparative Empirical Analysis." *Comparative Political Studies,* Vol. 21, No. 4 (January): 495–533.

Kraus, Vered, and Robert W. Hodge. 1990. *Promises in the Promised Land: Mobility and Inequality in Israel.* New York: Greenwood Press.

Liebman, Charles S. 1989. "Conceptions of 'State of Israel' in Israeli Society." *State, Government, and International Relations,* No. 30 (Winter): 51–60. (Hebrew)

Lipset, Seymour M., and Stein Rokkan. 1967. "Cleavage Structure, Party Systems, and Voter Alignments: An Introduction." In *Party Systems and*

Voter Alignments, eds. S. M. Lipset and S. Rokkan, 1–64. New York: Macmillan.

Liron, Ruth, and Shimon Spiro. 1988. "Public Participation in Planning and Management: Criteria for Evaluation and Their Application to Project Renewal." *Society and Welfare*, Vol. 9, No. 1:17–34. (Hebrew)

Mills, C. Wright. 1956. *The Power Elite*. New York: Oxford University Press.

Parsons, Talcott. 1951. *The Social System*. New York: The Free Press.

Plessner, Yakir. 1990. "Israel's Economy in the Post-Begin Era." In *Israel After Begin*, ed. G. S. Mahler, 291–306. Albany: State University of New York Press.

Rokkan, Stein, and Derek W. Urwin, eds. 1982. *The Politics of Territorial Identity: Studies in European Regionalism*. London: Sage Publications.

Shachar, Arie, and G. Lipshitz. 1981. "Regional Inequalities in Israel." *Environment and Planning A*, Vol. 13:463–73.

Shapiro, Yonathan, 1978. *Democracy in Israel*. Tel Aviv: Massada. (Hebrew)

———. 1985. "Political Sociology in Israel: A Critical View." In *Politics and Society in Israel*, Vol. III, ed. E. Krausz, 6–16. New Brunswick: Transaction Books.

Sharkansky, Ira. 1987. *The Political Economy of Israel*. New Brunswick: Transaction Books.

———. 1989. "The Overloaded State." *Public Administration Review*, Vol. 49, No. 2 (March/April): 201–4.

Shils, Edward. 1975. *Center and Periphery*. Chicago: University of Chicago Press.

Smooha, Sammy. 1978. *Israel: Pluralism and Conflict*. Berkeley: University of California Press.

———. 1988. "Internal Divisions in Israel at Forty." *Middle East Review*, Vol. 20, No. 4 (Summer): 26–36.

Sprinzak, Ehud. 1986. *A Law Unto Itself: Illegalism in Israeli Society*. Tel Aviv: Sifriyat Poalim. (Hebrew)

Swirski, Shlomo. 1981. *Orientals and Ashkenazim in Israel: The Ethnic Division of Labor*. Haifa: Mahbarot for Research and Criticism. (Hebrew)

Weiss, Shevach. 1979. *City, Region, and State: Local Government in Israel— Basic Problems*. Tel Aviv: General Federation of Labor. (Hebrew)

Yedioth, Ahronoth. 1989. March 1. (Hebrew)

Yishai, Yael. 1987. *Interest Groups in Israel: The Test of Democracy*. Tel Aviv: Am Oved Publishers. (Hebrew)

Yuchtman-Ya'ar, Efraim, and Yohanan Peres. 1991. "Public Opinion and Democracy after Three Years of Intifada." *Israeli Democracy*, Spring: 21–29.

PART I
■ The Arab-Jewish Cleavage

2 ■ Palestinians in the West Bank and the Gaza Strip: Contested Domains

Donna Robinson Divine

The conflict between Palestinians and Israelis in the West Bank and the Gaza Strip is more than a dispute over territory and the right for self-determination.[1] The Palestinians of the two regions are also ambivalent toward the modern Western values of the Jewish society. The rise of Islamic fundamentalism increases their militancy. Moreover, Palestinians and Israelis are locked in controversy over interests of economic development, water, agriculture, taxation, and fiscal management. The economy of the West Bank and the Gaza Strip is controlled by the Jewish center. Yet the static economy of the Intifada and rising unemployment forced the return to simple self-sufficient local and regional economies and less reliance on the Jewish economy.

Periods of intense conflict between Palestinians and Israelis have rarely been subjected to scrutiny in light of these issues. This essay posits the scope and intensity of conflict as the outcome of particular policies and the weakness of implementing administrative structures. An analysis of the dispute in light of institutional structures and policies may not stipulate the terms of a full resolution, but it certainly does suggest ways to mitigate hostility. In spite of the persistence of inherently conflicting political goals, the thrust of the argument presented here questions whether violence need endure.

This essay examines Israeli governance of the West Bank and the Gaza Strip and the kinds of human interactions that governance has forged. It describes the occupation policies of the Israeli government, explores their impact on the Palestinian population of the West Bank and the Gaza Strip and explains how these policies have often had unanticipated consequences. An official government policy which assumed the occupation would be temporary and minimally disruptive has turned into a prolonged period of Israeli rule. The great political

41

divide between Palestinians and Israelis has now become an economic, social, and cultural confrontation with the powers of the central government arrayed against the regions conquered in the 1967 war.

The primary impulse for the violence that has erupted periodically between Palestinians and Israelis in the territories stems from tensions produced by occupation policies. Occupation policies must heed a number of imperatives that often come into conflict with one another. Policies must serve local Palestinian interests in order to elicit support. They must contribute to the health of the Palestinian economy. Policies must also generate enough revenue to finance administrative and military operations. The precise way in which Israeli officials meet these imperatives is shaped by many factors. Among the most important are: the composition of the political coalitions on which they depend for support, the structure of the institutions which they establish to administer the occupation, and the regional and international balance of power.

Almost all policies have been unequal to the demands placed on them and have achieved far less than policymakers intended. Any policy successful at one time may be insufficient later as circumstances change, particularly as broader economic and political factors generate new problems or create new opportunities. Every regime has ended up pursuing policies which conflict with one another. Some policies, designed to reach accommodation with opposing political forces, actually stimulated increasing resistance. Often, the very policies that insured security stiffened resistance to Israeli rule. The deployment of army forces strengthens defense but also promotes political opposition. Policies intended to reduce local influence frequently provided an opening for leaders to gain prominence.

Although many Israeli policymakers typically assumed that simply by granting Palestinians access to more goods and services, a stable political order would be created, a higher standard of living has not produced a compliant population. Though policies were often effected in order to give Palestinians a choice between more goods and services without the possibility of sovereignty, on the one hand, or mobilization and risky political activities without economic security, on the other, the effects of policies could not be so closely regulated. Desirable policy consequences could be achieved—longer life-expectancy, lower infant-mortality rates—and still the harsh measures which alienated the population seemed necessary to preserve Israeli authority. By raising political consciousness, the very processes that sustained control could easily undermine security.

This essay examines Israeli occupation policies in light of strategic considerations, political goals, and administrative organization. Four distinct periods are isolated. The first is an initial period of consolidation from 1967 to 1974 where prevailing assumptions about the temporary status of the occupation shaped policies. The second period of rule, from 1974 to 1977, can be ascribed to the consequences of the 1973 war and a weakened regional position for Israel which placed the political leadership on the defensive. The third period coincides with the first term in office of Likud from 1977 to 1981 and the official endorsement of a new orientation toward the territories. The fourth period describes the civil administration from 1981 to 1987 and the administrative structures devised during that period. Thereafter, the economic and social consequences for the Palestinians are explored. The Palestinians have been subjected to substantial changes in policies and exposed, simultaneously, to dramatically different policymaking institutions. The Israeli occupation generated a sustained political crisis for Palestinians living in the West Bank and Gaza Strip. But it also provided the possibility for the emergence of new political movements and behavior. The essay concludes with an epilogue on the Intifada (December 1987–present) in light of the constraints and opportunities induced by the Israeli occupation.

CONSOLIDATING THE OCCUPATION, 1967–1974

In the immediate aftermath of the 1967 war, Israeli policymakers addressed the administration of the West Bank and Gaza Strip as a military problem. "As soon as it was occupied, the West Bank was placed under military administration, responsible to the Central Command of the Israel Defense Forces" (Lesch 1970, 5). The Military Governor was the first office established. The Labor party, which controlled the government in 1967, expected the occupation to be temporary and brief, anticipating a return of territory for peace with Jordan. However distinctive its military role, Israeli administration in the territories quickly acquired the characteristics typical of Israel's national bureaucracy: "pragmatism and an intuitive approach . . . flexibility and improvisation," with not entirely beneficial results. According to former State Controller Yitzhak Ernst Nebenzahl, Israeli bureaucracy is hindered by "a lack of respect for proper administration or at least indifference to the contribution which law and order can make to civilization" (Danet 1989, 95).

Israeli policies had the maintenance of law and order as a primary objective, but improvisation appeared the touchstone of their policy-making process. Administrative units were created and dismantled on short notice. Duties were not clearly defined. Policies were evaluated almost exclusively on the basis of cost: "Israel's security interests were linked to the territories, not to their inhabitants, and . . . Israel would not allow the territories to become a net budgetary burden" (Sandler 1988, 51).

The hierarchy of military authority started with the minister of defense and the chief of staff. Initial arrangements reposed enormous power on the minister of defense. In order to contain that power, the government established a ministerial committee on the occupied territories under the supervision of the minister of finance. The civil service staff for the administration came from various governmental ministries all of whom officially retained their original ministerial affiliations and responsibilities. In the early years of occupation, the civilian staff was relatively small (Lesch 1970, 11). A chain of command was effected with authority dispersed between military administration and the several ministries of government. Few legal restrictions constrained the authority of the military governor, whose powers have been compared to those of a head of state (Peretz 1986, 79). Underscoring the temporary nature of the Israeli occupation but contributing to the discretionary power of the military governor, no fully elaborated system of rule was introduced. The government applied Jordanian law unless superseded by subsequent decrees. Peretz (1986, 81) observes that the enormous number of military orders has "the cumulative effect of new legislation . . . [and] . . . provide[s] a record of legislation that many a parliament might envy." Given the overlap in administrative responsibilities and the absence of a consensus on the final status of the territories or on a political strategy for negotiating their return to Jordan, vital decisions could be taken at many levels, and they were.

On some issues, the power of individual ministers to forge policies was almost absolute. Minister of defense during the crucial first years of the Israeli occupation, Moshe Dayan often had a paramount role in the making of policies. For Dayan, employment, cash, and a substantial improvement in living conditions constituted the best safeguard against the mounting of a serious, broad-based Palestinian challenge to Israeli military control (Nisan 1978, 70; Yishai 1987, 65). Dayan introduced the concept of "open bridges" to insure that trade with Jordan and via Jordan to other Arab countries would continue unhampered. Jordan cooperated and benefited from this venture to the point where at least one scholar designated the first decade of the occupation "the joint control system" (Sandler 1988, 49).

Comparable policies were put into effect for the Gaza Strip but with dramatically different results. Spared destruction, the Gaza economy, nevertheless, suffered from the war's decimating consequences because its trade ties with Egypt were instantly severed. For almost twenty years under Egyptian rule, Gaza had depended on the export of citrus and its status as a free port (Roy 1986, 1). Opportunities for economic growth were limited. The Israeli conquest cut off Gaza's markets and banned its unregulated trade activities. These changes took their toll; the fortunes of its richest merchants declined (Roy 1986, 2). Dayan's policy of encouraging Israeli employers to provide jobs for Palestinians was born of his hope to ameliorate the poverty in the refugee camps in Gaza, and thereby dampen the discontent of their residents. No Israeli policymakers addressed the economic interests of the wealthy or the middle class.

Benvenisti's (1984, 44–45) depiction of an absolutely centralized administration, molded to serve Dayan's policy of nonintervention, is understandable but still exaggerated. Dayan may have been known as the "king of the territories," but his power was not without its limits or its contradictions. Many policies—on water resources, press censorship, education, political activities, the scope and nature of Jewish settlements—reflected input from a number of ministries and agencies. These policies, touching the jurisdiction of several ministries, were hammered out in the Interministerial Committee on the Occupied Territories. "Along with the task of coordination, [that committee] also served, under certain ministers, as a means of limiting the absolute rule of the Minister of Defense in the territories, particularly the activities of Moshe Dayan as minister of defense" (Benvenisti 1986b, 63). When the interministerial committee rejected Dayan's proposal to issue a general permit to private individuals and corporations to purchase land in the territories, it also circumscribed the power of his office. The autonomy conceded to the Ministry of Defense had enabled Dayan to introduce substantial changes in the territories as a matter of maintaining order. The interministerial committee's refusal to accede to Dayan's proposal signaled the beginning of a new system of controls over his activities in the territories with policy proposals considered in light of their impact on political party interests.

It is important to note that while many of Dayan's actions evinced sensitivity to the human needs of the Palestinians, many did not. True, he granted concessions to Palestinian teachers and accorded local educational institutions substantial curricular freedom, but he also severely punished those who disrupted the school routine. Dayan's efforts to build bridges of communication between Israeli authorities and Palestinians coincided with his enforcement of measures, such as collective punishments and the demolition of houses, considered an anathema by the majority of the Palestinians. Thus although Dayan regarded his administration as sensitive to the legitimate needs and demands of the local population, he supported policies which according to Palestinians menaced their way of life. Moreover, he endorsed and facilitated a qualified expansion of Jewish settlement in the territories.

Nevertheless, under what was frequently referred to as a benign occupation, Israeli policies, in many respects, improved the quality of life for Palestinians. The standard of living for Palestinians rose in the first decade of the occupation. What would matter to Palestinians, according to Israeli policymakers at this time, was not whether it was an occupation, but rather whether it was a ruthless or intolerable occupation. Israelis spoke of their occupation with pride and stressed its bountiful consequences. The number of paved roads increased. Others were widened and improved. Electricity and telephone service were delivered to almost all villages. More schools were opened, followed by the founding of five universities and several vocational institutes. On the West Bank alone the student population doubled. Advances in health conditions were marked and resulted from "the introduction of advanced medical technology and expertise provided by Israeli medical teams; the expansion of existing training facilities for local Arab medical teams; the establishment of new hospitals, medical centers, nursing schools and paramedical schools; the training of local Arabs in Israeli hospitals; the introduction of new equipment; the expansion of immunization programs, the establishment of school health services; the collection of information on contagious diseases; the improvement of sanitation systems; the installation of running water; and the establishment of mother-and-child health care centers" (State of Israel, Ministry of Defence, Coordinator of Government Operations in Judea-Samaria and the Gaza District 1983, 27). During the first decade of Israeli rule, "the GNP increased three-fold in Judea-Samaria and 3.4-fold in Gaza. Israel's GNP increased only 1.4-fold in the same period, with an average annual rate of 8–9 percent in fixed prices, while the annual per capita increase was 7.85 percent. Private per capita income more than doubled during the same period, in real terms" (State of Israel, Ministry of Defence, Coordinator of Government Operations in Judea-Samaria and the Gaza District 1983, 3–4).

Unemployment, which had hovered around 50 percent under the Jordanians, was reduced, with villagers and refugees gaining access to large cash remittances as a result of the availability of work for unskilled laborers in Israel. Sociologist Salim Tamari (1981, 56) spelled out the advantages for the rural hinterland: "In Ras al-Tin, for example, an average peasant family used to eat meat once a month in the sixties; today, once or twice a week. An average worker used to buy a new pair of trousers every year; today each worker has between five and eight pairs. There has also been a substantial increase in the number of durable goods in peasant households (in 1979, thirty percent of all Ras al-Tin households had TV sets, run on small generators and on batteries)."

That same study formed the basis for Tamari's conclusion that Palestinians prefer to work in Israel and face what he called a "daily routine of national humiliation [rather] than work for an Arab employer in the West Bank . . . [at] equal wages [because in Israel] payment for jobs takes place promptly and according to the conditions stipulated in the written contract" (Tamari 1981, 48–49). Despite the loss of land to Jewish settlements, to this day Palestinians have been able to hold on to all their cultivated land. Despite the determination of a segment of the Israeli power elite, the formal status of the West Bank (except for East Jerusalem) and Gaza territories remained unaltered.

Although hardly grateful for the bounties bestowed upon them, Palestinians seemed to find in many Israeli policies the means to strengthen their own cultural and social institutions. Censorship may have banned "books by the thousands" (Said 1989, 24), but the number and circulation of newspapers and journals increased (Shinar 1987, 41). Many Palestinians found in popular literature a calling in harmony both with their own political spirit and that of the times. The expansion of the school system created the need for more teachers and a zeal for education (Anabtawi 1986). The reliance of the military government upon the mayor and town or city council to disburse funds for local agricultural development or for the improvement of roads and services imposed on these offices both an unprecedented burden of political responsibility and for the first time, considerable authority (Lesch 1970, 32). The stimulating effect of the occupation on these offices became clear even before the municipal elections in

1976 when candidates proved their worth by identifying with the Palestine Liberation Organization.

RELAXED CONTROL, 1974–1977

The shifting of power relationships within the Labor party eventually activated new administrative arrangements for the territories. Moshe Dayan left office in 1974 tarnished by public dissatisfaction with the military's performance in the 1973 war. The circumstances of his departure had the effect of unsettling administration in the territories and weakening Israel's status in the territories. Competition between factions and rivals within Israel's ruling Labor party erupted into open quarrels and eroded the government's capacity to take decisive action. Taking advantage of political divisions, Jewish militants in the newly founded Gush Emunim mounted protests to compel the government to build more Jewish settlements on the West Bank. When the government did not respond, people affiliated with the movement occupied land often in areas densely populated by Arabs. Jewish militants generally stood their ground even against military troops sent out to dismantle their settlements, forcing the government to bow to many of their demands.

At the same time, the 1974 Arab summit in Rabat accorded the Palestine Liberation Organization (PLO) status as the sole, legitimate representative of the Palestinian people. The organization assumed a more commanding presence and its prestige in the territories climbed. The impression of a hesitant and ambivalent Israeli political leadership reinforced the PLO's position. With enhanced legitimacy and a substantial endowment, the PLO disbursed funds for local development. The altered regional balance of power and wealth elicited a more resolute behavior from local Palestinian leaders. The developments gave rise to what Moshe Ma'oz (1984, 117) called "the gravest wave of violent demonstrations and riots, school and business strikes . . . [which] also involved the blocking of roads, stoning of IDF soldiers, and the use of explosives against Israeli targets." Palestinian political leaders may not have had a single goal in mind, but they did assume the existence of shared economic interests. Mayors and local town councilors began to refrain from requesting funds from the Israeli budget for local municipal or town expenses. They turned to external Arab sources—the Arab oil producing states or the PLO—for financial grants. With its own fiscal problems creating the need for budgetary retrenchment after the 1973 war, the Israeli government readily accommodated the increased Palestinian desire for financial autonomy. The emphasis placed by the PLO on the situation in the territories, which assumed an unprecedented prominence, signaled promise for challenging the status quo. From the Palestinian perspective, Israel, in the aftermath of its second war in six years, seemed to be in a mood of retrenchment.

THE LIKUD'S FIRST TERM OF OFFICE: 1977–1981

The 1977 elections shook the confidence of Palestinians in the territories. In an atmosphere charged with militance, Israel brought to power a political party determined to retain the West Bank. But the rise to power in 1977 of the Likud in spite of its explicit endorsement of the historic right of the Jewish people to sovereignty over the West Bank, injected less rather than more clarity into Israeli occupation policies. Leading members of the government did not hold identical views on how to rule the territories, particularly during the Likud's first term of office from 1977 until 1981. Menachem Begin, prime minister and founder of the Herut movement, affirmed the principle of Jewish entitlement to the land of Israel without insisting that the political status of the territories be formally altered. Ezer Weizman, minister of defense until 1980, was prepared to make territorial concessions in return for peace. Ariel Sharon did not join the 1977 Likud coalition in support of expanding Jewish settlements, and it took him some time as minister of agriculture to revamp his ministry's budget in order to underwrite the expansion of Jewish settlements in the West Bank. Israeli policymakers did not speak with one voice on the subject of the occupation, and bureaucratic practices only escalated inconsistencies in lines of policy.

Occupation policies were no longer anchored primarily in the Ministry of Defense. New political circumstances had enhanced the power of staff officers as policymakers which formed the basis of Benvenisti's (1986b, 198) conclusion that "staff officers exercise the authority of the Jordanian crown, cabinet, judicial system, statutory authorities, and have supervisory authority over statutory and other bodies, including the power to enact by-laws." Unrest in the territories was met by a great variety of policy responses. Minister of Defense Ezer Weizman interpreted political developments in the territories— even the violence—as stemming from a legitimate impulse for more power. Orders were issued to relax political controls and permit Palestinians to create more grassroots organizations (Ma'oz 1984, 180). In contrast, staff officers sought to induce political restraint by curtailing privileges and by compelling Palestinians to endure more stringent fiscal controls and bear the harsher discipline of a new administrative order. Their administrative authority to issue rules and regulations began to acquire a punitive aspect. The issuance of licenses and permits was delayed in order to impose hardships on vocal and articulate opponents of the occupation. Export permits were rescinded for agricultural products grown in areas where anti-Israel violence erupted (Graham-Brown 1983, 188).

THE CIVIL ADMINISTRATION, 1981–1987

In March 1981, Israel introduced a civilian administration in addition to the military government with the declared purpose of "preparing the ground for the implementation of the autonomy of residents plan endorsed by the Camp David Accords" (Benvenisti 1986b, 23). To this view was counterposed a cynical interpretation of the civil administration as an attempt to forestall "American-Egyptian pressure to implement the West Bank autonomy proposals stipulated in the Camp David Accords" (Tamari 1983, 42). Whatever the intention of its architects, the civil administration's three branches—economics, administration and services, and resources and taxes—required a larger number of staff officers and significantly broadened their activities. The ministries accepted responsibilities once assumed in an ad hoc way by the military government. The military government transferred all power to establish guidelines on water usage to Mekorot, the Israeli Water Company. Supplying credit for irrigation passed from the offices of the military governor to the ministry of agriculture which had authority to stipulate budgetary expenditures for agricultural development in the territories. The Ministry of Social Welfare supervised the programs sponsored by foreign countries and international agencies. These organizations—some religiously affiliated, some run by the United Nations, and others by the American government or private American philanthropies—had both challenged Israeli hegemony in the territories and were vulnerable to it. Decisions by the Social Welfare Ministry staff redirected funds to or away from specific groups depending on the calculated political impact of their activities.

On the explosive problem of the availability of land for Jewish settlements, aggressive activities by the Ministry of Agriculture replaced
the modest role assumed earlier by the Ministry of the Interior. For
Palestinians, no issue was more sensitive than that of land acquisition.
Before 1977, the military government had used the strategic approach
of the Allon Plan as its reference base for confiscations, and the number of Jewish settlements had remained small and generally confined
to sparsely populated areas (Benvenisti 1984, 31). Jewish settlements,
set up outside of the plan's directives and without permission, were
typically declared illegal by the Israeli courts, dismantled, and/or
moved. In the first decade of occupation, Palestinians successfully
used the Israel High Court of Justice to challenge confiscations that
could not be justified for security purposes or public need. In effect,
when Labor controlled the government, Israeli legal institutions
helped secure Palestinian entitlement to land, even in the absence of
formal records and deeds.

After the 1977 elections brought the Likud to power, the party
introduced a change in the regulations governing land acquisition
which made it much less likely that Palestinians could take to the
courts for redress. Reaffirming the Jewish right to stewardship over
these lands, the government proclaimed "all land as national patri-
mony, except what the [Arab] villagers can prove is theirs under the
narrowest interpretation of the law" (Benvenisti, 1984, 32). This
policy subjected over two-thirds of the land on the West Bank to the
possibility of seizure. Only visible signs of cultivation inhibited con-
fiscation. Responding to the hunger for private property as well as
to its own creed warranting the historic right of the Jewish people to
settle the land of Israel, the Likud also lifted its restrictions against
private land purchases in September 1979. Israeli land speculators
bought tens of thousands of acres of Arab land. The strong market for
land sales promoted further administrative expansion because the interest in land purchases suggested that government policies could have
an impact on the size of the Jewish population in the territories. Staff
officers from the ministries of Housing and Agriculture, as well as
representatives from the Jewish Agency produced a number of blue-
prints to attract Jews to the territories. The term "settlements" may
"nowhere be found in annual budget proposals," but expenditures for
Jewish settlements increased dramatically and were dispersed by "all
government ministries" (Yishai 1987, 33).[2] The eruption of a national
scandal over land sales in the territories only obliged the government

to undertake more supervision and increase its intervention in the affairs of the territories. The Ministry of Justice set more rigorous standards for private land sales and assumed more administrative responsibilities.

During the Likud's second term (1981–84), Jews in the territories won new rights as well as privileges from the Likud-led government. Israeli law was formally extended to Jewish settlers in the territories. Their status as citizens of a Jewish state was no longer compromised by their residence in an area under military control. This measure facilitated the organization of municipal and regional councils which were then quickly invested with local authority. Ministerial programs were crafted and refined under the guidance of these local Jewish councils. With funds from the ministries of education and social welfare, the Jews built local institutions. In addition to their newly transformed status, Jewish settlements continued to enjoy special privileges. Subsidies for housing and education were earmarked for Jewish settlements. The cost of public services from water usage to electricity was lower for Jewish settlers than for their Palestinian neighbors. As frontier outposts, military obligations could be discharged by guard duty in the settlements, an incentive for orthodox Jews whose religious needs often deterred them from completing regular army service.

The Likud sought to effect a self-rule compatible with the continuation of the Israeli occupation. Ultimately, the civil administration rested not only on administrative arrangements but was grounded in particular economic and political conditions. Israeli occupation policies, once justified in light of strategic considerations and the economic rewards it bestowed upon the Palestinians population, acquired a new purpose.

Menachem Milson, the first chief of the civil administration, conceived the new approach in consideration of what he called the failure of the old stance of nonintervention. He attributed the rise of PLO influence in the territories to Israel's political passivity. Milson (1981) stressed the importance of assembling support for the occupation. Instead of reacting to events, he urged the government to take the initiative and enlist allies. Milson wanted to bring together those segments of the Palestinian population whose interests differed from those of the militant nationalist supporters of the PLO, and whose aims could be met, he claimed, without diluting Israeli control over the territories. Milson contended that patronage could be manipulated to serve Israeli interests. To the extent that Palestinians could help their friends and families and inflict harm on their enemies, they could be induced to back the Israeli occupation. Juxtaposing village and urban elites as irreconcilable political opponents, Milson identified the former as potentially amenable to serving Israeli political purposes. Milson further suggested the organization of village leaders into a regional network of Village Leagues and, in order to assure their credibility as leaders, gave a ringing endorsement to their empowerment.

The civil administration conveyed economic benefits to village leaders and also influence over the issuance of drivers' licenses, family reunion permits, travel passes to Jordan, and authorization for new construction. Village League members had the right to bear arms and arbitrate local disputes. Their intercession on behalf of prisoners carried weight with Israeli authorities. In order to function as patrons and deliver services to their clients in the villages, however, the group required substantial long-term financing. In this regard, Milson had in mind a sizable development budget for villages. He argued that the delivery of goods and services to villages could be made to yield political benefits. Roads could be built with security considerations in mind. Electricity could be brought to villages and towns under the aegis of the Israel Electric Authority. After the establishment of the civil administration, a more pronounced pattern of Israeli involvement in the internal affairs of the Palestinian population could be discerned.

Milson failed to take into account the Likud's determination to expand the Jewish population in the territories and the financial consequences of such a settlement policy. The common need for government support opposed the interests of Jewish settlements and Palestinian villages. In the competition for relatively scarce resources, Palestinian villagers ultimately waged a losing battle. On the particularly scarce resource of water, the interest of Jewish settlers almost always prevailed over those of Palestinians. Funds allotted by the PLO for the territories were blocked, but no comparable domestic resources existed to compensate for the lost revenues. Stringent Israeli budgetary cutbacks eventually worsened conditions and threatened both projects and jobs. The interplay of economic and political forces and sporadic violence convinced Israeli policymakers to dismiss the mayors of several large towns and cities, who supported the PLO and were seen as doing too little to combat terrorism. Their dismissal and the subsequent failure to find replacements aggravated the general economic disorder. Finally, the Village Leagues could never command respect unless they had the power to deny land for Jewish settlements.

On this point, the Likud could not break faith with its own political principles by agreeing to limit the historic right of the Jewish people to the land of Israel.

The Israeli occupation not only produced serious policy contradictions; it also triggered opposition between administrative structures. The amount of property utilized for Jewish settlements or the acceptable cost of holding these territories was often determined on the basis of distinct institutional interests and goals. Staff officers tried to breathe life into the civil administration by expecting to elicit full cooperation from Palestinians for their policies. Military governors generally had compliance in mind when they issued regulations.

On the issue of law and order, the asymmetry of military and civil administrative approaches was particularly striking. Undaunted by the emergence of political dissent within the Village League association, military officials allowed the formation of the Democratic Movement for Peace whose charter called for "internationally supervised elections in the West Bank and Gaza to determine the true leaders of Palestine" (Tamari 1983, 387). When the movement's leader, Mohammed Nasr, tried to hold a conference, however, civil administrator, Shlomo Ilya, had him and his close advisors arrested.

How the placement, if not the very existence of Jewish settlements, fits along the grip of a low-cost stable occupation was never fully determined. Policymakers were absorbed by issues of security, but there were serious differences over whether Jewish settlements compromised or strengthened Israel's defense. Citing experiences in Israel's earlier wars, particularly in 1947–48, some policymakers insisted that a Jewish population in the territories created a first line of defense against an invasion of Israel's population centers. Others challenged this view. Building their case on the need to evacuate Jewish settlers from the Golan Heights in the 1973 war, these policymakers claimed that such a defense network was now militarily obsolete: "In an era of modern warfare that includes Soviet advanced missiles such as FROG and Scud, border settlements can hardly arrest the enemy's advance. There are also women and children living in the settlements who have to be hastily evacuated" (Yishai 1987, 31).

Nor was a policy consensus ever forged on how to maintain law and order in the territories. Demonstrations have provoked authorities to close down schools on the West Bank while in the Gaza Strip the local school system is considered as having a limited effect on the outbreaks of violence directed against Israeli rule. Municipal elections have been held on the West Bank but never in the Gaza Strip. There are also striking inconsistencies with respect to currency regulations. The policy process seems beset by conflicting goals and procedures. The contrast in administrative agendas has distinct consequences for Palestinians. Palestinians have no representation in Israel's parliament nor can they elect officials to Israel's highest offices of state. No formal government channel permits them to press for budgetary funds to meet their needs. No wonder Palestinians have been unable to acknowledge the legitimacy of any one of the institutions involved in the occupation. However, they have been able at times to play one administrative structure against the other. While each institutional branch of the occupation is viewed as an instrument of oppression, Palestinians have developed techniques for utilizing the authority and policy interests of some institutions to protect possessions, livelihoods, and resources. The multiplicity of administrative structures and aims has forced many Palestinians to concentrate on particular economic or social issues. It has also enabled them to find in the context of the occupation the means for communal survival. Occupation policies may have inhibited Palestinians in their capacity to organize on a regional basis, but they have encouraged active involvement at a local level.

The creation of the civil administration broadened the influence of organized interests in determining Israel's occupation policies. Ministries in Israel have traditionally been allied with specific economic interests and have endorsed policies to accommodate them. Some of Israel's major interests enjoy access to ministries responsible for the occupation: citrus cultivators, textile manufacturers, and producers of durable goods. As their responsibility for the occupation grew, ministries have had the opportunity and the tendency to consider proposals with respect to their impact on their constituents. The longer the occupation has lasted the more its policies were bent to the service of Israeli economic interests.

Although policies never embraced the idea of developing the economy of the territories, policies came increasingly to reflect private Israeli interests as opposed to the Palestinian public sector. Agricultural products from the territories can be sold in Israeli markets only with a permit issued by the relevant agency. Pressure has been applied to insure that agricultural goods grown in the territories do not flood Israeli markets. Israeli grape cultivators in 1981 convinced the Israel Fruit Council to withdraw a permit from Hebron grape cultivators to sell their fruit in Israel (Graham-Brown 1983, 188). Water usage is fixed at the 1967 level which constrains agricultural production. The additional limits placed on the export and sale of fruits and vegetables have an extremely adverse impact on agricultural conditions and are responsible for the general economic stagnation in the territories, particularly since 1977. Problems created by Israeli policies are particularly acute for the Gaza Strip which possesses few natural resources and limited opportunities for growth. Restrictions are placed on manufactured products which might undersell items already produced in Israel. By contrast, goods manufactured in Israel have privileged access to markets in the territories.

Israel has allowed normal contacts between Palestinians and Jordanian officials or private businessmen and hence permitted the unrestricted flow of Arab capital into the territories. Fiscal policies, however, imposed constraints on banking services which operated to impede large-scale agricultural improvements and almost all significant industrial development. "The number of workers employed in industry has remained constant at 15,000 since 1970. In 1984 only 9,550 (9% of the total employed in the West Bank) were employed in industrial plants. . . . Of 2,000 enterprises only five employ more than 100 workers" (Benvenisti 1986a, 112). Numerous financial barriers blocked the formation of industries whose products might compete with Israeli manufactures. Political circumstances and confining economic policies combined to direct investment funds into the service sector.

The intersection of Israeli political and economic interests impelled Palestinians to respond in kind and use political stratagems to attain economic objectives. For Palestinians, Israeli administrative regulations were nothing more than political weapons wielded by the Israeli government against their struggle for independence. Palestinians amassed their own political arsenal. Their international leverage has been mobilized to extract concessions from Israel. Palestinians found allies in the highest offices of the world's most powerful states who were able to dispense lucrative benefits through international agencies or foreign aid programs.

Recent decisions of the European Economic Commission (EEC) have sustained in Palestinians the conviction of the correlation between political and economic power. After years of negotiation, Palestinians have won the right to export citrus products and avocadoes directly, outside of Israeli marketing agencies, to the EEC. Written agreements between the Israeli government and two independent Palestinian agricultural organizations established the terms of this European trade. The successful conclusion of Israel's own lucrative and vital agreements with the EEC depended on its willingness to accede to Palestinian demands. "Clearly, there had been a quid pro quo, and the European Economic Commission and the government of Israel were eager to move ahead and normalize their relationship" (Laufer 1989, 17).

ECONOMIC AND SOCIAL CONSEQUENCES OF OCCUPATION

Israeli political leaders have always assumed their governance posed no critical threat to Palestinian society and culture. But so central has the occupation become to the collective consciousness of Palestinians, that social changes were bound to occur in its wake. Even when the same people dominated local affairs, political behavior changed. But for the most part, the occupation marked the emergence of new faces and classes in politics. The political class became less socially homogeneous. Politics was no longer the domain of the landowners. Professionals and merchants were prominent in the cities. Combinations of old and young ran the villages. The political class was not just new relative to the men who held positions under the Jordanian regime; the class was repeatedly renewed as occupation policies foreclosed regionwide activities and narrowed political opportunities to local areas. The opening of the Israeli economy to Palestinian labor provided cash to a marginal sector of the population and afforded their families new opportunities. Expanded trade increased the standard of living in the villages.

If Israeli rule has not heralded the dawn of a new age for the Palestinian population in the territories, it has disrupted old traditions. Israel granted Palestinian women access to both the vote and jobs which they had never possessed. In rural areas, women may be in charge of tasks never before entrusted to them. Village women must fill the economic gaps men leave behind when they go off to work in Israel. If the occupation has not dispossessed men from their patriarchal primacy, it has certainly weakened the mechanisms through which they once exercised their control. Inspired by exposure to a new set of freedoms, women have founded more voluntary organizations than ever before. They felt as much need as Palestinian men to challenge Israeli authority. Their resolute behavior in the many strikes and demonstrations has been sharply etched in the minds of Palestinians. "During the Intifada [uprising in the territories which began on December 1987 in Gaza]," Edward Said (1989, 38) has written, "women came to the fore as equal partners in the struggle. They confronted Israel [male] troops; they shared in decision-making; they were no longer left at home, or given menial tasks, but they did what the men did, without fear or complexes. Perhaps it would be still more accurate to say that because of the Intifada the role of men was altered, from being dominant to being equal."

At the outset of occupation, the West Bank and the Gaza Strip were traditional societies based on an agrarian economy, with the family pivotal as a social institution. A commercial and service sector operated in some of the larger cities, notably Jerusalem and Gaza, where tourists provided foreign exchange. A small manufacturing sector existed, stemming from the processing of food and raw materials. Lacking significant investment, the industrial base did not expand during the period of Jordanian rule.

Israel's policies have cast Palestinians into the throes of modernization without a corresponding economic development. Agriculture has declined, its contribution to the gross domestic product was decreasing since 1983. "The value of agricultural production in 1984 was about $250 million, compared with about $300 million in 1983 and $320 million in 1982" (Benvenisti 1986a, 1). The bulk of the population is no longer employed on the land and the land no longer confers security or necessarily designates position (Tamari 1981, 43). A number of factors now influence the composition of the elite. Money confers power. Property no longer guarantees status (Tamari 1981). Because of cash remittances from Jordan and the PLO to municipalities and social service organizations, political considerations have an important bearing on material well-being, opportunities, and influence. The projects funded by external sources sometimes comprise the only jobs commensurate with training or skill for professionals and skilled workers, all of whom have few employment opportunities in the territories and virtually none in Israel. Participation in social service organizations provides access to funds. The compartmentalization of organizations into pro-Jordanian and pro-PLO does not do justice to the interplay between them with respect to economic or social consequences (Ibrahim 1989, 1 and 12). Boundary lines between them are fluid. International agencies have also contributed to the improvement of conditions in the territories. They, too, acknowledge the link between the workers' economic conditions and their anomalous political circumstances.

Although occupation policies have enabled many Palestinians to earn high wages, the triumph of a higher standard of living was not without its darker consequences. Opportunities for unskilled labor are far greater than for professional or skilled workers. But "workers who depended on intermittent piecework inside Israel for their livelihood faced daily reminders of their subservient status; they were paid less than Jewish workers, they had no union to support them, they were required to be kept under lock and key anytime they stayed overnight inside the Green Line" (Said 1989, 24). The occupation has significantly increased wages for Palestinian villagers, but they work and live in an atmosphere charged with social tension. Many Palestinians have become subcontractors, responsible for finding employment and laborers. The subcontractor's profit depends on his contacts with Israeli employers and his ability to estimate time requirements for the job as well as to project its final costs. On construction sites, Palestinians have little contact with Israelis, but they are immersed in its modern consumer society (Tamari 1981, 49). By providing employment particularly in the construction sector or service economy to relatively underdeveloped areas, Israeli policies could not preserve traditional Palestinian hierarchies or organizations.

The Israeli occupation set the Palestinian population in motion. Palestinians have been uprooted from their land, homes, work habits, and customs. The lure of cash salaries has drawn peasants away from working the land and into Jewish cities where they have had to contend with the disorienting effects of an open consumer society. Palestinians may have found employment opportunities in modern, industrialized settings, but they have also been exposed to life-styles and secular values which appear foreign and threatening. By transporting Palestinians into this new world, the Jewish state also seems to bear some responsibility for weakening the force of sacred tradition.

For Palestinians, education and employment in Israel were the only ways to fulfill their ambitions and meet their daily needs. Both options could leave them without security and with unsatisfactory employment. The one might lead to jobs not commensurate with educational achievement; the other offered income but was insufficient to assure status. Villagers often utilized their new incomes to give their children an education, but which increasingly failed to improve their earning potential. "Workers . . . net an average monthly wage of 5,000 pounds, from which nothing is deducted since they are not registered workers. This should be compared to the salary of a school

teacher in the West Bank holding a B.A. degree, which amounted during the same period to 4,000–5,000 pounds per month" (Tamari
1981, 48). Still, a formal education became not only the core but also
the common experience of the Palestinian young in village and city.
Under the auspices of Israeli rule, "students [might be] . . . forced to
endure the extended closing of schools and universities" (Said 1989,
24), but their education furnished them with a shared political language and a new sense of community.

Population growth and dramatically improved conditions have
spawned a society with many more young than old (Benvenisti and
Khayat 1988, 27). The expansion of schools at all levels has generated
dramatically different life-cycle experiences for young and old. Most
of the male population under the age of twenty has spent or will spend
a considerable amount of time in nonfamilial settings. Households or
extended family networks no longer comprise the only domain where
crucial interactions occur.

For young Palestinians, schools and youth movements have become principal arenas for forging political and social outlooks. A
static local economy in the West Bank or the Gaza Strip had induced
those with high school or college diplomas to leave their homes long
before the advent of Israeli rule. Emigration to other Arab states had
always served as an outlet for a population which could not be fully
absorbed by its domestic economy. Many work in Israel; many who
do not work at all have acquired the kind of education which in the
past guaranteed them high prestige jobs in government or the service
sector. Occupation policies offered possibilities for personal enrich-
ment and a higher standard of living, but they did not expand the
range of personal opportunities for Palestinian society. Population increases overwhelmed limited resources. There was less room on the
land and in the cities for the surplus population coming of age under
Israeli rule. No wonder that the occupation was viewed as the primary
reason for economic distress and social disorganization.

Schools have increasingly taken on the task of transmitting Palestinian identity. But the line of thinking which suggests that students
and graduates have weakened their ties with Israeli society and government is misleading. Their very attendance at school has brought
them into contact with the Israeli government in the territories. Although there is a growing population of Palestinians with a strong nationalist commitment, it must also be acknowledged that this
population has been more involved than its forebears with Israeli
bureaucracy.

The housing shortage exemplifies the changes in Palestinian society and captures the central predicament of the occupation. Traditional Palestinian households often contained several generations. Limited economic opportunities made it understandably difficult and costly for newly married couples to build their own separate dwelling. For most Palestinians, the long wait for a home of their own could easily be legitimized by tradition. Palestinians have always turned their houses into symbols of value. A house confers status on its owner; it signifies position. The building of a house measures the unity in village or among kin who contribute essential labor or material (Tamari 1981, 41–42). Higher education, restricted to a small segment of the privileged under the Jordanian regime, nevertheless, provided access to privileged jobs and a home of one's own.

In contrast, the Israeli occupation altered life trajectories for Palestinians. It expanded the opportunities for a university education without enhancing the prospects for employment or for self-sufficiency. Many Palestinians now interpret their large extended households as symbols of deprivation. They are discontent because of the asymmetry between their impoverished villages and the expensive housing developments in nearby Jewish settlements. "The standard of living of Palestinians in the West Bank remained relatively high, but at the same time lower than the Israeli standard of living by a ratio of 4:1" (Benvenisti 1986a, 199). The standard of living has not improved at all since 1980.

EPILOGUE: THE INTIFADA

The crisis which erupted in the territories in December, 1987 is not simply a battle for land. It is also a political and economic struggle. Its origins lie in a set of changes Palestinians have experienced during the Israeli occupation which led to significant population growth and substantial economic upheaval. The population growth combined with drastically reduced numbers emigrating to other lands placed pressure on local resources at the same time that international and domestic political factors have weakened Israel's own capacity to meet these demands.

If the impulse for the Intifada originated in a spontaneous outrage against the conditions of the occupation and the sense of being manipulated by Israeli authorities, the demonstrations and the violence have not simply been unplanned explosions of anger. The Intifada has been sustained by careful though limited organization. The local focus in village and neighborhood has proved to be its source of strength. The protestors are school comrades, neighbors, and kin, all of whom have multiple ties with one another. The population has been tutored in the amenities of nation-building through Israeli policies and through participation in local voluntary groups and societies. "Is it not the fear that the Palestinians in the territories will build a voluntary communal structure, modeled on the embryo Zionist state under the British, that impels Israelis to close down labour unions and women's associations, and arrest voluntary activists?" (Benvenisti 1989, 18).

The political aspirations behind the Intifada have been forged in the modern world, but the mode of organization is highly traditional. In order to sustain their struggle, Palestinians have had to try to reconstruct their age-old economies: self-sufficient household farms with little reliance on the market for manufactured goods. Yet the struggle is conducted by means of the most modern of technologies, utilizing television, video, and xerox facilities to communicate demands and coordinate political activities. Even Palestinian militants have become attuned to the virtues of the "newsbite" and concerted political action.

If political opportunities created by the Intifada still seem too distant to realize, the economic effects for both Israelis and Palestinians have been immediate. The Intifada has disrupted life in the territories and forced Israel to pay a higher cost for its occupation. Financial burdens have replaced economic benefits. By appealing to common political aspirations and shared national grievances, Palestinian laborers have heeded periodic calls for strikes and have been able to cause considerable dislocation to the Israeli economy. Israeli manufacturers have felt the pinch of a declining market in the territories and reduced purchasing power for Israeli goods. It may be totally outside the realm of political possibility for Palestinians to force an Israeli withdrawal from the territories, but they have been able to shift the burdens of occupation in spite of their lower socioeconomic status, rising unemployment, and scarce resources.

The Intifada has not fostered a united front among the several institutions responsible for the occupation. A chastened and more sober political, military, and administrative leadership has not meant one more united in political orientation or in policy implementation. Soldiers have been deployed in greater numbers to curtail political activities. The minister of defense until 1990, Yitzhak Rabin, architect of what has been described as the rough treatment meted out by soldiers, also endorsed the need for a political resolution of the conflict and of elections.

Unrest in the territories arose from both occupation policies and a framework of Israeli rule which never achieved even conditional acceptance from the Palestinian population. Authority was fragmented among several civil and military institutions, none of which provided Palestinians an arena in which to press for their own interests. Over time, Israeli offices of state became less accessible to Palestinians. Without a transformation of local structures of power, it is difficult to imagine ending the current wave of violence. The drama of the Intifada in its first months has now given way to a routine of civil unrest which has persisted far beyond the worst nightmare of Israeli political leaders.

The West Bank and the Gaza Strip territories may be contested domains, but domains can be contested in different ways. For the confrontation to soften, power must be decentralized in such a way as to accord Palestinians some measure of control over their own lives. Undoubtedly from the perspective of many members of the Likud, a decentralized framework of authority, based on the 1979 Israeli-Egyptian Autonomy Agreements, threatens the hope of expanding the Jewish population in the territories. But the increasing economic toll of the uprising has lowered that hope by substantially raising the cost of building Jewish settlements. If reposing authority over land and other resources saddles Jewish settlers with many constraints, it also affords Palestinians the prospect of exercising control over local and scarce resources.

Plagued by economic uncertainty, fiscal distress, and a lack of consensus, the Israeli occupation faces a problematic future. However painful the impasse, the Intifada has also presented new political opportunities. By their very unanticipated success in transforming the economic structure of the territories, Israeli occupation policies have also dissolved the social bases upon which traditional alliances were built and maintained. New leaders have come of age during Israeli rule and have grown sensitive to the collective pleasures given by a modern society. Such commonalities between Israelis and Palestinians have not thus far brought civic harmony. But they may, someday, perhaps, ease the strains and eventually provide the urgency to reach an accommodation and the willingness to operate according to its terms.

64   DONNA ROBINSON DIVINE

Notes

1. The West Bank is a mostly mountainous region of 2,100 square miles located in the east-central area of Israel, west of the Jordan River. Its western border, only about thirty miles from the river, is also known as the "Green Line." Between the "Green Line" and the Mediterranean Sea is the narrow coastal zone, densely inhabited by two-thirds of Israel's population. The southern and northern portions of the West Bank are also known by most Israelis as Judea and Samaria respectively. The Gaza Strip, 140 square miles, is a narrow area of shoreline that extends some twenty miles along the Mediterranean coast to the Egyptian border. Benvenisti and Khayat (1988, 28, 33, 113) estimate the Arab population as 1,067,873 in the West Bank and 633,562 in the Gaza Strip; and the Jewish population as 67,000 (in 107 small settlements) and 2,506 (14 settlements) respectively. The West Bank Arab population is distributed among some 25 towns and cities and 425 villages. There are less than ten Arab towns and villages in the Gaza Strip.

2. Benvenisti and Khayat (1988, 32) estimated the investments in Jewish settlements in the West Bank as follows: "during the first decade [of the occupation] U.S. $750 million . . . [while] during the second decade—U.S. $1.67 billion or double the previous average annual investment." Total military government development budget in the Gaza Strip for the years 1983–87 was U.S. $186 million (Benvenisti and Khayat 1988, 109).

References

Anabtawi, Samir N. 1986. *Palestinian Higher Education in the West Bank and Gaza: A Critical Assessment.* London: KPI.

Benvenisti, Meron. 1984. *The West Bank Data Project.* Washington, D.C.: American Enterprise Institute.

———. 1986a. *1986 Report: Demographic, Economic, Legal, Social and Political Developments in the West Bank.* Washington, D.C.: American Enterprise Institute.

———. 1986b. *The West Bank Handbook.* Jerusalem: The Jerusalem Post.

———. 1989. "The Morning After." *The Jerusalem Post International Edition,* 4 March, pp. 8, 18.

———, and Shlomo Khayat. 1988. *The West Bank and Gaza Atlas.* Jerusalem: The Jerusalem Post.

Danet, Brenda. 1989. *Pulling Strings: Biculturalism in Israeli Bureaucracy.* Albany: State University of New York Press.

Graham-Brown, Sarah. 1983. "The Economic Consequences of the Occupation." In *Occupation: Israel over Palestine,* edited by Naseer H. Aruri, 167–222. Belmont: Association of Arab-American University Graduates.

Ibrahim, Youssef M. 1989. "Jordan's West Bank Move Upsetting Daily Life." *The New York Times*, 18 October.

Laufer, Leopold Yehuda. 1989. "A Lesson in Conflict Resolution." *The Jerusalem Post International Edition*, 14 January, p. 17.

Lesch, Ann Mosely. 1970. *Israel's Occupation of the West Bank: The First Two Years*. Santa Monica: The Rand Corporation.

Ma'oz, Moshe. 1984. *Palestinian Leadership on the West Bank*. London: Frank Cass.

Milson, Menahem. 1981. "How To Make Peace with the Palestinians." *Commentary*, Vol. 71, No. 5 (May): 25–35.

Nisan, Mordecai. 1978. *Israel and the Territories: A Study in Control 1967–1977*. Ramat Gan: Turtledove.

Peretz, Don. 1986. *The West Bank*. Boulder: Westview Press.

Roy, Sara M. 1986. *The Gaza Strip: A Demographic, Economic, Social and Legal Survey*. Boulder: Westview Press.

Said, Edward. 1989. "Intifada and Independence." *Social Text* 22 (Spring): 23–39.

Sandler, Shmuel. 1988. "Israel and the West Bank Palestinians." *Publius: The Journal of Federalism* 18 (Spring): 47–62.

Shinar, Dov. 1987. *Palestinian Voices: Communication and Nation Building in the West Bank*. Boulder: Lynne Rienner.

State of Israel, Ministry of Defense, Coordinator of Government Operations in Judea-Samaria and the Gaza District. 1983. *A Sixteen Year Survey (1967–1983)*. Jerusalem: State of Israel, Ministry of Defense.

Tamari, Salim. 1981. "Building Other People's Homes." *The Journal of Palestine Studies*, Vol. 11, No. 1 (Autumn): 31–66.

———. 1983. "Israel's Search for a Native Pillar: The Village Leagues." In *Occupation: Israel over Palestine*, edited by Naseer H. Aruri, 377–90. Belmont, CA: Association of Arab-American University Graduates.

Yishai, Yael. 1987. *Land or Peace: Whither Israel?* Stanford, CA: Hoover Institution Press.

3 ■ The Changing Strategies of
Mobilization among the Arabs in
Israel: Parliamentary Politics, Local
Politics, and National Organizations

Majid Al-Haj

THE MINORITY STATUS

After the 1948 war, only 156,000 Arabs remained in Israel. They
constituted 13 percent of the total population. The Arabs were a
weak and isolated group, cut off from their kin who became refugees
in the Arab countries of the Middle East. The vast majority, 80 percent, were villagers. The bulk of the urban Arab middle- and upper-
class—merchants, professionals, and the clergy—was evacuated as a
result of war and exodus (Al-Haj and Rosenfeld 1990, 24). Only 6
percent of the 200,000 Arabs who formerly lived in cities remained
there after the war (Lustick 1980). In addition, some 20 percent of the
Arab population in Israel became "internal refugees." They were
forced to move to new communities after their original villages were
destroyed during and immediately after the war (Al-Haj 1988a).

Since the 1950s, the Arab population has quadrupled because of
high fertility and decreasing mortality rates. In 1988 there were
678,000 Arabs in Israel (excluding East Jerusalem) constituting approximately 16 percent of the total population. Among the Arab population, 75 percent were Sunni Muslims, 15 percent were Christians
of several denominations, and 10 percent were Druze (Central Bureau
of Statistics 1989).

The Arabs are dispersed throughout Israel in seven cities, three
towns, and 148 villages. They are concentrated in three areas: the
Galilee, the Little Triangle, and the Negev. About 85 percent of them
live in homogeneous Arab villages and towns and 15 percent live in

seven mixed Jewish-Arab cities. However, even in these mixed communities, the Arabs live in segregated neighborhoods.

The Arabs in Israel have experienced a conspicuous modernization process. It is reflected in the rise of the level of education, the improvement of the standards of living, the intensive politicization process, and the social modernization in terms of attitudes and lifestyles (Smooha 1989; Central Bureau of Statistics 1989, 608–9; Ministry of Education 1988, 24).

Although modernization has increased the Arabs' aspirations for socioeconomic mobility, ethnic stratification in Israel has placed mobility limits on them. The educational gap between Arabs and Jews, though decreased, is still wide. In 1988 the median years of schooling among the Arab population was 8.6 as compared to 11.8 among Jews (Central Bureau of Statistics 1989). While the proportion of Arabs in the Israeli population is one in six, only one in sixty senior government positions is occupied by an Arab (Shipler 1986, 439). Arabs are situated in the class of low and moderate income. The rise in their standard of living has not resulted in diminishing the gap between them and the Jewish population. This gap still exists in several areas and in some cases it has widened (Lewin-Epstein and Semyonov 1986).

The modernization process among the Arabs in Israel was influenced by internal and external factors. Arabs started from a low point of development. The fact that Israel was created by the Jews and for Jews placed Arabs outside the modern nation-state building (Lustick 1980). The bond between the Israeli Arabs and the Arab world, and particularly with the Palestinians, has placed Israeli Arabs in a status of a "hostile minority." This factor has strongly affected the conflict of values and the nature of relations between Arabs and Jews in Israel. These relations are characterized as formal, asymmetric, and leading to estrangement and tension (Smooha 1989).

Despite the restrictions on their political development, the Arabs in Israel employed a number of strategies of political mobilization in order to penetrate the Israeli power structure and to improve their bargaining position over resources. Parliamentary politics was the first strategy of political mobilization to be used by the Arabs in Israel after the establishment of the state. But it has proven to deliver only minor returns from the Jewish center. Unlike parliamentary politics, the second strategy, local politics, has become a central political activity and a very important means for political mobilization. In both strategies, however, internal political competition is evident. The

Arab vote is split over ideological, religious, kinship, and other local issues. In order to bridge the internal contradictions among Arab political groups, the Arabs have developed a third strategy of political mobilization through extraparliamentary national organizations. The importance of this strategy is gradually increasing in light of the political localization of the Arab population and the growing national and religious consciousness among them. All the three strategies are affected by the internal structure of the Arab community, the extent of access that Arabs have to national-level social and political opportunities, and the nature of the political culture of Israel as a state with an ongoing Israeli-Palestinian conflict.

Each of the three strategies of political mobilization is analyzed in one section below. We begin with parliamentary politics. We then continue with two other strategies: local politics and extraparliamentary national organizations.

MOBILIZATION THROUGH PARLIAMENTARY POLITICS

As citizens of Israel, the Arabs were granted from the outset the right to vote in free democratic elections for the Israeli parliament, the Knesset. Nevertheless, the share of the Arabs in the national power was restricted from the very beginning. The lack of an urban middle class and national leadership in the aftermath of Israeli independence, together with a low political consciousness, prepared the ground for the localization of politics and leadership among the Arabs. That facilitated the control of the Israeli government over the entire population via a few key local leaders while simultaneously preserving internal divisions among the Arabs so as to counteract the formation of a collective national identity or any rapprochement with the extreme left-wing parties (Rosenfeld 1978).

The Israeli military administration suppressed national-level activities, as well as attempts to revive the traditional leadership among the Arabs (Cohen 1965; Lustick 1980). Mapai (later Labor), the ruling party, controlled the military apparatus that gave it a stronghold in the Arab communities and a tremendous influence in their local governments. The military administration excluded the local leadership that showed resistance to the establishment. In many cases new *mukhtars* (community leaders) were created in addition to those already serving, so as to foster new leadership and, in turn, to increase the competition between the various factions and reinforce the trend of cooperation with the Israeli authorities (Al-Haj and Rosenfeld 1990).

At the national level, the partisan participation among Arabs was minor. The Arab citizens were not eager to join existing parties and to enter national politics (Landau 1969). The main reason for this trend was lack of a political organization that could appeal to Arabs. They were not accepted as members in the Zionist parties nor could they identify with the basic ideology of these parties (Nakhleh 1975).

Arab affiliated lists were one of the most efficient instruments of channelling Arab votes, especially until the late 1960s (Abu-Gosh 1972). These affiliated lists were initiated and backed by Zionist parties, primarily the Labor party, which was the principal force in the Israeli establishment until 1977 (Shokeid 1982, 122). The purpose of these lists was not political mobilization of the Arab population but rather the catching of Arab votes through traditional means of persuasion (Landau 1969). The structure of the Arab affiliated lists was tailored to fit the deep social territorialization of the Arab population and its traditional character (Nakhleh 1975).

These lists claimed the representation of the several factions of the Arab population. Their candidates were carefully selected in order to encompass the main divisions among the Arab citizens: geographic region, religious group, prominent *hamula* (extended family), and large Arab localities (Landau 1969; Lustick 1980).

Until the seventh Knesset elections (1969) the Arab affiliated lists with Labor were the major political framework among the Arab minority. During that period their power ranged between 28–55 percent of the Arab votes (table 1).

Since the early 1970s Labor's Arab affiliated lists decreased in power. In the tenth Knesset elections (1981) they did poorly and none of them were represented in the Knesset (Al-Haj and Yaniv 1983). Since then the affiliated lists have disappeared from the national political scene.

Zionist parties, without exception, always sought to share the Arab vote (Shokeid 1982; Nakhleh 1975). The parties' approach toward the Arab population was paternalistic and based on individual interests (Ben-Rafael 1982, 215). Hence, they maneuvered through local Arab *hamula* heads and notables. Thus they minimized their costs and maximized their gains. Along the electoral campaigns from 1951 to 1988 they received between 26–50 percent of the Arab vote

Table 3.1. Arab Vote, 1949–1988 (percentage)

	Arab Voters		Breakdown of Arab Vote				
Knesset Elections	Percent of Arab Voters	Voting Turnout	Communist Party After 1977: DFPE	PLP	Arab Lists Affiliated with Labor	Labor	Total Zionist Parties
1st, 1949	6.6	79	22	—	28	10	—
2nd, 1951	7.5	86	16	—	55	11	26
3rd, 1955	8.2	90	15	—	48	14	23
4th, 1959	7.9	85	11	—	42	10	26
5th, 1961	8.3	83	22	—	40	20	29
6th, 1965	8.6	82	23	—	38	13	27
7th, 1969	8.4	80	28	—	40	17	27
8th, 1973	8.5	77	37	—	27	13	29
9th, 1977	8.9	74	50	—	16	11	21
10th, 1981	9.8	68	37	—	12	29	45
11th, 1984	10.4	72	32	18	—	26	50.4
12th, 1988	12.0	74	34	14	11 (ADP)	17	42

Source: Based on Al-Haj, Majid and Henry Rosenfeld 1990, 71.
Abbreviations:
DFPE—Democratic Front for Peace and Equality
PLP—Progressive List for Peace
ADP—Arab Democratic Party

(table 3.1). At the inception, Zionist parties aimed to recruit the Arab votes without accepting Arabs as party members (Landau 1969). Mapam was the first Zionist party to open its ranks in 1954 to Arab members and to integrate them into its activities (Al-Haj and Rosenfeld 1990). However, the fact that Mapam was a Zionist party and part of the establishment of Labor Zionism, impeded its activity among the Arab minority.

Maki, the Israeli Communist Party, was the only non-Zionist party with which the Arabs could identify. Indeed, this party began its activity among Arabs during the British Mandate, earlier than any other party (Landau 1984). It should be noted that the voting for the Communist party had symbolized for Arabs a protest at two levels. At the national level it had channelled the feelings of frustration and resentment of the Arab population against the government's policy (Abu-Gosh 1972; Rekhess 1986). At the local level it had absorbed the protest of the young Arab generation and the peripheral groups in the Arab villages against the local traditional leadership and the estab lished prominent *hamulas*.

Since the early 1970s several factors have deepened the politicization process among the Arab population and have increased their tendency to take part in the competition over the national power system. The aforementioned modernization process experienced by Arabs in Israel has increased political consciousness among them including the awareness of their potential power and the available democratic means for the promotion of their status. The growing proportion of the Arab voters, as a result of high fertility and the change in the age structure, has increased the political value of the Arab sector. In the last Knesset elections (1988) Arabs constituted some 12 percent of the total eligible votes. Therefore, the large parties counted on Arab voters for determining the close competition between the right and left wings (*Maariv*, 30 March 1988).

The abolishment of the military government and the growing accessibility of the Jewish population have facilitated the contact between Arabs and the Jewish center. The increasing level of education and the growing number of the young Arab generation have increased the awareness of Arabs to the rules of the "political game" and decreased the power of the traditional methods of persuasion (Rosenfeld 1978; Smooha 1989).

In the early 1970s a strong national awakening was observed among the Arab minority in Israel. Several factors led to this trend, among them: the renewed contact between the Arabs in Israel and their brethren in the West Bank and Gaza Strip after the 1967 war; the rise of the Palestinian national movement and the increasing international recognition of the PLO; and the results of the 1973 war which boosted the feelings of dignity among the Arab minority (Rekhess 1989a).

The national awakening, which is called by some scholars "Palestenization" (Smooha 1984), has been accompanied by increasing tendency among the Arabs for integration in the Israeli society. The growing perception of the Arabs in Israel for their future as firmly linked to the state of Israel has in turn increased their attempts to participate in the decision-making regarding their affairs, including the allocation of resources and the shaping of their political future (see Smooha 1989; Al-Haj 1988b).

The government and the political parties alike had attempted to absorb and utilize the new trend among the Arab population. The Israeli officials viewed the new trend among the Arab population as worrisome. Thus, they sought the means to localize the national feelings and to direct them to the citizenship matters and to the day-today life (Mari 1978). The Israeli government declared its intentions to improve the conditions of the Arab population and to speed its integration. To accomplish this goal, several ministerial committees were formed in order to investigate the services given to the Arab population. The Ministry of Education formed the Peled Committee for the planning of Arab education towards the 1980s. The Ministry of Interior formed a special committee chaired by Sami Geraisy (later to be called the Geraisy Committee) to investigate local services and municipal budgets in the Arab localities. The advisor of the prime minister for Arab affairs initiated a study to explore the situation of Arab University graduates and the possibility of their absorption in governmental offices. Policy-oriented research investigated the planning of housing assistance to the Arab villages in Israel (Kipnis 1982). In the wake of the first Land Day strike, which was organized by the Arab population in 1976, a special ministerial committee was formed to deal with the needs of the Arab citizens.

The Communist party sought to utilize the new changes in the orientation of the Arab citizens for expansion of its power. It tried to fill the gap that resulted from the diminishing power of the traditional Arab leadership with the intention of becoming the sole representative of the Arab population (Rekhess 1989a). In this sense, the party started to establish itself as the "informal establishment" among the Arab minority in Israel. For this purpose the party initiated a number of extraparliamentary national Arab organizations. In 1977 the Communists established a wider Arab-Jewish party called the Democratic Front for Peace and Equality (DFPE). In addition to the Communist leadership, it included noncommunist Arab and Jewish public figures (Al-Haj and Yaniv 1983). Backed by the PLO and Palestinian national leadership in the West Bank and Gaza, the DFPE gained a sweeping victory in the 1977 Knesset elections, receiving about 50 percent of the Arab vote (Rekhess 1989a).

The structure of the DFPE has been repeatedly criticized by some of its noncommunist Arab partners. The first signs of split occurred in Nazareth when some of the university graduates broke away following a dispute with the Communist partners over the control of the party. The breakaway faction then founded the Progressive Movement in Nazareth which ran in the 1983 municipal elections and won 20 percent of the vote (Al-Haj and Rosenfeld 1990). Subsequently, the Progressive Movement sought to increase its effect on the nationwide politics. It established the Progressive List for Peace (PLP) together with a Jewish group called "Alternative." This list was the main competitor of the DFPE in the 1984 Knesset elections and won 18 percent of the Arab vote. In the 1988 elections it decreased to 14 percent (table 1).

It should be mentioned that the main competition among the Arab population in the 1988 Knesset elections was between the three predominantly Arab parties: the DFPE, the PLP, and the newly formed Arab Democratic Party (ADP). Having a similar political platform, they based their dispute, to a large extent, on personal issues. Although they received together about 60 percent of the Arab vote, they wasted nearly two Knesset seats by failing to form an agreement between them for the division of the extra votes (*Davar*, 11 January 1989). This result outraged many of the Arab voters who pressured these parties to minimize their disputes and to form a framework for cooperation. The pressure accelerated the formation of the joint Jewish-Arab list for the 1989 Histadrut (General Federation of Labor) elections. However, this list, which included for the first time representatives of all the three predominantly Arab parties, did not appeal to the Arab voters. It received only 35 percent of the Arab votes (*Al-Sinnarah*, 17 November 1989).

The Zionist parties traditional tactics was to argue that only through establishment parties can Arabs promote their case. This approach was mainly adopted by the Labor party (Shokeid 1982). The National Religious Party (Mafdal) adopted a particularistic approach. The party's long-standing control of the Ministry of Interior and the Ministry of Religions allowed it to penetrate the Arab communities through its connections with traditional leadership (Al-Haj and Rosenfeld 1990). The Likud, unlike other Zionist parties, sought from the beginning to concentrate on two main groups: the Druze and the Bedouins.

The Labor party (later the Alignment) has maintained its position as the central Zionist party among Arabs, despite its gradual decrease in votes since the 1981 Knesset elections. In 1981 it received 29 percent of the Arab vote, 26 percent in the 1984 elections and 17 percent in the 1988 elections. The fact that the 1988 elections were held under the shadow of the Palestinian Intifada, and the role of the Labor minister of defense, Rabin, in repressing the Intifada, weakened the stand of the Labor party in the Arab sector. Nevertheless, it appears that the Labor party is in the process of regaining its power among the Arab population. In the 1989 Histadrut elections it received 43.3 percent of the Arab vote (*Al-Sinnarah*, 7 November 1989). Against the gradual decline of the Arab affiliated lists, the Alignment sought since the early 1980s to directly include Arab candidates in its list for the Knesset elections. Indeed, two Arab Knesset members were elected on the Alignment slate in the 1981 and 1984 elections and one in the 1988 elections (Rekhess 1989a).

In the 1988 elections the Civil Rights Movement (Ratz) quadrupled among Arabs from 1 to 4 percent, and Mapam received nearly 4 percent of the Arab votes, for the first time as a separate list from Labor (Al-Haj and Rosenfeld 1990). In the recent Histadrut elections (1989) Ratz received 7.2 percent and Mapam 8.6 percent of the Arab votes (*Al-Sinnarah*, 7 November 1989).

It seems that the Zionist parties have a potential support among two types of the Arab population called by Smooha (1989, 166) the "accommodationist type" and the "reservationist type." The former believes that "by accepting the Jewish consensus and working through the system they can best extract concessions from the Jews." The latter is caught between the Zionist establishment and the non-Zionist opposition.

Despite the aforementioned politicization of the Arab minority and its eagerness for political integration in the nationwide political system, Arabs do not share the national power center (Rosenfeld 1978; Lustick 1980). This led to a growing process of political localization.

One major factor responsible for the political localization of the Arab minority in Israel is the exclusion of Arabs from Israel's nation-state building. It has been repeatedly emphasized that the formal policy towards the Arabs in Israel is based on three main contradicting principles: the democratic character of the state, the Jewish-Zionist character, and security concerns (Smooha 1980; Lustick 1980; Rouhana 1989). While the first principle calls for equality and integration of Arabs, the other two promote exclusion. When these principles are juxtaposed, it is clear that national and security considerations gain the upper hand (Carmi and Rosenfeld 1988). As a result, Arabs have only "partial membership" in Israeli society (Ben-Rafael 1982, 206). They are excluded from the main national organizations in Israel and from its core political culture (Lustick 1980). While non-Zionist ultra-Orthodox parties are considered legitimate partners in the government coalition, the Arab parties are not (Galnoor 1989, 40).

The trend of political localization of the Arab minority is also affected by the nature of Arab-Jewish relations in Israel. Most of the interpersonal relations between Arabs and Jews are formal, technical, and characterized by asymmetric minority-majority relations (Mari 1988). This asymmetry is also reflected in the political sphere. While

large-scale well-organized Jewish parties and associations continuously penetrated the Arab minority, there occurred no corresponding
effective penetration of the Jewish majority by the predominantly
Arab parties (Cohen 1965).

Despite the fact that the leadership of the DFPE and the PLP was
almost equally divided between Jews and Arabs, the support they received from the Jewish population was negligible. Upon the formation
of the Joint List in the recent Histadrut elections (1989), the DFPE
insisted that a Jewish member of the Communist party chair the list
(*Al-Ittihad*, 26 November 1989). This might have affected negatively
the popularity of this list among the Arab population without bearing
any fruits from Jewish voters (*Haaretz*, 20 November 1989).

Since the Likud came to power in 1977, a more pragmatic
approach is noted among the leadership of the predominantly Arab
parties. Fear of expansion of right-wing parties has driven the DFPE
and later (1984) the PLP to cooperate with the Alignment and to support its candidates as against those nominated by the Likud or the
other right-wing parties. Such was the case of the election of Hillel
(Labor) as the speaker of the Knesset in 1984 (*Al-Hamishmar*, 25 February 1990).

The predominantly Arab parties took an unprecedented step in
1988 in their efforts to become a legitimate partner in the establishment. They declared their willingness to participate in a coalition led
by the Alignment and the other leftist Zionist parties under certain
conditions (Al-Haj 1990). The required conditions, such as a commitment to the promotion of the peace process with the Palestinians and
to the equality of the Arab citizens in Israel, were vague. In fact, these
conditions were also declared by the leftist Zionist parties during their
electoral campaign among the Arab population.

Darawsheh, the head of the ADP, went further in his pragmatic
approach. Throughout his electoral campaign he emphasized his intention to be included in the political consensus in Israel as a legitimate partner with Zionist parties (*Haaretz*, 10 November 1989).

Against the pragmatic tendency of the predominantly Arab parties, the Zionist parties, including the Labor Alignment, never offered
the Arab parties any chance of becoming a genuine legitimate partner
in a coalition government. Instead, the Alignment counted on the support of the Arab parties to block the possibility that the Likud might
form a coalition (Ozacky-Lazar 1989). The formation of the National
Unity Government (1984–90) further weakened the bargaining power
of the predominantly Arab parties. The maneuvering power of these

parties is limited. Unlike the Jewish orthodox parties, their potential partnership is limited only to the left-wing parties led by the Alignment (Galnoor 1989). After the fall of the National Unity Government in March 1990, the small parties proved to be of crucial importance in light of the delicate balance between the Likud and the Alignment. This situation should have given the Arab parties a boost. But once again the Alignment counted on their support "from the outside," not as integral partners in potential coalition (*Haaretz,* 20 March 1990). The orthodox parties, with whom the Alignment negotiated, also showed their opposition for a coalition dependent on the Arab parties (*Maariv,* 20 March 1990).

Although political localization was forced on the Arab minority in Israel, some Arab political groups have voluntarily refrained from participation in parliamentary politics and established themselves as extraparliamentary organizations. Most prominent among them are Abna el-Balad (the Sons of the Land) and the Islamic Movement. Having rejected the right of Israel to exist as a Zionist-Jewish state, Abna el-Balad has repeatedly declared that the Israeli parliament and its elections are illegitimate (Al-Haj and Yaniv 1983). Abna el-Balad has not succeeded yet in expanding its base among the Arab population. For the time being it has been a marginal group even in local Arab politics (Rekhess 1989b, 350).

Unlike Abna el-Balad, the Islamic Movement has been considerably more powerful among the Arab population. Although participating in local politics, the Islamic Movement has refused thus far to be involved in the parliamentary elections. However, the leader of the movement, Nemir Darwish, made contradictory statements regarding the intentions of the Islamic Movement to run in the next Knesset elections (*Al-Ittihad,* 26 November 1989; *Maariv,* 14 March 1990).

The stand of the Islamic Movement concerning the Histadrut elections (1989) was vague at the beginning. Subsequently, the movement made it clear that Muslims should not vote for non-Muslim candidates. Thus, while abstaining from voting to the Histadrut general assembly, they voted for the Muslim slates which competed for the local Labor Councils in Taibe and Nazareth (Mansour 1989).

On the eve of the March 1990 coalition crisis in the Israeli government, the leader of the Islamic Movement announced the formation of a new party called "the United Arab Party" (*Hadashot,* 18 March 1990). He indicated that this party will include all Arab political groups and public figures, excluding the Communist party. He added that his step came after consultations with Muslim spiritual leaders inside and outside Israel. Undoubtedly, if such a party is to be established it would increase the political activity of the Arab citizens in Israel, though it might not change their political localization.

Our discussion shifts now from parliamentary politics to two other mobilization strategies of the Arab minority. These are local politics and extraparliamentary national organizations. We will discuss three key questions. What is the impact of political localization on a national minority that already has achieved a considerable level of individual modernization? What is the alternative strategy that arose due to the lack of access to the national power center? What are the future implications of the widening gap between expectations and reality among Arab citizens?

MOBILIZATION THROUGH LOCAL POLITICS

Upon the establishment of Israel in 1948 there were only three Arab localities with local councils that originated in the British Mandate. During the next decade, the Israeli authorities took initial steps towards establishing local authorities in the Arab settlements. The three Arab local authorities from the British Mandate were reactivated. In addition, eight local authorities were set up in the large Arab villages in the northern and central regions.

The request of Arab communities for their own local governments has increased over time. Currently, two-thirds of the Arab settlements are administered by local governments including three towns, fifty-eight local councils, and thirty-eight regional councils (Al-Haj and Rosenfeld 1990).

Local government became the central political system and the most important means for the mobilization of the Arab minority in Israel. Several factors contributed to this. Taking into consideration the political localization of the Arab population in Israel, local government became the only political framework in which Arabs appear to have a direct impact. Arab nationalist political parties cannot be established in Israel. Therefore, local politics was effective as a legal means for organizing on a nationalist base. The "voluntary localized" Arab political organizations saw local government as the only official framework that did not contradict with their ideology. The involvement in local politics and leadership had a major impact on the votes that the parties received in the Knesset elections.

The limited local economic resources among the Arab population, as a result of dependency on the Jewish center, further increased the importance of the local government as a channel for allocation of resources and benefits. The failure of the government ministries to hire Arab university graduates turned the local government into a major employer for them. They were forced to compete for jobs in their own communities. The projects carried out by the local governments also became an important source of livelihood for local contractors and entrepreneurs.

Israeli policymakers declared that the establishment of local governments in the Arab settlements aims to improve the level of services and to give the Arab population an opportunity to increase their involvement in running their internal affairs. It was also intended to promote relations between the Arab population and the central government as well as to create a "safety valve" for feelings of frustration caused by the sudden transformation from the status of majority to that of minority (Landau 1969, 217).

As the Arab settlements gained their own local government, the *hamula* has become of major importance in local politics (Nakhleh 1975; Cohen 1965; Habash 1977). Most of the slates in local elections are *hamula*-based. Coalitions are deeply affected by *hamula* interests (Abu-Gosh 1972). The *hamula* has adapted to the local political system and has been well integrated into the political life of the Arab settlements. However, the modernization process among Arabs in Israel has deeply changed the basis of the *hamula* functioning and the dynamic of its internal and external relations. Hierarchical relationships dominated by *hamula* interests were replaced by pragmatic considerations of the *hamula* members (Al-Haj 1987). While traditionally the individual was controlled by the *hamula* and behaved according to its expectations, at present the *hamula* is utilized by its members as a framework for political and social adjustment. The kinship system has become flexible and adaptable to the new changes (Rosenfeld 1980).

Since the mid-1960s conspicuous political changes occurred in local political competition. The system was politicized and local concerns were simultaneously coupled with national issues. The political campaign for the last local elections (1989) is of special interest. Many of the lists in these elections were directly backed by parliamentary parties or Arab extraparliamentary organizations. The disputes among the political parties in the Knesset elections were transferred to local politics.

Table 3.2. Results of the Local Elections in the Arab Settlements by
Party Affiliation of the Elected Mayor, 1983 and 1989[a]

Political Affiliation	1983	1989
Democratic Front for Peace and Equality	20	14
Labor Party	14	4
Likud	3	1
Islamic Movement	1	5
Arab Democratic Party	—	3
Progressive List for Peace	—	2
Civil Rights Movement	—	2
Independent	12	14
Total	50	45

a. This table relates only to the settlements in which elections were conducted, including Druze local authorities.

The rise in the power of the Islamic Movement may be one of the most salient features of the recent local elections. While in the 1983 elections only one mayor was affiliated with the Islamic Movement, in the 1989 elections it gained the mayorship in five local governments and was represented in the local councils of another nine settlements. One of its most important achievements took place in Aum el-Fahim, the second largest Arab town in Israel. The former mayor, affiliated with the DFPE (Communist party), was replaced by the candidate of the Islamic Movement who received 75 percent of the vote (*Al-Sirat*, March 1989).

While in 1983 twenty of the elected mayors were affiliated with the DFPE, their number decreased to fourteen in the 1989 elections. As a result, the status of the DFPE among the Arab population was shaken. At the same time, the impetus gained by the Islamic Movement turned it into the main competitor of the DFPE in the Arab sector (*Yideot Aharonot*, 2 March 1990).

The PLP ran in these elections and gained the mayorship of one of the largest Arab villages in Galilee (Arabe). It was also represented in a number of local councils. The ADP, encouraged by its success in the Knesset elections, also sought to penetrate Arab local politics. Three of its candidates were elected as mayors (table 3.2).

The main loser in the 1989 elections was the Labor party. Only four of the elected mayors were affiliated with this party as compared to fourteen in the 1983 elections. These results are consistent with the drastic decrease in the power of the Labor party among the Arab population in the twelfth Knesset elections (1988).

Mapam and Ratz used the momentum gained in the parliamentary elections to further establish their position in Arab settlements. Candidates affiliated with Ratz captured the mayorship in two Arab localities while candidates of Mapam were elected as members in several Arab local councils.

The partisan identification of Arab mayors, however, is not always straightforward. Those affiliated with the DFPE are usually more committed to their party and well organized as a distinct group. Some of the so-called independent mayors are, in fact, linked to this party or another with informal relations. Their independent status allows them to maneuver and, if needed, to shift alliance from one party to another in order to maximize their gains. Therefore, the results of the local and the national elections, though related, do not necessarily coincide (Al-Haj and Rosenfeld 1990).

MOBILIZATION THROUGH EXTRAPARLIAMENTARY NATIONAL ORGANIZATIONS

The National Committee for Heads of Arab Local Authorities became the major representative of the Arabs in Israel. Interestingly, upon its foundation in 1974, the National Committee gained the sympathy and even the support of the central government (Al-Haj and Rosenfeld 1990). Based on our earlier analysis, it is reasonable to assume that by encouraging the creation of this committee, the government aimed to channel the national awakening among Arabs to local issues and, in addition, to create a counterbalance for the growing power of the Communist party. However, the cooperation between the National Committee and the government did not last. After the first Land Day strike (1976) the National Committee was declared an independent organization. While the founders focused at the inception merely on local services, after the first Land Day they shifted their emphasis to national issues.

The national committee was involved in issues such as budget allocation, planning, construction, land, industrialization, and the development of local services. The National Committee's strife over these issues led to a number of confrontations with the government agencies, sometimes prolonged and accompanied by strikes. Only in rare instances did these strikes meet with understanding on the part of the government. In most cases the government emphasized that these actions were unjustified, needless, and politically motivated (*Haaretz*, 30 December 1981; *Davar*, 13 July 1986).

In order to continue its struggle on a more sophisticated basis, the National Committee established a network of professional committees for specific areas. The first was the Follow-up Committee for Arab Education, which was established in 1984. This committee was composed of Arab academics, educators, students, mayors, and representatives of several public bodies dealing with education. Since its inception the committee has been in charge of the negotiations with the Ministry of Education and other official bodies concerned with the promotion of the Arab educational system. It has focused on changes in both the goals and the curriculum of Arab education, which have been deprived of any Arab-Palestinian national content (Follow-up Committee for Arab Education 1988).

In 1986 a special conference was held in Nazareth to deal with the situation of health services in the Arab settlements. A follow-up committee was set up in the wake of this conference to trace the implementation of its recommendations and to lobby for the improvement of medical and health conditions of Arab citizens. The Follow-up Committee for Health Services was composed of Arab physicians, professionals, and public figures (Follow-up Committee for Health Services 1986).

In 1987 a third professional committee was founded by the National Committee to deal with social services in Arab localities. This committee was composed of social workers, psychologists, and public representatives. Since its formation, it led the negotiations with government officials for the improvement of welfare services. In addition, it organized a campaign among the Arab citizens against drug abuse and juvenile delinquency (Follow-up Committee for Social Services 1987).

In 1984 the National Committee issued its political guidelines, which have become the cornerstone of the consensus among Arabs in Israel regarding national and citizenship issues, emphasizing that

> the Arab masses in Israel are an integral part of the Palestinian Arab nation, and it is important for them that they realize their legitimate national rights. . . . At the same time, the conference emphasizes that the masses of Arabs in Israel are an integral part of the state, that they share a common fate with the Jewish masses in Israel in a common homeland. (National Committee of Heads of Arab Local Authorities, Minutes, 8 February 1984)

The National Committee, supported by its affiliated follow-up committees, made tangible achievements concerning services and budget allocations to Arab communities. While in the 1970s the average ratio between the budgets of the Jewish and the Arab local governments was 13:1 in favor of the former, this decreased to 2.5:1 in the 1980s. Education and health and social services improved in Arab localities, although their level of delivery still does not meet the expectations of the Arab populations (Al-Haj and Rosenfeld 1990, 136–37). No less important, these committees have emerged as a unifying power among the Arab population. Furthermore, the National Committee became the only body capable of speaking in the name of Arab citizens and authorized to decide on their nationwide policies. This created a considerable competition among the different Arab political groups over the control of the National Committee. Some of them complained of not being represented in it, mainly Abna el-Balad and the Islamic Movement. To overcome these disputes, the National Committee was expanded in 1987 to become the "Supreme Surveillance Committee of the Arab Affairs." It included the representatives of all the public bodies and political parties as well as Arabs affiliated with Zionist parties (Supreme Surveillance Committee, Minutes, 24 June 1987).

The Supreme Committee and the bodies participating in it are often called the "parliament of the Arabs in Israel" and the "institutions of autonomy" (*Haaretz*, 18 December 1986; *Haaretz*, 11 September 1987). This is yet another indication of their importance and representation of the Arab minority in Israel. Indeed, since its formation the Supreme Committee led a number of demonstrations and general strikes as a means of mobilizing the Arab population over citizenship and national issues. The main ones were: the "Day of Equality" (24 June 1987); the "Day of Peace" (21 December 1987); the "Day of Housing" (15 November 1988); and the annual commemoration of the "Day of Land."

CONCLUSIONS

This paper discussed the political mobilization strategies of the Arab citizens in Israel. We showed that the development of the Arab population in Israel was not affected only by typical processes associated with modernization, but also by competing, and to a large extent conflicting, citizenship and national identities based on the status of a national minority excluded from the process and institutions of nation-state building.

Sociodemographic changes among the Arabs accompanied by deep politicization and awareness of the rules of national politics, have intensified the tendency to seek available democratic means for political mobilization. Three major strategies have been adopted for this purpose: parliamentary activity, local politics, and extraparliamentary national organizations. While parliamentary activity seems to be the most plausible instrument for bargaining and affecting the national power center in a democratic state, it has proven to be of minor help for the Arabs in Israel. In all three strategies, however, the conflict of interests with the Jewish center revolved around local-level issues such as budget allocation for local services and education as well as issues of local planning and construction.

The Jewish-Zionist character of the state of Israel, the asymmetric and tense Jewish-Arab relations, the internal contradictions within the Arab community, and its ambivalency towards the modern Western values that are prevalent in Jewish society, have all led to the political localization of the Arab minority in Israel. At the same time, the Arabs remain with little share in national decision-making.

The "integration strategy" adopted by the Arabs since the early 1970s has brought considerable results, but it has failed to meet the Arabs' expectations and needs. The national Jewish power center remained tightly closed. Under these circumstances, mobilization through local politics and extraparliamentary organizations has gained prime importance. By developing these frameworks, the Arabs sought to minimize the control of the majority, to utilize the increasing Arab consensus concerning citizenship and national issues, and to resolve the internal conflict among the Arab political groups.

Nevertheless, the Arabs are still dependent on the Jewish center and are not likely to relinquish their endeavor for mobilization through parliamentary activity. Moreover, some options for parliamentary organization have not been exhausted yet. These are: the formation of a Muslim fundamentalist party or Arab party dominated by the Islamic Movement; the establishment of a genuine joint Arab list to the Knesset; and the formation of a broad-based Jewish-Arab leftist party, including Ratz and/or Mapam. Nevertheless, as long as the existing core state ideology and trends in the political culture of Israeli society continue, none of these options is capable of changing the status of Arabs as a localized national minority. This, in turn, will increase the process of social and political segregation between Jews and Arabs in Israel.

The Arabs in Israel will continue to search for alternative mobilization strategies in order to improve their status and to maximize their bargaining power. Taking into consideration the state of political localization imposed on them, Arabs are more likely to demand some sort of autonomy within the state of Israel. If this materializes, the characteristics of this autonomy and the Israeli response to it will become the central issues of the public debate.

References

Abu-Gosh, Subhi. 1972. "The Election Campaign in the Arab Sector." In *The Elections in Israel*, ed. Alan Arian. Jerusalem: Jerusalem Academic Press.

Al-Haj, Majid. 1987. *Social Change and Family Processes: Arab Communities in Shefar-Am*. Boulder: Westview Press.

————. 1988a. "The Arab Internal Refugees in Israel: The Emergence of a Minority Within the Minority." *Immigrants and Minorities* 7, 2(July): 149–65.

————. 1988b. "The Socio-political Structure of Arabs in Israel: External vs. Internal Orientation." In *Arab-Jewish Relations in Israel: A Quest in Human Understanding*, ed. John Hofman, 92–122. Bristol, IN: Wyndham Hall Press.

————. 1990. "Elections under the Shadow of the Intifada in the Arab Sector in Israel: Advertisement and Results." In *The Elections for the 12th Knesset among the Arab Population in Israel*, ed. J. Landau. Jerusalem: Jerusalem Center for Israeli Studies.

————, and Henry Rosenfeld. 1990. *Arab Local Government in Israel*. Boulder: Westview Press.

————, and Avner Yaniv. 1983. "Uniformity or Diversity: A Reappraisal of the Voting Behavior of the Arab Minority in Israel." In *The Elections in Israel—1981*, ed. A. Arian, 139–64. Tel Aviv: Ramot Publishing, Tel Aviv University.

Al-Hamishmar. 25 February 1990. (Hebrew)

Al-Ittihad. 16 November 1989; 26 November 1989. (Arabic)

Al-Sinnarah. 7 November 1989. (Arabic)

Al-Sirat. March 1989 (Arabic)

Ben-Rafael, Eliezer. 1982. *The Emergence of Ethnicity: Cultural Groups and Social Conflict in Israel*. Westport, Conn.: Greenwood Press.

Carmi, Shulamit, and Henry Rosenfeld. 1988. *Changes in Class-National Relations in Palestine-Israel: A Political Economy Perspective*. Tel Aviv: International Center for Peace in the Middle East.

Central Bureau of Statistics. 1989. *Statistical Abstract of Israel, 1989*. No. 40. Jerusalem: Central Bureau of Statistics.

Cohen, Abner. 1965. *Arab Border Villages in Israel*. Manchester: Manchester University Press.

Davar, 13 July 1986; 11 January 1989. (Hebrew)

Follow-Up Committee for Arab Education and the National Committee for Arab Local Authorities. 1988. *Identity Co-existence and Education Content.* Report from a Study Day, 22 August 1988. (Arabic)

Follow-Up Committee for Health Services. 1986. *Report on the Conference for Health Services.* Nazareth. (Arabic)

Follow-Up Committee for Social Services. 1987. *Report on the Conference for Social Services.* Nazareth. (Arabic)

Galnoor, Itzhak. 1989. "The Israeli Elections: The Flight from Freedom and Responsibility." *Tikun* 4, 1: 38–40.

Haaretz. 30 December 1981; 18 December 1986; 11 September 1987; 10 November 1989; 20 November 1989; 20 March 1990. (Hebrew)

Habash, Awni. 1977. *Processes of Change and Modernization in the Arab Family: A Survey in an Arab Village in Israel.* Jerusalem: Hebrew University, Institute for Labor and Welfare (Mimeographed, Hebrew).

Hadashot. 18 March 1990. (Hebrew)

Kipnis, Baruch. 1982. *Planning Housing Aid Policy for the Urbanizing Arab Villagers of Israel.* Monograph Series on the Middle East No. 1. Haifa: The Jewish-Arab Center, University of Haifa.

Landau, Jacob. 1969. *The Arabs in Israel: A Political Study.* London: Oxford University Press.

———. 1984. "The Arab Vote." In *The Roots of Begin's Success: The 1981 Israel Elections,* ed. Dan Caspi, Abraham Diskin, and Emanuel Sultman. London: Croom Helm.

Lewin-Epstein, Noah, and Moshe Semyonov. 1986. "Ethnic Group Mobility in the Israeli Labor Market." *American Sociological Review* 51 (June): 342–51.

Lustick, Ian. 1980. *Arabs in the Jewish State: Israel's Control of a National Minority.* Austin: University of Texas Press.

Maariv, 30 March 1988; 14 March 1990; 20 March 1990. (Hebrew)

Mansour, Attallah. 1989. "The Troops of the Joint List." *Haaretz,* 11 November 1989.

Mari, Sami. 1978. *Arab Education in Israel.* Syracuse, N.Y.: Syracuse University Press.

———. 1988. "Sources of Conflict in Arab-Jewish Relations in Israel." In *Jewish Arab Relations in Israel: A Quest in Human Understanding,* ed. John Hofman, 21–44. Bristol, IN: Wyndham Hall Press.

Ministry of Education. 1988. *Report.* (Mimeographed, Hebrew). Jerusalem: Ministry of Education.

Nakhleh, Khalil. 1975. "The Direction of Local Level Conflict in Two Arab Villages in Israel." *American Ethnologist* 23 (August): 497–516.

National Committee of Heads of Arab Local Authorities. Minutes, 8 February 1984.

Ozacky-Lazar, Sarah. 1989. "A New Approach to the Question of Israeli Arabs." *New Outlook* 3 (October–November): 36–37.

Rekhess, Eli. 1986. "Between Communism and Arab Nationalism: Rakah and the Arab Minority in Israel (1965–1973)." Ph.D. dissertation, Tel Aviv University. (Hebrew)

———. 1989a. "The Arabs in Israel and the Territories: A Political Linkage and National Solidarity (1967–1988)". *Hamezrah Hehadash:* 165–191. (Hebrew)

———. 1989b. "The Arab Nationalist Challenge to the Israeli Communist Party (1970–1985). *Studies in Comparative Communism* 22,4(Winter): 337–50.

Rosenfeld, Henry. 1978. "The Class Situation of the Arab National Minority in Israel." *Comparative Studies in Society and History* 20, 3 (July): 374–407.

———. 1980. "Men and Women in Arab Peasant to Proletariat Transformation." In *Theory and Practice,* ed. Stanley Diamond, 195–219. The Hague: Mouton.

Rouhana, Nadim. 1989. "The Political Transformation of the Palestinians in Israel: From Acquiescence to Challenge." *Journal of Palestine Studies* 18, 3 (Spring): 38–59.

Shipler, David. 1986. *Arab and Jew: Wounded Spirits in a Promised Land.* New York: Times Books.

Shokeid, Moshe. 1982. "The Arab Vote and the Israeli Party System." In *Distant Relations: Ethnicity and Politics among Arabs and North African Jews in Israel.* New York: Praeger.

Smooha, Sammy. 1980. "The Control of Minorities in Israel and Northern Ireland." *Comparative Studies in Society and History* 22, 2 (April): 256–80.

———. 1984. *The Orientation and the Politicization of the Arab Minority in Israel.* Haifa: The Jewish-Arab Center, University of Haifa.

———. 1989. *Arabs and Jews in Israel, Conflicting and Shared Attitudes in a Divided Society,* vol. 1. Boulder: Westview Press.

Supreme Surveillance Committee. Minutes, 24 June 1987.

Yideot Aharonot. 14 November 1989; 2 March 1990. (Hebrew)

PART II
■ The Ethnic-Class Cleavage

4 ■ Oriental Jews in the Development Towns: Ethnicity, Economic Development, Budgets, and Politics

Efraim Ben-Zadok

Following its establishment in 1948, the state of Israel launched a national policy of building new towns. They were called "development towns." Numerous studies were conducted to evaluate the towns. Most of the studies approached the development towns from a national-level perspective. In urban and regional planning, for example, the towns were evaluated in light of the principles of Zionist ideology and its national goals such as security and defense (e.g., Spiegel 1967; Shachar 1971). In anthropology and political sociology, the economic dependency of the towns on the central government and the political parties was marked (e.g., Deshen 1970; Aronoff 1974; Cohen 1974; Swirski 1981). In spite of the extensive literature, the towns were not studied as a regional phenomenon. An exception is a study by Gradus (1984) which argues that the emergence of regional consciousness in the towns expressed a protest against the political center.

The development towns are actually more than a simple regional phenomenon. They are concentrated in two regions in Israel. The two, north and center/south (fig. 4.1), also include other communities. Moreover, the towns are largely populated by Oriental Jews from a lower socioeconomic background. Consequently, the towns have distinct demographic, social, cultural, economic, political, and electoral characteristics. Both the regional concentration and the distinct characteristics of the development towns prepare the ground for their conflict with the larger Israeli society and the central government. This conflict is the subject of this chapter.

To some extent, the conflict between the towns and the larger society and the government reflects the widely documented (e.g., Ben-Rafael 1982; Smooha 1988) national-level ethnic-class cleavage between Oriental Jews, mostly working-class, and Ashkenazic Jews, largely middle-class. (The ethnic-class definition of the two groups will be provided later.) In fact, in the third section of this chapter the conflict is analyzed around social and cultural values mainly in the terms of the national cleavage. Namely, it is essentially an ethnic conflict between the values of the relatively more traditional group, the Orientals, and the relatively more modern group, the Ashkenazim, whose Western-oriented values dominate the larger society. The conflict around economic interests is analyzed in the fourth and fifth sections. The economic tensions between the development towns and the larger society, and between the towns and the central government, are analyzed as evolving mainly around local and regional issues such as industrial growth and unemployment. Much of the economic tension is actually generated by class issues between working-class Orientals, the vast majority of the towns' residents, and middle-class Ashkenazim who dominate the Israeli economy and power structure. The political process, in the sixth section, encompasses both the ethnic conflict over social and cultural values and the class conflict over economic interests. The concluding section maintains that in the future the conflict of values may decrease while the intensity of the conflict of interests will probably increase. It also contends that the development towns are becoming a powerful force in Israeli politics.

The chapter begins with background description. In the first section, a spatial-social definition of the towns is developed. In the second section, their demographic and social characteristics, in comparison to those of the general Israeli population, are analyzed.

THE DEVELOPMENT TOWNS:
SPATIAL-SOCIAL DEFINITION

Between 1948 and 1952, the policy of building development towns was targeted towards populating and enlarging abandoned or semi-abandoned historical towns such as Beer Sheva and Tiberias. Thereafter, new towns were built from scratch. All but two of the thirty-three development towns discussed here, and listed in table 4.1, were established by 1957; Arad and Karmiel were founded in 1962–63. All the thirty-three towns were included in the postindependence development towns policy.[1]

One of the major goals of the policy was population dispersion. While some 90 percent of Israel's 1948 population lived in the narrow congested coastal plain between Haifa and Tel Aviv, large areas in the north (Galilee) and the south (Negev) were uninhabited. However, dispersion towards these areas was not only important for the achievement of a demographic-regional balance. It also aimed to provide a labor force for these undeveloped areas and, more importantly, to support another major goal of the new towns policy—security and defense. Specifically, many of the towns were built in frontier areas along the borders and the presence of population there was assumed to strengthen national security.

Table 4.1 indicates that the population dispersion goal was equally implemented at least in terms of the number of towns founded in each of the two regions: sixteen were built in the north and seventeen in the center/south. Moreover, in each of the two regions fifteen towns were concentrated within clearly defined boundaries (fig. 4.1). Thus, although by definition the development towns are spread nationwide, they are actually concentrated in two regions. This spatial affiliation is one important reason for these communities to pursue common economic and political interests.

A second reason is the similar demographic and social characteristics shared by almost all the development towns. The vast majority of the residents are working-class Oriental Jews, or Sephardim, who originate in the Islamic countries of North Africa and the Middle East. They were part of the mass immigration of refugees to Israel throughout the 1950s. Indeed, immigrant absorption, an acute problem at the time, was one of the major goals of the new towns policy. The history of this immigration wave, described briefly below, is instructive to understand the social background shared by the residents of the development towns.

Oriental Jews immigrated from traditional societies in North Africa and the Middle East to a relatively modern and Western-oriented culture in Israel. As poor refugees with limited property, economic means, and skills to cope with the new situation, they had little opportunity to choose their residence. They were located in the development towns, mostly peripheral communities that were all sponsored by the central government.[2] Upon improvement of their economic situation, some of them moved into the metropolitan areas of the coastal plain. But most of them, with no other choices, stayed behind and remained dependent upon the provision of employment, education, housing, and social and welfare services by the government.

The comfort of economic dependency and the opposite desire for independence, gradually led to an ambivalent relationship between the development towns and the central government. Since the 1970s this relationship became increasingly tense, reflecting the national-

Table 4.1. The Development Towns by Size of Population (1987) and Region

Population	North	Center/South
Less than 5,000	Rekhasim Shelomi	Mizpe Ramon
5,001–10,000	Hazor Ma'alot Or Aqiva Yoqneam Ilit	Netivot Sederot Yeroham
10,001–20,000	Bet She'an Karmiel Migdal Ha'emek Qiryat Shemona Safed	Arad Bet Shemesh Ofakim Qiryat Mal'akhi
20,001–40,000	Afula Akko Nahariya Nazerat Ilit Yavne	Dimona Eilat Qiryat Gat Tiberias
40,001–75,000		Ashdod Ashqelon Lod Ramla
More than 75,000		Beer Sheva
Total Number of Towns	16	17

Source: Central Bureau of Statistics 1989a.

level conflict between Oriental and Ashkenazic Jews. The latter are largely middle-class, immigrants of European (mostly) and American origin who control the government and dominate the country's political and social life. This ethnic-class division explains, to a great extent, the relationship between the towns and the Israeli society and government. But before this relationship is analyzed, it is important to provide a brief demographic and social review of Israel's two ethnic-class groups, and of the development towns in relation to the country's general population.

Figure 4.1

Israeli Development Towns by Size of Population, 1987

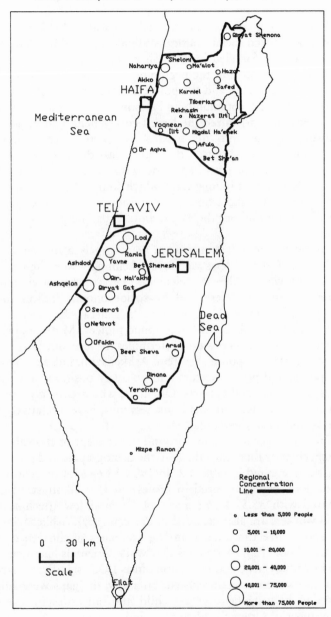

DEMOGRAPHIC AND SOCIAL CHARACTERISTICS

The Oriental immigrants who entered Israel after 1948 met a cohesive and centralized social-political system controlled by Ashkenazim. The system was founded by a small group of East European Jews who came to Palestine at the beginning of the century. They quickly became the social elite and the political establishment of the Yishuv, the pre-state Jewish community in Palestine. They led this community to independence, organized the Israeli government, and infused their socialistic ideology into the masses who entered throughout the 1950s. Thus, from the outset, the ethnic-class division between Ashkenazic and Oriental Jews had to do with the latter not being part of the early waves of immigration which founded the Israeli system. By the late 1950s, the ethnic-class division was formed, and it remained firm throughout the 1970s and 1980s, the period under discussion here.

During the period, Ashkenazim were largely affiliated with the middle-class. Oriental Jews were overwhelmingly working-class with a growing lower middle-class element. (The concept of class in this chapter is basically determined by socioeconomic indices such as housing, education, and occupation). In general, Ashkenazim rank higher than Orientals on socioeconomic indices. More importantly, an upper or lower class position determines the level of control of that class over the social-political system. Ashkenazim, indeed, control Israel's public and private sectors and hold key positions in all major parties, academia, and the arts. Orientals, who are mostly employed in blue-collar service and small-business jobs, have a relatively small share of control in these areas.

The rough generalizations around the concept of class above are more specifically illustrated through the demographic and social characteristics presented in table 4.2. In 1987, 58.6–68.4 percent of Ashkenazic Jews were employed in professional or administrative jobs compared with 35.5–43.2 percent of Oriental Jews (technical and clerical workers are also included in this category). Ashkenazim were represented three times more among graduates of thirteen or more years of school. Table 4.2 shows that while Orientals had made clear gains in employment and education since 1975, significant gaps between the two groups still existed. Similarly, the gaps were still significant in housing density and child allowance despite the great improvement of Orientals along these indices since 1975.

Table 4.2. Demographic and Social Characteristics of Israel's Ethnic Groups (percentage for 1972, 1975, and 1987)

Demographic/ Social Characteristic	Total Jews	Ashkenazic Jews		Oriental Jews	
		Born in Europe or America	Born in Israel, European or American Origin	Born in Asia or Africa	Born in Israel, Asian or African Origin
Representation in the Jewish Population					
1972	100	44.2ᵃ		47.4ᵃ	
1987	100	37.0ᵃ		42.5ᵃ	
13 or More Years of School					
1975	17.7	22.9	34.7	7.0	7.3
1987	26.2	32.0	48.8	12.9	16.4
Employed in Professional or Administrative jobsᵇ					
1975	43	47.2	64.3	25.3	36.7
1987	51.2	58.6	68.4	35.5	43.2
Density of 2 or More Persons per Room					
1975	26.2	12.2	11.6	47.2	38.5
1987	8.0	2.8	5.0	12.7	13.1
Families Receiving Child Allowance					
1975ᶜ	15.9	13.6		47.4	
1987ᵈ	34.8	16.8		29.8	

Sources: Central Bureau of Statistics, 1976, 1988a; Achdut and Yaniv 1988, 218.

a. This figure does not include children of Israel-born parents. When such third generation Israelis are included, the 1987 Oriental population is estimated at 55 percent.

b. Professional—scientific, academic, professional, and technical workers. Administrative—administrators, managers, and clerical workers.

c. For three or more children.

d. For one or more children (after the reform in the system).

The national-level ethnic-class gaps in employment and education are generally reflected in table 4.3, where the development towns, with a population of three-quarters Orientals, are compared with the total Jewish population.[3] Yet a closer examination reveals a mixed picture here. Indeed, the 1983 percentage of the towns' residents employed in professional or administrative jobs in table 4.3 (40.4), and the 1987 national figures for Orientals in this category in table 4.2 (35.5–43.2), are similar. But, interestingly, the 1983 percentage of residents with thirteen or more years of school (21.8), which almost tripled since 1972, clearly exceeds the 1987 national figures for Orientals in table 4.2 (12.9–16.4). Thus, the residents of the development towns markedly improved their education level, which is currently higher than that of Orientals in the rest of the country.

On the other hand, social welfare indices point out a problematic situation in the development towns. Borukhov and Werczberger (1981, 425) report that 9.3 percent of the 1972 households in the towns, compared with a national average of 5 percent, were dependent on welfare payments. A more troubling picture is evident in table 4.3. In 1978 and 1983 the towns included a significantly higher percentage of families with three or more children compared with the total Jewish population. Furthermore, 36.6 percent of Israel's unemployed adults in 1978 and 40.1 percent in 1987 lived in the towns. The towns comprised 17.2 percent of Israel's 1987 total population (Jews and non-Jews). This extremely high rate of unemployment is a continuous problem which attracted much public and media attention. With respect to other indices in table 4.3, while the number of motor vehicles in the towns more than doubled between 1978 and 1987, the gap with the national rate, 159.7 to 200.0 or about 40 vehicles per 1,000 people, still remained in 1987. Crime was also significantly higher compared with the national rate.

Overall evidence for the class gap between the development towns and the country as a whole can be found in a classification of ninety-five local governments in Israel (Dori et al. 1988). Eighteen of the thirty-three towns are among the twenty-three local governments which scored lowest according to the socioeconomic characteristics of their population in 1983. Furthermore, 25 and 28 of the towns are respectively among the 41 and 50 governments that scored lowest.

The intersection of lower socioeconomic status and Oriental ethnicity is very powerful when one considers the towns' relative size in Israeli society (table 4.3). The towns comprise one-fifth of the total Jewish population and one-third of the Oriental population. Orientals, three-quarters of the towns' population, are clearly overrepresented. Orientals currently have a slight numerical majority over Ashkenazim in the total Jewish population (table 4.2).

Despite their significant representation in Israeli society, their successful contribution to the national objective of population dispersion

Table 4.3. Demographic and Social Characteristics of the Development Towns versus the Total Population, 1972–1987

Demographic/Social Characteristic	Development Towns	Total Population	Development Towns as Percentage of the Total Population
TOTAL JEWISH POPULATION			
1972	545,700	2,686,700	20.3
1987	756,520	3,612,900	21.0
Percentage of Oriental Population[a]			
1972	75.4[b]	47.4	32.3
1983	68.4	44.1	32.9
Percentage of Families with 3 or More Children[c]			
1978	46.3	32.5	—
1983	43.0	31.4	—
Percentage of Population with 13 or More Years of School			
1972(towns); 1975(total)	7.8[d]	17.7	—
1983(towns); 1987(total)	21.8[e]	26.2	—
Percentage Employed in Professional or Administrative Jobs			
1983(towns); 1987(total)	40.4	51.2	—
ISRAEL'S TOTAL POPULATION (JEWS AND NON-JEWS)[f]			
Unemployed Adults			
1978	6,785	18,527	36.6
1987	15,028	37,468	40.1
Crime Rate per 1,000			
1978	84.5	56.5	—
1983	76.9	59.8	—
Motor Vehicles per 1,000			
1978	71.2	115.9	—
1987	159.7	200.0	—

Sources: Central Bureau of Statistics 1973, 1984, 1988a, 1989a; Borukhov and Werczberger 1981; Dreifuss 1987.

a. Children of Israel-born parents of Oriental origin (third generation) are not included. When included, these figures will increase (e.g., 68.4 to 75–80, 32.9 to 36–39).

b. Reported for 29 towns, with standard deviation of 18.4, by Borukhov and Werczberger (1981, 424).

c. Based on data from 30 towns.

d. Based on data from 18 towns.

e. Based on data from 23 towns.

f. Based on data from 30 towns.

(Shachar 1971), and the 38 percent growth of their population between 1972 and 1987, the development towns still remained small communities. In 1987 all but five of them had a population of less than 40,000 people (table 4.1) and the average size per town was 22,925 people. Moreover, while their natural population growth at that time, 17.7 per 1,000, is close to the national average (16.0), their migration balance (in-migration minus out-migration) is only 1,024 people (data compiled from Central Bureau of Statistics 1989a). This figure is especially troubling since a number of studies consider the towns' ability to attract migrants as an indicator of successful development (Kirschenbaum and Comay 1973; Ya'ar and Heller 1977; Borukhov and Werczgberger 1981).

The lower socioeconomic status and Oriental ethnicity of the residents of the development towns are related to their values. These values further contribute to the conflict between the towns and the larger society. The conflict of values is the subject of the following section.

CONFLICT OF VALUES

The broad ethnic dichotomy discussed earlier between Ashkenazim and Oriental Jews is not so simple. Differences are still prevalent among Jews from Germany, Poland, Hungary, or Argentina as well as among Jews from Morocco, Egypt, Syria, Iraq, or Yemen. Yet, while the specific European-American ethnic origins are gradually vanishing and a single broad category, Ashkenazim, has been formed, the distinct ethnic frameworks are more pronounced among Oriental Jews. Much of the Orientals' distinctiveness centers around their traditional patterns of religious practice, culture, and community and family life. The vast majority of Orientals practice religion and view the local synagogue as an important communal institution; they consider the neighborhood as the focus of social activities; and their social relations are based upon family and kinship ties (Weingrod 1979, 58–62).

The original intent of the Ashkenazic founders of the state, however, was to build a European-style homogeneous national culture. Ethnic distinctiveness was considered to be divisive and impeding the creation of the new national culture. The state emphasized an ideology of "ingathering of exiles" and applied strong pressure for cultural homogenization through the public schools and the universal conscription to the army. The goal was to create an autonomous Israeli culture which is in contrast to the previous discredited Jewish "exile mentality" (Goldberg 1977, 170). The traditional culture of Oriental Jews, and their relatively late entry to Israel with poor skills and little experience in bureaucratic institutions, were viewed by the Ashkenazic establishment as inhibiting the Orientals' integration into the emerging Western-style modern democratic society. The temporary cultural gap was supposed to fade away as part of the absorption process. The Orientals were expected to transform their modes of behavior into modern European style. An integrated society was to emerge from the "melting pot."

To some extent, Oriental Jews conformed to the pressure and adopted the European-style Israeli culture. At the same time, their own Middle Eastern culture, which dominated the larger region, impinged upon the Ashkenazim. Eventually, the mutual infusion resulted in a certain degree of mix. Consequently, social barriers in socializing, child-rearing, life-style, and intermarriage were reduced. But beyond this partial integration process, the salient feature mentioned before remained: Ashkenazim emerged as a broad and dominant culture category, while Orientals were far more persistent in maintaining their traditional unique ethnic frameworks.

This trend continued and was reinforced in the early 1970s. Suppressed by the ideological pressures of the establishment for two decades, Oriental ethnicity then surfaced, often as a form of resistance to the mainstream Western culture. Partially absorbed into the new society, the immigrants became secure enough to expose their cultural roots. The establishment itself began to view cultural pluralism as less threatening to the system and more legitimate. This change came about as a result of the easing security, economic, and immigrant absorption pressures. The newly pronounced ethnic and cultural identity took many forms. Most popular was the revitalization of ethnic celebrations such as the Moroccan Mimouna and Kurdish Se'eranna festivals (Goldberg 1977; Weingrod 1979).

The revival of ethnicity intersected with class. Although in the 1950s and 1960s the dominant socialistic ideology attempted to minimize gaps in income, occupation, and education; class stratification, closely linked with ethnicity, has been observed since the 1970s by numerous studies. Weingrod (1979), for example, reports on the emergence of an Israeli version of "working-class culture." Its members are blue- and white-collar Oriental Jews who have specific preferences regarding clothing styles, songs, and sports. Hasson (1983), in a study on the lowest stratum of this class, observes feelings of ethnic deprivation and frustration along with the demand to preserve the Oriental heritage. Smooha (1988, 27) describes Orientals as the overwhelming majority of the Jewish proletariat, uneasy and somewhat alienated from the dominant Western-oriented culture, and fairly content with Mediterranean or Arab culture. Intertwined with their lower- and working-class base, the growing ethnic and cultural consciousness of the Orientals increased their group solidarity and pride.

The manifestations of their class, ethnicity, culture, and group solidarity and pride were especially strong in Oriental communities that, though linked among themselves, were spatially and socially isolated from their neighbors. Well-known examples in the 1970s were the poor neighborhoods of Jerusalem where members of the Black Panthers and the Ohalim Movement transformed their feelings of injustice and discrimination into a series of violent, confrontational, and cooperational acts (Hasson 1983). In the case of the development towns, these communities were not only physically, but also socially isolated due to their homogeneous composition, which was mostly working-class Oriental Jews. The Orientals, as mentioned before, did not have much choice in selecting their residence when they moved to Israel. In addition, the towns could not attract significant numbers of middle-class Ashkenazic immigrants or veteran Israelis. Although these new towns were considered standard-bearers of the national "melting pot" ideal, the reality was that no standards were set for planning their ethnic or socioeconomic composition. Ironically, they became homogeneous communities, spatially isolated from their neighbors and fairly detached, socially, from the larger Israeli society.

The territorial confinement reinforced the preservation of traditional ethnic and cultural patterns. In turn, it increased the towns' resistance to the attempts of the establishment to impose a European style. A prominent example of this conflict of values was the tense relationship between the development towns and their neighboring kibbutzim, originally a local/regional conflict which escalated into a national-level conflict in the 1980s. The content of the conflict was the clash between the traditional and religious values of the towns' residents and the Western-oriented values and socialistic ideology of which the kibbutzim were the national spearhead. The conflict is documented in a number of studies which focus on social and psychological problems as well as mutual images and stereotypes (e.g., Hareven 1981; Fovin et al. 1985).

An important source of the conflict of values with the larger society was the threat that the mainstream culture posed to the traditional family structure of the towns' residents. In his country of origin the Oriental father was the breadwinner and the source of authority; in the new society he became unskilled, frequently unemployed, and dependent on public assistance. To complement his low income, his wife and children were forced to work. Subsequently, the father's status in the family dropped as he could no longer care for its basic needs. The family became increasingly disorganized and problems of crime and juvenile delinquency were not unusual. This process was followed by some resentment and bitterness towards modern Western values. This was later translated into organized economic and political demands, which will be discussed in the following sections.

CONFLICT OF INTERESTS: TENSIONS DUE TO PLANNING AND IMPLEMENTATION SHORTCOMINGS

It was described earlier that the particular economic and social circumstances at the time of the Oriental immigration to Israel clearly contributed to the lower socioeconomic status of the development towns. Moreover, this status was reinforced by a series of shortcomings in the planning and implementation of the new towns policy. This section begins with an analysis of these shortcomings which impeded economic development, maintained the lower socioeconomic status, and subsequently contributed to class conflict over economic interests between the towns and the larger society and between the towns and the central government. The conflict itself is analyzed later in the section. It focuses on problems of lagging industrial growth, unemployment, "negative selection" of population, and out-migration.

The principles of Zionist ideology clearly dictated the planning and implementation of the new towns policy. The policy was designed with much emphasis on the national goals of security and defense, population dispersion, and immigrant absorption (Spiegel 1967; Berler 1970). At the same time, the policy failed to provide sufficient attention to the economic goals of efficiency, growth, and the provision of a wide range of economic activities (Shachar 1971; Altman and Rosenbaum 1973). This economic failure originated in the spatial distribution of the towns.

As mentioned earlier, the goal of dispersing population from the congested coastal zone to the uninhabited frontier areas was designed not only to accelerate their development, but also to strengthen national security and defense. Furthermore, decreasing the economic and social dominance of the largest city, Tel Aviv, while increasing the importance of agricultural settlements and smaller communities in the hinterland, was compatible with the anti-urban bias of Zionist ideology.[4] Accordingly, the new towns policy was based on the integration of agricultural settlements, namely kibbutzim and moshavim, with medium-to-small-sized urban service centers, the development towns, which were fully sponsored by the government. The towns were supposed to serve as the intermediary links between the small rural settlements and the large cities (Brutzkus 1964).

Implementation, however, was problematic. Most of the development towns were small and therefore could develop neither a wide range of urban services nor a sufficient level of service delivery. In addition, the agricultural settlements continued their tradition of receiving services, and buying and selling in the large cities. Thus, they bypassed most of the towns and the latter did not become service and market centers as planned (Borukhov and Werczberger 1981, 422). This process significantly impeded the economic growth of the towns.

When it became evident that the goal of centralizing services in small communities could not provide the base for economic growth, the policy was changed towards manufacturing, such as textiles, a nongrowth industry characterized by unskilled labor (Gradus and Krakover 1977). Many of the towns developed such an industry, which due to their small size remained the single one in town, suffering from shortage of skilled workers as well as a lack of managerial and technical expertise. The plants themselves were dispersed among the different towns and remained far away from their markets in the coastal zone (Shachar 1971, 367). The government, nevertheless, continuously tried to attract industries to the towns through grants, subsidies, loans, investment credits, tax exemptions, and training programs.

Despite all these financial incentives, industrial growth and service delivery to the agricultural hinterland have been sluggish. Economic efficiency and growth in industrial production, and in service and commerce activities, could not be achieved due to the towns' small size and their wide spatial distribution. The overriding national goals continued to dictate such dispersal which, in itself, was a successful policy. Namely, population growth in the densed coastal zone was reduced through the establishment of medium-to-small-sized urban centers, the development towns. Yet the option of fewer—but larger—towns, though considered, was never implemented.

These shortcomings in planning and implementation had severe implications for industrial growth in the development towns. The lag in industrial growth is a major problem which illustrates that the national dispersal policy is not necessarily compatible with the interests of the towns. The dispersal policy frequently resulted in a single manufacturing plant in town, specializing in textiles, clothing, diamonds, wood, or paper and dependent on an unskilled workforce. When the plant was closed, due to its lack of growth potential and the conditions of the national economy, the whole town faced major economic difficulties including severe unemployment. Such an unstable economic environment, which also lacked local entrepreneurs and capital for developing a modern industry, tended to rely on external ownership. The dependency on owners of single plant from the developed urban centers in the coastal zone, or on a government and Histadrut (General Federation of Labor) multiplant firms with head offices there, was a constant source of conflict between the owners and the towns.

In their study of the factors that affect the closure propensity of industrial plants in the development towns, Razin and Shachar (1987) elaborate on the problem of external ownership and the tension engendered by it. Accordingly, while the locally owned plants, 15 percent of the plants in 1983, were relatively small and indeed with a short life span and a high closure propensity, the nonlocal single-plant firms, 30 percent, had the highest closure rate. For market, communication, and social reasons, the inexperienced managers of the nonlocal firms preferred to live and to establish headquarters in the large urban centers of the coastal zone. Moreover, they considered their jobs in the remote towns as a stepping-stone towards better positions in the urban centers. Much more stable were the nonlocal multiplant firms, 45 percent of the total in 1983, which employed 68 percent of the total industrial labor in the towns. Such government- and Histadrut-owned plants were managed in accordance with national interests, with less emphasis on purely economic considerations and more sensitivity to public opinion. At the same time, the owners of these plants and the residents of the towns clashed over the latter's demand for increased financial incentives, jobs, and local control. Interestingly, the highest stability was found in plants owned by the rural-cooperative sector, the kibbutzim. These plants enjoyed long-range planning and their owners were sensitive to the dismissal of workers from the neighboring development towns.

The problem here, however, was the tense social relationship between the kibbutz-member administrators and the unskilled manual workers from the towns.

The lagging industrial growth was the main reason for the extremely high rate of unemployment (table 4.3) in the development towns (Borukhov 1988). Unemployment, and the different policies to overcome this problem, emerged as highly controversial issues between the towns and the central government during 1989–90.[5] The towns demanded significant increases in the funding of grants, subsidies, tax exemptions, and for covering their budget deficits. Their mayors protested in Jerusalem and asked for emergency cabinet meetings on these acute issues. The reluctant government, though sympathetic, had somewhat different national economic priorities.

The problems of industrial growth and unemployment eventually determined the social composition of the towns' population. The towns did not attract high technology or more sophisticated growth industries which tend to employ the better educated and professionals. They remained homogeneous communities with a vast majority of working-class Oriental Jews. The process of "negative selection" was reinforced as the better educated and upwardly mobile residents of the towns tended to move to the urban centers on the coast while the unskilled and the poor were left behind. Stereotyped as the "Second Israel," a housing shelter for the uneducated and economically dependent, the towns could not attract middle-class residents and have suffered high rates of out-migration. As mentioned earlier, they remained small communities with a low in-migration balance.

The process of "negative selection" of population and out-migration has resulted in tension between the development towns, small communities attempting to improve their size and social composition, and the much wealthier urban centers of the coast. The tension is centered on the towns' interests regarding economic development. The towns try to attract and maintain middle-class residents. The latter tend to stay in the coastal zone or, if already residing in the towns, to move to the coast. Because the towns are much weaker, they become economically dependent on the urban centers of the coast. Swirski (1981) describes this relationship as another expression of the "ethnic division of labor" between Oriental Jews and Ashkenazim.

On a further note, the formation of isolated and socially homogeneous communities plagued with economic problems contradicts the original national goal of the new towns policy—immigrant absorption and integration into Israeli society. This contradiction is a constant source of tension between the towns and the central government, especially in regard to the allocation of budgets from the center, as shall be apparent in the following section.

CONFLICT OF INTERESTS: BARGAINING OVER BUDGETS

To overcome the problems of industrial growth, employment, and social composition, the towns pressure the government to increase their budget. The bargaining over budgets, between the towns and the central government, is another manifestation of the class conflict. The towns demand to increase their budgets to cover huge deficits, to fund investment credits and tax exemptions, to build new industrial plants, to reduce unemployment by creating new jobs, and to improve the quality of their schools. In general, each town's budget allocation is based on the rank of its level of economic development by the government. The ranking, thus, in terms of whether it is economically weak or sound, becomes an important part of the political bargaining. The towns are striving to receive the ranking which guarantees maximum funding. This process is further complicated by the fact that each ministry (e.g., Housing and Construction, Industry and Commerce) has its own system of ranking.

The development towns' demands for the central government to increase their budgets, as mentioned earlier, became especially acute during 1989–90. Mayors and residents protested against the government, blaming it for their deficits, high unemployment, and for the negligence of Israel's deprived populations in the frontier areas. A major target of their criticism was the high priority the government accorded to the new settlements in the West Bank. On the other hand, some critics (e.g., *Ha'aretz*, 30 June, 1989) called on the government "to dismantle the development towns," describing them as ideologically driven projects lacking any economic rationale.

There are different estimates of the allocations granted to the development towns by the government and quasi-government agencies. Beyond budget politics, three methodological reasons might explain why the estimates varied. First, there have been different accounts of the number of towns (e.g., 33, 29, or 25; see note 1). Second, there have been different accounts of indirect sources of quasi-government funding such as from the Histadrut, the Jewish Agency, and Project

Table 4.4. Total Revenues of the Development Towns as Percentage of Total Revenues of All Israeli Municipalities for 1969/70, 1979/80, and 1985/86

Fiscal Year	Ordinary Budget	Extraordinary (Development) Budget
1969/70	17.8[a]	23.3[b]
1979/80	21.5	24.5[c]
1985/86	18.8	14.0

Sources: Central Bureau of Statistics 1971, 1982, 1988c.
a. Based on data from 32 towns.
b. Based on data from 17 towns.
c. Based on data from 25 towns.

Table 4.5. Expenditure on Services and Deficit: The Development Towns as Percentage of All Israeli Municipalities, Ordinary Budget for 1985/86

Expenditure on all state services	23.4
Expenditure on welfare services	27.1
Expenditure on Religious services	23.3
Annual Deficit	40.1

Source: Central Bureau of Statistics 1988c.

Renewal, rendering any calculation highly complicated. Third, government funding fluctuates from year to year and can increase greatly in an election year. These three reasons might explain why Torgovnik (1987, 72), for example, provides data that are inconsistent with the budget analysis of this study, which is presented below. First, Torgovnik focuses on only sixteen development towns. Second, he indicates a roughly four-fold higher central government expenditure per capita in the towns compared with developed settlements.[6] Third, he reports that government funding ranges between 63 to 89 percent in an election year (1980–81).

The following results of the budget analysis take into account the thirty-three towns, their ordinary and extraordinary (development) budgets, and nonelection years only. When the towns are calculated as a percentage of all Israel's municipalities or population, in regard to several budget items, a slightly favorable treatment for the towns is observed. It is expressed in 6–7 percent above the 17 percent (namely 23–24 percent) that the towns comprise of Israel's population throughout the years in question. These items are extraordinary bud-

Table 4.6. Social Welfare Indicators: Development Towns versus Israel's Population, 1987ª

Indicator	Development Towns	Israel's Population	Development Towns as Percentage of Israel's Population
Families Receiving Child Allowance	102,413	513,345	20
Number of Clients of Social Services	85,583	372,481	23
Clients of Social Services as Percentage of the Population	11.3	8.4	—

Source: Central Bureau of Statistics 1989a.
a. Based on data from 30 towns.

Table 4.7. Local Revenues of the Development Towns and All Israeli Municipalities as Percentage of Total Revenues, Ordinary Budget for 1969/70, 1979/80, and 1985/86

Fiscal Year	Development Towns	All Israeli Municipalities
1969/70	51.7	56.4
1979/80	19.4	29.6
1985/86	47.6	59.6

Sources: Central Bureau of Statistics 1971, 1982, 1988c.

get (1969/70 and 1979/80 in table 4.4), expenditure on all state and (particularly) religious services (1985/86 in table 4.5), and number of clients of social services (1987 in table 4.6). Similarly, a 10 percent preferential treatment (namely 27 percent) is noted in expenditure on welfare services (1985/86 in table 4.5). The striking difference, however, is in the towns' 1985/86 deficit which comprises 40 percent of the deficit of all Israeli municipalities (table 4.5). A clear difference is also noted in the percentage of clients of social services in 1987: 8 and 11 percent of the country's and the towns' population, respectively (table 4.6). Finally, the towns are consistently 5–12 percent lower than all Israeli municipalities in their locally raised revenues (1969/70, 1979/80, and 1985/86 in table 4.7). Namely, they receive a somewhat higher proportion of external funding, mainly from the central government.

In summary, ordinary budget deficit (table 4.5) and unemployment (see also table 4.3) are two focal points of budget bargaining between the development towns and the central government, especially since the mid-1980s. On both the deficit and unemployment, the towns account for 40 percent of all Israel's municipalities or population, that is, 2.3 times more than their 17 percent representation in the population. The deficit is a continuous problem despite the towns' higher proportion of central government funding; in 1985/86 the towns raised locally only 47 percent while the national average was 59 percent (table 4.7). Similarly, unemployment is an acute problem which is followed by higher expenditure for welfare services as well as a higher percentage of clients of social services.

POLITICS

The preceding sections described the conflict of values, essentially centered on ethnic differences, and the conflict of interests, essentially centered on class issues. All of these conflicts between the development towns and the larger society and the central government are ultimately handled in the political arena. The political process in which the towns participate is the subject of this section. The process is analyzed with the focus on Knesset (parliament) and local elections in the towns, the power leverage of the towns in the Knesset and the cabinet, and their attempt to influence legislative and executive policymaking.

The most salient feature of the political process in the 1950s and 1960s was the overwhelming economic dependency of the development towns on the central government and its budget policy. At the time, the Israeli central and local governments, cabinet, Knesset, and the Histadrut, were all controlled by Labor (earlier Mapai), a moderate socialistic party. In exchange for their votes, the towns' residents, many of them with little means of their own, accepted jobs, public contracts, licenses, and other material favors from the ruling party. These inducements were offered through the local government—specifically the local council, and the mayor and city administration—as well as through industries owned by Histadrut companies. The Histadrut was not only a federation of unions. It was also one of the biggest employers in the country, and it provided a variety of local services in education, culture, health, welfare, housing, banking, and insurance. A similar exchange of votes for material favors, though on a much smaller scale, was offered to the towns' residents by the National Religious Party (NRP) in the municipalities under its control.[7]

The NRP, though much smaller than Labor in its ability to deliver material favors, appealed to the Oriental immigrants because their vast majority upheld religious and traditional values. The party was ideologically committed to religious beliefs, delivery of religious services, and traditional life-styles. The ideological commitment to Labor, on the other hand, was fairly weak. Nevertheless, the residents of the development towns responded, to some extent, to the pressures of the party ideology and adopted modern Western values. The ideology maintained that such adoption would reinforce social integration and national unity. This ideology dominated the larger society throughout the 1950s and 1960s.

The economic dependency of the towns' residents on the NRP, and especially on the Labor party, was significantly reduced throughout the 1970s for three major reasons. First, the Israeli welfare state took over more economic and service functions; since the pre-state period these functions had been delivered by the parties and the Histadrut. Second, a greater number of immigrants, especially younger and educated ones, were absorbed into the job market, and there was less need for party-arranged public jobs. Third, because transportation was improved and the towns became less isolated, more residents commuted to work out of town, and less residents held local jobs.

The increasing economic independence was followed by protest against the paternalism of the party that represented the establishment. Labor was blamed by the residents of the development towns, as well as by the larger working-class Oriental immigrant community, for their (still) inferior class position and relative deprivation vis-à-vis the Ashkenazim. Oriental Jews believed their situation was a direct result of Labor's mistakes made in their absorption during the 1950s and 1960s. In the 1970s, this was one important reason for Oriental Jews to switch their support from Labor, which had become a middle-class Ashkenazic party, to the main opposition party, the right-wing Likud. Two other reasons were the Likud's more favorable attitudes towards traditional and religious values, and its hawkish foreign policy (Shamir and Arian 1982). The growing Oriental support for the Likud sharpened the national-level ethnic-class cleavage,[8] and simultaneously increased the tension between the towns and the larger society.

The above political developments are reflected in the results of Knesset and local elections in the development towns presented in ta-

Table 4.8. Results of Knesset Elections in Development Towns and Nationwide (percentage of valid votes for 1965, 1981, and 1988)

| | Political Bloc | | | | | Voting |
	Labor	Likud	Religious	Other	Total	Turnout
Development Towns						
1965[a]	53.8	20.1	13.1	13.0	100	81.0
1981	29.2	48.9	9.2	12.7	100	77.5
1988	27.4	40.8	20.0	11.8	100	78.1
Nationwide						
1981	36.6	37.1	10.9	15.9	100	78.5
1988	32.5	31.1	14.6	21.7	100	79.7

Sources: Central Bureau of Statistics 1966, 1981, 1988a, 1988b, 1989b.
a. Based on data from 30 towns.

bles 4.8, 4.9, and 4.10.[9] Namely, since the 1970s, a sharp decline was observed in the Labor vote and a significant increase in the Likud vote. Within this broad trend, there are some smaller, though also important, tendencies which require further explanation. To begin, the decrease in the Labor vote to the Knesset and the electoral shift to the Likud was stronger in the towns than nationwide (table 4.8). This was due to the large proportion of Oriental Jews in the towns. The Likud was very effective in capturing Labor's votes to the Knesset in the towns. Between 1965 and 1988, Labor lost one-half of its votes while the Likud doubled its electorate (table 4.8). In the elections for local councils, however, despite Labor's dramatic decline, the Likud registered only a moderate growth of 11 percent between 1965 and 1989 because many Labor supporters switched to local lists (table 4.9). The growing support for local lists was also the reason for the lower vote for both Labor and Likud local council candidates in the 1980s (table 4.9), when compared with that of their candidates for the Knesset (table 4.8). Finally, while the Likud took many Labor votes and rose significantly in the 1989 local elections, its mayoral candidates were much more attractive and successful than its candidates for the local councils (table 4.9 and 4.10).

Another broad trend was the strong increase in votes for local lists to the councils. This increase was gradual from one election year to another. But overall, between 1965 and 1989 the increase was very dramatic, from 3 to over 33 percent, respectively (table 4.9). The growing power of local lists in the councils had no parallel, however,

Table 4.9. Results of Local Elections for Council and Mayor in Development Towns (percentage of valid votes), 1965-1989

	Political Bloc					
	Labor	*Likud*	*Religious*	*Local*	*Other*	*Total*
Council						
1965	52.8	16.8	19.9	3.1	7.4	100
1969	40.5	25.5	20.1	8.7	5.1	100
1973	39.3	21.7	18.8	11.5	8.5	100
1978	29.2	25.9	18.8	18.8	7.3	100
1983	27.7	22.1	21.5	26.6	2.1	100
1989	18.9	27.8	17.8	33.7	1.8	100
Mayor						
1978	33.2	33.7	10.4	18.2	4.2	100
1983	30.7	26.9	12.6	29.0	0.8	100
1989	23.8	43.5	7.3	24.9	0.5	100

Sources: Central Bureau of Statistics 1966, 1970, 1974; Ministry of the Interior 1979; Goldberg 1984; Reshumot-Yalkut Ha'pirsumim 1989.
Note: Results for Mayor do not include the runoff elections.

Table 4.10. Results of Local Elections for Mayor in Development Towns, 1978 and 1989

	Political Bloc					
Election Year	*Labor*	*Likud*	*Religious*	*Local*	*Other*	*Total*
1978	15	9	5	4	—	33
1989	10	18	1	4	—	33

Sources: Ministry of the Interior 1979; Reshumot-Yalkut Ha'Pirsumim 1989.
Note: Results include the runoff elections.

in elections for mayors. In both 1978 and 1989, only four mayors were elected from local lists (table 4.10).

This discrepancy in the vote for councils and mayors points out the limited ability of mayoral candidates from small local lists, with no national visibility and little financial backing, to succeed in personal elections (for mayors) in a system dominated by parties that compete for proportional representation (for councils and Knesset elections). Nevertheless, Labor's loss to the local lists reflects the trend of the 1970s and 1980s, namely, the transition from politics based on national ideology to politics based on territoriality (Elazar 1975). In the development towns, this transformation is spearheaded by the more educated and younger generation, the children of the immigrants. They represent local interests and grassroots action for autonomy and growing liberation from all the major parties that promote national-level ideological platforms.

One more broad trend was the stability of the religious bloc in the development towns in both Knesset and, especially, local councils elections (tables 4.8 and 4.9). The exception was the 1988 Knesset elections when this bloc recorded a dramatic gain at the expense of the Likud. It rose to 20 percent, from 9 percent in 1981, which is far more than the nationwide results (table 4.8). A reverse tendency, however, was noted in elections for mayors. The religious loss, from five mayors in 1978 to one in 1989, is clearly registered as the Likud's gain (table 4.10).

This last observation demonstrates again the limited attractiveness of mayoral candidates from smaller parties in the Israeli elections system. Beyond that, the stability of the religious bloc in the development towns is nourished by the legitimacy of its religious and traditional platform. Its cultural and spiritual significance stands in contrast to the material exchange offered by Labor to its voters. Despite Labor's financial and organizational advantages, its power declined sharply when the towns increased their economic independence. While the religious vote remained steady, in the absence of an ideological commitment to Labor and political socialization of the residents into this party, they turned against it. To conclude, Labor's material exchange with the voters was effective in the short-run yet unproductive in the long-run (Goldberg and Ben-Zadok 1988).

Labor voters shifted to the Likud, a party which offered a more religious, traditional, hawkish, and anti-establishment platform. Enjoying the massive support of Oriental Jews, two out of every three of its voters in the 1977, 1981, and 1984 elections, the Likud then rose to power in the development towns and nationwide. After three decades in opposition, the Likud formed its first government in 1977 and remained in power until 1992. Nevertheless, the Likud's loss of some of the Oriental vote to the religious bloc in 1988, in the towns even more than nationwide, points out again the solid ideological base of the religious bloc. The protest against the mainstream culture, the pronounced and restored Oriental ethnicity, are still more naturally integrated into the traditional platform of the religious bloc.[10]

Beyond the ideological platform of the Likud, the party offered broad channels of political mobility, which were denied by Labor, to the younger generation of the towns, and enabled them to represent their own ethnic and local interests. Throughout the 1970s, local Likud leaders replaced the Labor leaders that were traditionally controlled by, or even sent from, the party headquarters in the urban centers of the coastal zone. The new leaders, similar to those from the local lists, were more sensitive to local needs and enjoyed grassroots support in their effort to increase local autonomy. Supported by masses of residents, and relying on steady, large voter turnouts (table 4.8), the more ambitious of them used their local, frequently mayoral, positions as stepping-stones to national politics, and became members of the Knesset. The most ambitious entered into the top corridors of power of the Israeli government, as members of the cabinet.

The penetration from local to national leadership positions was rapid. Two Knesset members in 1969, nine in 1981, and fourteen in 1988 were from the development towns. Out of them, one in 1969, five in 1981, and six in 1988 represented the Likud; respectively to those years, only one, three, and four represented Labor; and none, one, and four were from the religious bloc. In 1988, the towns' delegation, led by a Likud majority, comprised 12 percent of the Israeli legislature. Furthermore, members of the delegation were included in all key Knesset committees: two in foreign affairs and defense; two, including the chairman, in finance; and four in social welfare. Finally, in 1981 and 1988, two Likud members from the development towns were appointed as cabinet ministers. In 1990, after the dismanteling of the Likud-Labor National Unity Government and the establishment of a narrow right-wing cabinet, this number increased to three. All three were heading powerful ministries: foreign affairs, economics, and transportation.

The Knesset members from the development towns tend to emphasize the local issues of their communities in their legislative work.[11] They also collaborate in an informal forum, across their (opposing) party lines, attempting to promote their common local and regional interests. In a legislature which still gives much attention to national-level priorities, and is strongly bound to party discipline and loyalty, this is an unusual strategy. The forum exerts much influence on executive policymaking, mainly by ensuring its members the positions of ministers and deputies in offices that are vital to economic development and financing of the towns. These are the ministries of economics, transportation, housing, labor, welfare, immigrant absorption, and religious affairs. Furthermore, the appointment of David Levy from Bet She'an, a northern development town, in 1981 to deputy prime minister and in 1990 to minister of foreign affairs, indicates that the development towns intend to affect the whole range of national-level policymaking.

The local and regional interests of the development towns, promoted by their representatives in the Knesset and the cabinet, clash from time to time with the interests of three other sectors in Israel. These are the kibbutzim, the Palestinians in the West Bank and Gaza Strip, and the Jewish settlements in the West Bank. The conflict between the towns and each of these sectors is rooted in ethnic-class issues.

The conflict with the kibbutzim is actually more complicated than what was discussed earlier. Indeed, the towns supply workers to the industrial plants that are owned by the kibbutzim in their regions. Furthermore, the kibbutzim are socially closed societies, populated by Ashkenazim; almost all of them are affiliated with the Labor party. The friction between the employees and their white-collar managers symbolizes, to the former, the exploitation of Orientals by Labor and their lack of occupational mobility (Yishai 1982, 236–37; Gradus 1984, 93–94).

Another conflict centering on employment and occupational mobility is between the towns' residents and the Palestinians. Peled (1990) conceptualizes it in terms of "split labor market" theory. Accordingly, Orientals compete with Palestinians for the lower-level jobs in the occupational ladder. The towns' residents are threatened by that and fear decline in wages and unemployment. Subsequently, they develop exclusionary sentiments against Palestinians and tend to support extreme right-wing religious parties.

Lastly, there is the tension between the towns and the mostly middle-class Ashkenazic West Bank Jewish settlement. The friction here is around the central government allocation of budgets for development. The representatives of the towns complain that they are relegated to a lower position by the government and protest the negligence of the towns due to the ideological saliency of the settlement in the West Bank.

CONCLUSIONS

Since the early 1970s, the development towns emerged as a powerful force in Israeli politics. In protest against the neglect of the towns by the government, the children of the immigrants formed a new leadership. They grew up in the towns and they understood the needs of their communities and the residents. The younger and educated leaders rose from local positions to the corridors of power in the Israeli parliament and cabinet in Jerusalem. As an organized group, they exerted much influence on legislative and executive policies, attempting to promote their local and regional interests.

Their considerable leverage and bargaining position in national politics is based on at least two major sources. One, comprising about one-fifth of Israel's population, the thirty-three towns represent a powerful demographic and voting force. Two, their geographic concentration, in the north and center/south, positions them in a leading role in the policymaking of the two regions. Furthermore, if electoral reform materializes, based on elections of Knesset candidates from districts, the towns' potential to influence government policies in their regions and nationwide would increase due to their geographic concentration.

The development towns enjoy a high degree of social cohesiveness which reinforces their organized action and political effectiveness. Their cohesiveness is based on the number of demographic and social characteristics shared by most residents. The vast majority of the residents are working-class Oriental Jews with a similar level of education, occupation, income, and housing conditions. Their relatively traditional values are brought from their countries of origin. They all share a problematic experience of absorption into the new society. These common characteristics create a fairly unified and homogeneous social base that enables this group to make strong economic and political demands from the society and the central government.

One may argue that the social cohesiveness of the Oriental community, particularly in the development towns, although less so in Israel in general, will prolong the conflict of values with the larger society. Nevertheless, a reduction in tension over values is possible in the future. The main reason for this reduction is the increasing tolerance on the part of Ashkenazim to the traditional cultural and religious patterns of Oriental Jews coupled with increasing recognition of cultural pluralism in the Israeli public. Moreover, the dominant Western-oriented culture is gradually opening up to the culture of the region, that is, Middle Eastern patterns. Simultaneously, Orientals continue to make some adaptation to the European style. These mutual cultural infusions are primarily transmitted through the schools, military service, media, leisure activities, and ethnic intermarriage. These exchanges might reduce the conflict of values in the future.

This general societal trend should be qualified with respect to the development towns. Specifically, the towns might be slower when it comes to cultural exchange. Despite the reputation of the towns

as national projects and their accessibility due to the small size of
the country, modern communication technology, and transportation,
the towns are still relatively isolated and peripheral communities.
Mutual cultural infusions are less likely to occur, and distinct ethnic
frameworks are more likely to be preserved, in homogeneous communities that are distant from large urban areas. Thus, the boundaries of Oriental ethnicity, and the conflict of values that revolves
primarily around ethnic issues, will probably remain more significant
in the towns.

The conflict of interests is mainly centered on class issues and its
future direction seems highly problematic. The towns are constantly
struggling with overwhelming problems of industrial growth, unemployment, and budget deficits. Consequently, the class gaps with the
larger society, in education, income, and standard of living, are not
being closed. If this economic situation is not improved, the conflict
of interests with society will endure. The conflict is not heightened
at present to its maximum level because the towns hold significant
political power which assures higher than average funding from the
central government. In light of the huge investments in these communities, however, and the severe problems of the Israeli economy in
general, government funding could be reduced in the future. The
smaller and less developed towns might even be dismantled. Moreover, their increasing local and regional political autonomy, an important ideological demand of the development towns, could backfire if
the government reacts to it by weakening the economic dependency
ties. Indeed, political independence cannot be achieved in the absence
of a self-sufficient economic base.

Notes

1. The government-sponsored "development town" status was originally
conferred to all the 33 communities, yet 29 held this status in 1970 and only
25 continued to receive government assistance throughout the 1980s.

2. Oriental immigrants were also settled in most of the 300 agricultural
communities, *moshavim*, which were built in the 1950s as part of the national
rural policy. At that time, lower-class Oriental immigrants also moved into
the pre-1948 urban settlements and inhabited the poor neighborhoods that
after 1977 constituted the national Project Renewal.

3. Generally, in tables 4.1–4.10, quantitative data are drawn from all
the thirty-three development towns. When a smaller number of the towns is
mentioned, (e.g., in table 4.3), this number should be viewed as representing
all of them.

4. On this bias, see Cohen (1970).

5. A detailed coverage of this controversy is available in Israel's daily newspapers. See for example *Ha'aretz* 21 and 30 June 1989; 4, 18, and 24 July 1989; 24 May 1990. See also *Ma'ariv* 30 June 1989; 4 and 5 July 1989.

6. An examination, based on a report of the Central Bureau of Statistics (1988c), shows that in income per capita in 1985/86 ordinary budget, only 14 of the 33 development towns were included among the top twenty Israeli localities for total budget; for government participation only, 17 of the 33 towns were included among the top twenty.

7. A detailed description of the exchange of votes for material favors in the towns, and its first conceptualization under the "party political machine" theory, is available in Ben-Zadok and Goldberg (1983).

8. For more on this cleavage and its electoral patterns, see for example Yishai (1982), Torgovnik (1986), and Roumani (1988).

9. One general comment on the concept of "political bloc" in tables 4.8, 4.9, and 4.10. The most effective way to understand Israel's diversified multiparty system is to classify the many parties and lists under major political blocs. Accordingly, the "Labor" bloc includes Mapai, later the Labor party or Alignment, and Mapam, a junior partner. The "Likud" bloc includes Gahal (Herut and the Liberal party), later Likud. Each of the two blocks might also include another one or two minor parties, depending on the election year. The components of the "Religious" bloc are the National Religious Party (NRP), Agudat Israel, and, depending on the election year, Tami, Shas, and smaller parties. "Other" includes numerous small parties and lists that are clearly left of Labor, right of Likud, and at the center. "Local" indicates genuine local lists with no affiliation, formal or informal, to any of the parties classified under the blocs above.

10. For more on that, see, for example, Freedman (1989).

11. For more on that, see Ben-Zadok and Goldberg (1983, 62).

References

Achdut, Lea, and Gideon Yaniv, eds. 1988. *National Insurance Institute Annual Survey, 1987*. Jerusalem: National Insurance Institute.

Altman, Elizabeth, and Betsy R. Rosenbaum. 1973. "Principles of Planning and Zionist Ideology: The Israeli Development Town." *Journal of the American Institute of Planners*, Vol. 39, No. 5 (September): 316–25.

Arnoff, Myron J. 1974. *Frontier Town: The Politics of Community Building in Israel*. Manchester: Manchester University Press.

Ben-Rafael, Eliezer. 1982. *The Emergence of Ethnicity: Cultural Groups and Social Conflicts in Israel*. Westport, Conn.: Greenwood Press.

Ben-Zadok, Efraim, and Giora Goldberg. 1983. "A Sociopolitical change in the Israeli Development Towns: An Analysis of Voting Patterns of Oriental Jews." *Plural Societies*, Vol. 14, No. 1/2 (Spring/Summer): 49–65.

Berler, Alexander. 1970. *New Towns in Israel*. Jerusalem: Israel University Press.

Borukhov, Eli. 1988. "Industry in Outlying Development Regions, *Environmental Planning*, No. 37–38: 44–54. (Hebrew.)

——, and Elia Werczberger. 1981. "Factors Affecting the Development of New Towns in Israel." *Environment and Planning A*, Vol. 13: 421–34.

Brutzkus, Eliezer. 1964. *Physical Planning in Israel*. Jerusalem: Ministry of the Interior.

Central Bureau of Statistics. 1966. *Results of Elections to the Sixth Knesset and to Local Authorities, 2.11.1965*. Special series no. 216. Jerusalem: Central Bureau of Statistics (Hebrew).

——. 1970. *Results of Elections to the Seventh Knesset and to Local Authorities, 28.10.1969*. Special series no. 309. Jerusalem: Central Bureau of Statistics (Hebrew).

——. 1971. *Local Authorities in Israel, 1969/70*. Special series no. 348. Jerusalem: Central Bureau of Statistics (Hebrew).

——. 1973. *Population and Housing Census 1972*. Stage B. Jerusalem: Central Bureau of Statistics.

——. 1974. *Results of Elections to the Eight Knesset and to Local Authorities, 31.12.1973*. Special series no. 461. Jerusalem: Central Bureau of Statistics (Hebrew).

——. 1976. *Statistical Abstract of Israel, 1976*. No. 27. Jerusalem: Central Bureau of Statistics.

——. 1981. *Results of Elections to the Tenth Knesset, 30.6.1981*. Special series no. 680. Jerusalem: Central Bureau of Statistics (Hebrew).

——. 1982. *Local Authorities in Israel, 1979/80 Financial Data*. Special series no. 687. Jerusalem: Central Bureau of Statistics (Hebrew).

——. 1984. *Localities: Population and Households Demographic Characteristics*. Census 1983 No. 3. Jerusalem: Central Bureau of Statistics (Hebrew).

——. 1988a. *Statistical Abstract of Israel, 1988*. No. 39. Jerusalem: Central Bureau of Statistics (Hebrew).

——. 1988b. *Monthly Bulletin of Statistics*. Vol. 39, No. 12 (December 1988) Jerusalem: Central Bureau of Statistics (Hebrew).

——. 1988c. *Local Authorities in Israel, 1985/86 Financial Data*. Special series no. 830. Jerusalem: Central Bureau of Statistics (Hebrew).

——. 1989a. *Local Authorities in Israel, 1986/87 Physical Data*. Special series no. 841. Jerusalem: Central Bureau of Statistics (Hebrew).

——. 1989b. *Results of Elections to the Twelfth Knesset, 1.11.1988*. Special series no. 856, vol. B. Jerusalem: Central Bureau of Statistics (Hebrew).

Cohen, Erik. 1970. *The City in Zionist Ideology*. Jerusalem: Institute of Urban and Regional Studies, Hebrew University.

————. 1974. "The Power Structure of Israeli Development Towns." In *Comparative Community Politics*, ed. T. Clark, 179–201. New York: John Wiley and Sons.

Deshen, Shlomo A. 1970. *Immigrant Voters in Israel: Parties and Congregations in Local Elections Campaign*. Manchester: Manchester University Press.

Dori, Issachar, et al. 1988. "Classification of Local Authorities according to the Socio-Economic Characteristics of the Population in 1983." Jerusalem: Ministry of Interior (Hebrew).

Dreifuss, Benjamin, ed. 1987. *Social Profile of Cities and Towns in Israel*. Jerusalem: Ministry of Labour and Social Affairs.

Elazar, Daniel. 1975. "The Local Elections: Sharpening the Trend toward Territorial Democracy." In *The Elections in Israel, 1973*, ed. A. Arian, 219–37. Jerusalem: Jerusalem Academic Press.

Fovim, Abraham, et al. 1985 "Kibbutz Members and Development Towns' Residents: Relations, Images, and Willingness to Cooperate." Tel Aviv: Sapir Center, Tel Aviv University.

Freedman, Robert O. 1989. "Religion, Politics, and the Israeli Elections of 1988." *Middle East Journal*, Vol. 43, No. 3 (Summer): 406–22.

Goldberg, Giora. 1984. "The Local Elections in Israel—1983." *Electoral Studies*, Vol. 3, No. 2 (August): 203–6.

————, and Efraim Ben-Zadok. 1988. "Ethnic Rebellion Against the Political Machine: The Case of Oriental Jews in Israel." *Ethnic Groups*, Vol. 7, No. 3: 205–26.

Goldberg, Harvey. 1977. "Introduction: Culture and Ethnicity in the Study of Israeli Society." *Ethnic Groups*, Vol. 1, No. 3 (February): 163–86.

Gradus, Yehuda. 1984. "The Emergence of Regionalism in a Centralized System: The Case of Israel." *Environment and Planning D*, Vol. 2: 87–100.

————, and S. Krakover. 1977. "The Effect of Government Policy on the Spatial Structure of Manufacturing in Israel." *Journal of Developing Areas*, Vol. 11: 393–409.

Ha'aretz. 21 and 30 June 1989; 4, 18, and 24 July 1989; 24 May 1990.

Hareven, Shulamit, ed. 1981. "Neighbors or Partners? Relations between Development Towns and Kibbutzim." Jerusalem: The Van Leer Jerusalem Foundation (Hebrew).

Hasson, Shlomo. 1983. "The Emergence of an Urban Social Movement in Israeli Society—An Integrated Approach." *International Journal of Urban and Regional Research*, Vol. 7, No. 2 (June): 157–74.

Kirschenbaum, A., and Y. Comay. 1973. "Dynamics of Population Attraction to New Towns—the Case of Israel." *Socio-Economic Planning Sciences*, Vol. 7: 687–96.

Ma'ariv. 30 June 1989; 4 and 5 July 1989.

Ministry of the Interior. 1979. *Results of Elections to Local Autorities, 7.11.1978*. Jerusalem: Ministry of the Interior (Hebrew).

Peled, Yoav. 1990. "Ethnic Exclusionism in the Periphery: The Case of Oriental Jews in Israel's Development Towns." *Ethnic and Racial Studies*, Vol. 13, No. 3 (July): 345–67.

Razin, E., and Arie Shachar. 1987. "Ownership of Industry and Plant Stability in Israel's Development Towns." *Urban Studies*, Vol. 24, No. 4 (August): 296–311.

Reshumot—Yalkut Ha'pirsumim. 1989. 9, 12a, 12b, 13, 21, 22, 23a, 23b, 26, 30 March 1989; 6, 14 April 1989. Jerusalem: State of Israel (Hebrew).

Roumani, Maurice M. 1988. "The Sephardi Factor in Israeli Politics." *Middle East Journal*, Vol. 42, No. 3 (Summer): 423–35.

Shachar, Arie S. 1971. "Israel's Development Towns: Evaluation of National Urbanization Policy." *Journal of the American Institute of Planners*, Vol. 37, No. 6 (November): 362–372.

Shamir, Michal, and Asher Arian. 1982. "The Ethnic Vote in Israel's 1981 Elections." *Electoral Studies* 1:315–31.

Smooha, Sammy. 1988. "Inernal Divisions in Israel at Forty." *Middle East Review*, Vol. 20, No. 4 (Summer): 26–36.

Spiegel, Erika. 1967. *New Towns in Israel*. New York: Praeger.

Swirski, Shlomo. 1981. *Orientals and Ashkenazim in Israel: The Ethnic Division of Labor*. Haifa: Mahbarot for Research and Criticism (Hebrew).

Torgovnik, Efraim. 1986. "Ethnicity and Organizational Catchall Politics." In *The Elections in Israel, 1984*, ed. A. Arian and M. Shamir, 57–77. Tel Aviv: Ramot Publishing Co.

———. 1987. "Urban Policy in Israel." In *Local Government in Israel*, ed. D. Elazar and C. Kalchaim. 55–85. Jerusalem: Jerusalem Center for Public Affairs (Hebrew).

Weingrod, Alex. 1979. "Recent Trends in Israeli Ethnicity." *Ethnic and Racial Studies*, Vol. 2, No. 1 (January): 55–65.

Ya'ar, Efraim, and A. Heller. 1977. "Absorption Capacity of Development Towns and Other Urban Settlements in Israel." Jerusalem: Ministry of Absorption (Hebrew).

Yishai, Yael. 1982. "Israel's Right-Wing Jewish Proletariat." *The Jewish Journal of Sociology*, Vol. 24, No. 2: 87–97.

5 ■ The Integration of Renewal Neighborhoods into the Mainstream of Israeli Society: Illusion or Reality?

Hana Ofek

Since 1977 ninety neighborhoods in Israel became part of a nationwide rehabilitation project—Project Renewal. The project was declared by the government "a major national priority." The aim of the project was to rehabilitate distressed sections of towns and cities or whole settlements, and to help residents improve their quality of life. The intent was to tackle physical and social problems simultaneously through the coordination of government and local authorities, and to reduce social and economic disparities between groups. At the beginning, about half of the project's budget was invested in physical improvements, mostly in housing and infrastructure. The Ministry of Housing and Construction, the major governmental sponsor of the program, sought to increase the stock of affordable housing for low-income groups.[1]

The renewal strategy in Israel has three stages. The first stage, rehabilitation and construction, seeks to reduce distress and to supply the means for adequate social functioning in all spheres. It requires massive action in housing, public facilities, education, employment, and health services. The second stage, growth and renewal, includes stimulating residents' awareness and motivating them to participate in renewal activities, while establishing a realistic level of expectations. The third stage strives for the ultimate goal of the project—independence and integration. Accordingly, to enter the

I would like to thank Hagit Hovav (Social Policy Team, Ministry of Housing and Construction) for providing me with useful information about Project Renewal. I would also like to thank Zvi Weinstein and Sara Levitov (Tel Aviv University) for their assistance in data collection.

mainstream of society, neighborhoods must attain local independence, self-confidence, and self-esteem.

The residents of these neighborhoods, the target population of the renewal strategy, are immigrants of the 1950s. They were first placed in transition camps and fringe areas of cities. Apartments built later to house them permanently were of low standard, with large families squeezed into tiny apartments. Neglect and decay soon became the marks of most immigrant neighborhoods, in which a culture of poverty inevitably developed. The residents in these deprived neighborhoods felt increasingly hopeless about the possibility of improving their situation.

Project Renewal sought to provide a comprehensive solution to the multidimensional problems of deprivation that prevail among residents of these low-income neighborhoods. Neighborhoods have joined the Project at different stages since its inception in 1977. A decade later, the project has reached ninety neighborhoods throughout the country, thereby affecting 700,000 residents, or about 19 percent of Israel's Jewish population.

Renewal neighborhoods were selected according to several criteria: housing conditions; the state of the physical infrastructure; population density; conditions of public and educational institutions; the ratio of the dependent population (residents under 19 years and over 65 years) to independent population; the rate of out-migration; number of children per family; the educational level of heads of households; the number of young couples on welfare; and the number of minors with criminal records. Consideration was also given to social problems resulting from dependence on social services and to declining cultural and educational standards (Jewish Agency for Israel 1986, 6).

According to Ginor (1979, 7), three forms of inequality could create a conflict between the renewal neighborhoods and the larger society: social differences in status and prestige, economic differences in the standard of living, and political differences stemming from distribution of power and level of participation in decision-making. Similarly, and more symbolically, Hazan (1990, 73) maintains that a neighborhood inclusion in Project Renewal implies ethnic labeling, economic deprivation, and political powerlessness. He further elaborates that in the context of the Israeli culture these attributes invariably involve a whole gamut of stigmatic images ranging from educational backwardness through poor hygiene and violent behavior to present-oriented gratification and reliance on the state.

Whether the potential conflict is substantive, symbolic, or both, it clearly evolves around the three following areas mentioned by Ginor and Hazan: (1) around differences in social values as they are related to status, prestige, and ethnicity; (2) around differences in standard of living and economic development; and (3) around differences in political interests as they are related to power distribution and level of participation. The three areas are obviously connected. Political power is used to obtain social status and economic advantages. Economic power can serve as a stepping-stone to political power and it enhances social status. Social status can be a precondition to obtaining political power, but there is also a clear distinction between the two.

This chapter attempts to explore the differences, gaps, and tensions between Project Renewal neighborhoods and the larger Israeli society in the three areas mentioned above. The chapter identifies and analyzes the social, economic, and political changes in renewal neighborhoods. It then compares the neighborhoods to the larger society before and after the implementation of Project Renewal.

The first section of the chapter, on socioeconomic characteristics, reviews differences in standard of living and economic development (the second area above). These differences are also covered in the second section which discusses class and housing issues. The second section also analyzes differences in social values as primarily derived from ethnicity (first area). The third and fourth sections discuss differences in political interests as related to power distribution and level of participation in decision making (third area).

SOCIOECONOMIC CHARACTERISTICS

The socioeconomic characteristics of the population of renewal neighborhoods such as age, size of household, quality of housing, income, education, and employment are discussed below. The demographic trends of the population of renewal neighborhoods are compared to the total Israeli Jewish population. The analysis is based on data from the 1972 and 1983 Census of Population and Housing (1983 is the latest available).[2]

To sum up, the data indicate that the population in renewal neighborhoods aged faster than in Israeli society in general. Between 1972 and 1983 family size decreased in renewal neighborhoods but it still remained higher than in the rest of the population. Housing conditions have improved since 1972 but in 1983 only 53.5 percent among renewal neighborhoods' residents owned their apartments, as compared with 71.8 percent of the total Jewish population. A significant gap of income level appeared between the population of renewal neighborhoods and Israeli society as a whole.

With respect to the data on education, two trends can be distinguished. First, a greater number of students finished high school in renewal neighborhoods since 1972, but it is still lower than the general population. Second, it is likely that most of the youngsters who finished high school left the renewal neighborhoods in search for better opportunities. The percentage of employed males decreased compared with the percentage of employed females in renewal neighborhoods. The high percentage of women in the work force suggests that the women acquired skills other than domestic ones. These socioeconomic changes are key descriptors of renewal neighborhoods. The discussion below covers each of these characteristics.

The Process of Aging

One of the remarkable demographic changes that has occurred in Israel since 1972 is the process of aging, especially in the renewal neighborhoods. Table 5.1 presents the changes in age configuration from 1972 to 1983 in renewal neighborhoods and in the total Jewish population. The population aged faster in the renewal neighborhoods than in the larger society. The median age increased in renewal neighborhoods by 3.3 years (from 22.0 to 25.3 years), compared to an increase of 1.5 years in the total Jewish population (from 25.1 to 26.6 years). In addition, the ratio percentage of the aged group of residents (65 +) increased from 6.1 to 8.5 percent during the years 1972 and 1983. A smaller increase occurred among the total population in the sixty-five-years-and-over category, from 7.7 to 9.5 percent.

These changes may be due to two critical phenomena that took place in the renewal neighborhoods. The first phenomenon is out-migration of young people because of the lack of job opportunities in the renewal neighborhoods in the years before Project Renewal (or before 1977) and even after it.[3] The second phenomenon accounting for aging is the drop in the number of children per family. As a result, the percentage of the group aged 0–14 in renewal neighborhoods decreased from 35.0 percent in 1972 to 31.1 percent in 1983.

The Dependent Ratio Index in table 5.1 indicates how changes in age configuration might influence the level of demand for social ser-

Table 5.1. Age Distribution in Renewal Neighborhoods and Total Jewish Population, 1972–83 (%)

Ages	Renewal Neighborhoods 1972	Renewal Neighborhoods 1983	Total Jewish Population 1972	Total Jewish Population 1983
0–14	35.0	31.1	29.6	30.7
15–29	28.3	27.7	27.3	24.2
30–44	14.8	15.9	15.9	18.8
45–64	15.8	16.8	19.4	16.8
65 +	6.1	8.5	7.7	9.5
Total	100.0	100.0	100.0	100.0
Median Age[a]	22.0	25.3	25.1	26.6
Dependency[b] Index	1.114	0.945	0.934	0.932

Source: Central Bureau of Statistics 1973, 1985a.
a. Median age is calculated according to individual ages.
b. Dependency index is the ratio between the total of those aged 0–19, and those aged 65 and over, to those aged 20–64. This is the ratio of dependent and independent population.

vices (education, welfare, and health). This index consists of the ratio between the population that is dependent, which cannot be included in the labor force, and the independent population which might potentially be included in the labor force. The data (table 5.1) show that in renewal neighborhoods there was a decline in the dependent ratio between 1972 and 1983, from 1.114 to 0.945. Among the total population there was no change (0.93). This change in renewal neighborhoods is an important indicator for narrowing the gap between them and the rest of the society.

Family Size

Table 5.2 shows changes that took place in family size during the same period. Between 1972 and 1983 family size decreased in renewal neighborhoods. The average number of persons per household was 4.2 in 1972, and 3.6 in 1983. In the total population there was a small change of 0.4 between 1972 and 1983. The average family size in 1983 in the renewal neighborhoods almost equaled the family size in the larger society. There was an especially strong decline in the number of larger families (seven persons or more) in renewal neighborhoods, but a small gap still remained between these neighborhoods and the total population.

Table 5.2. Household Characteristics in Renewal Neighborhoods and Total Jewish Population, 1972–83 (%)

Characteristic	Renewal Neighborhoods		Total Jewish Population	
	1972	1983	1972	1983
Average number of persons per household[a]	4.2	3.6	3.6	3.2
Percentage of households with seven persons and more	16.6	8.2	8.2	4.2
Percentage of households with one person	11.0	17.4	12.8	18.6
Percentage of households with children under 17	59.3	50.6	50.6	49.5

Source: Central Bureau of Statistics 1973, 1985a.
a. The average number of persons per household is calculated by dividing the population living in households by the number of households.

Data from Hazan (1990, 50) show that 38 percent of the families consisted of 1–2 members, 30 percent consisted of 3–4 members, 20 percent of 5–6 members, and 12 percent of 7 or more members. With this decline in the population of the neighborhoods and particularly the decreasing of young families, the number of households with more than three or four children also dropped. The fact that 20 percent of the families consisted of at least six members is not necessarily related to the understanding of the problems incurred by "children-blessed" households. It might be related to factors such as age composition, participation in the work force, level of income, and division of labor.

Quality of Housing

The age distribution of the population and the family size in renewal neighborhoods are two key descriptors of renewal neighborhoods when comparing them to the entire society. Overcrowding, poor building quality, and inadequate infrastructure are the key features of physical distress in the neighborhoods.

Project Renewal was implemented in stages. In the first stage of implementation, a special effort was required to foster the confidence of the inhabitants in the establishment (the government) which is responsible for the project. To achieve this goal, the project emphasized physical renewal to obtain short-run effects. This is because social renewal is an investment with results that take a long time to surface. By the Israeli norms of the 1980s, there were too many substandard housing units in these neighborhoods. About half of the dwelling units had a floor space of only 300–600 sq. ft. The average size of a new dwelling unit was 1200 sq. ft. and living in units below this size was considered tantamount to living in distress even for a small family.

Table 5.3 displays data about the quality of housing and the standard of living in 1972 and 1983.[4] These data, concerning the standard of housing conditions in renewal neighborhoods as compared with the Jewish population as a whole in 1972 and 1983, indicate a significant improvement in renewal neighborhoods and a narrowing of the gap between them and the general population. The percentage of small apartments (1–2 rooms) in renewal neighborhoods is similar to that of the overall Jewish population (27.2 percent as compared with 22.2 percent), although there is still a difference in the percentage of large apartments (four rooms and more). Nevertheless, the data indicate that the breakdown of the inventory of apartments in renewal neighborhoods was relatively balanced in 1983 and enabled young expanding families to continue living there. In earlier years, these families had left the neighborhoods due to the lack of spacious apartments. An examination of average housing density per room in renewal neighborhoods indicates a significant improvement in 1983 over 1972. This improvement is the outcome of two processes: a reduction in the size of the average family in renewal neighborhoods, and a rise in the number of average rooms per apartment. It should be noted that the percentage of families in renewal neighborhoods who, in 1983, still lived in a housing density of three or more persons to a room (defined as substandard) was extremely low—3 percent.

Another area in which differences appear between households in Project Renewal and households in the general Israeli population is the home ownership rate. Only 53.5 percent in Project Renewal, as compared with 71.8 percent in Israel as a whole, own their apartments. Because private home ownership is known to result in better property maintenance, higher satisfaction with housing, and stability of residence, Project Renewal aimed at increasing the rate of owner-occupancy.

It was not until October 1981, however, that substantially higher incentives and better terms of purchase were offered to residents of Project Renewal neighborhoods, compared to those offered to residents of buildings owned by public companies in other neighborhoods. Towards the end of 1982, it was announced that 25 percent of

Table 5.3. Selected Data on the Quality of Housing in Renewal Neighborhoods and Total Jewish Population, 1972–83

Characteristic	Renewal Neighborhoods 1972	1983	Total Jewish Population 1972	1983
% of small flats, 1–2 rooms	46.5	27.2	39.0	22.2
% of 4 room flats or more	7.0	22.5	13.3	31.1
% of homeowners	44.6	53.5	67.2	71.8
Average density per room	1.7	1.2	1.4	1.0
% of 3.0+ density per room	13.8	3.3	8.0	1.2

Source: Central Bureau of Statistics 1973, 1985a.

Project Renewal loans for home purchase would not be linked to inflation, which has been a significant factor in Israel's economy (Carmon 1988). Beginning in late 1982, the residents of renewal neighborhoods had much to gain by purchasing their dwellings. The price paid for Amidar apartments (a public construction company) at the end of 1982 was about 10–20 percent of the market value of the apartment. At the end of 1983 the figure rose to 20–40 percent of the value of the apartment (Lerman, Borukhov, and Evron 1985). Despite these low rates the purchase program met with only limited success.

But the physical quality of life and the housing conditions of the inhabitants of renewal neighborhoods were improved by the investments of the project. From the start of Project Renewal in 1977 until the end of 1985 about 45,000 housing units were renovated, representing about 35 percent of all housing units deemed in need of physical renovation. In addition, about 13,000 housing units were enlarged.[5]

Distressed neighborhoods and development towns are characterized by a high percentage of rented rather than individually owned housing units, which is contrary to the overall Israeli pattern. In these neighborhoods and towns the percentage of rented dwelling units far exceeds the national average (King et al. 1987, 30). These units are mostly owned and managed by either Amidar, a subsidiary of the Ministry of Construction and Housing, or Amigur, a subsidiary of the Jewish Agency. It is estimated that 47 percent of distressed neighbor-

Table 5.4. Average Net Monthly Income in Renewal Neighborhoods and Total Jewish Population, 1983 (INS)

Income	Renewal Neighborhoods	Total Jewish Population	Difference in Percentages
Average net monthly income per household whose head is an employee[a]	32,804	40,300	22.9%
Average net monthly income per standard person, in household whose head is an employee[b]	10,581	14,100	33.2%

Source: Central Bureau of Statistics 1985a.
a. A family income is the sum of all incomes of all household members from work and other sources.
b. The income per household whose head is an employee is divided by the number of standard persons in the household, and not by the actual number of persons.

hood dwellings are rented, compared to a national average of less than 30 percent.

Average Income

Another important dimension for comparison between renewal neighborhoods and the overall society is the average income. Table 5.4 shows the average net monthly income per household, and per person, in 1983. A significant gap in income level exists between the population of renewal neighborhoods and the overall Jewish population. The average net monthly income per household is 23 percent lower than that of the total Jewish population. The average net monthly income per person shows a gap of about 33 percent.[6] One factor contributing to the gap is the average size of the family in renewal neighborhoods, which is higher than in the rest of the Israeli population.

Renewal neighborhoods include a high percentage of families with low income level. This is the result of family size, level of education, occupational skills, and working age. Family size reduces per capita income. A low level of educational attainment, an absence of necessary or marketable occupational skills, and a high percentage of residents below working age, reduce job opportunities.

Table 5.5. Education Variables in Renewal Neighborhoods and Total Jewish Population, 1972–83

Education	Renewal Neighborhoods		Total Jewish Population	
	1972	1983	1972	1983
Median years of schooling	8.1	9.7	9.8	11.5
Percentage of 0–4 years of schooling	23.9	18.5	13.6	9.0
Percentage of 9–12 years of schooling	32.8	47.3	42.6	49.2
Percentage of 13+ years of schooling	6.4	9.5	14.5	23.1

Source: Central Bureau of Statistics 1973, 1985a.

Education

One of the characteristics of modern Israeli society is the great emphasis placed on achievements in education, employment, and income. Differences in the social take-off point of individuals in society require differential investment of resources. Two channels have been found to be most promising: investment in education and investment in vocational training. Until recently, education received preference in Israel both in inputs and attitudes. In the last few years, efforts have also been directed toward increasing the importance of vocational training.

A major part of Project Renewal's resources are devoted to education. In 1983/84 over 18 percent of Project Renewal's total social budget was devoted to formal education, another 27 percent to informal education and leisure, and 14 percent to early child development (Ministry of Education 1983). The programs sponsored by Project Renewal should be seen in the context of a broader effort to narrow the gap in educational achievement.

Table 5.5 shows that in renewal neighborhoods the percentage finishing 9–12 years of schooling rose but is still lower compared to the overall society: in 1972, 32.8 percent in renewal neighborhoods compared to 42.6 percent in the total population; in 1983, 47.3 percent in renewal neighborhoods compared to 49.2 percent in the total population. The percentage finishing 13 or more years of schooling in

Table 5.6. Percentage of Employed and Unemployed in Renewal Neighborhoods, Ages 20–64, 1972–83

| | 1972 | | | | | |
| | General | | Males | | Females | |
Ages	Employed	Unemployed	Employed	Unemployed	Employed	Unemployed
20–29	58.2	41.8	70.1	29.9	45.5	54.5
30–44	59.7	40.3	93.2	6.8	27.4	72.6
45–64	54.3	45.7	88.7	11.3	23.4	76.6
	1983					
20–29	60.2	39.8	65.0	35.0	54.9	45.1
30–44	69.1	30.9	88.4	11.6	49.3	50.7
45–64	53.4	46.6	80.2	19.8	30.7	69.3

Source: Central Bureau of Statistics 1973, 1985a.

renewal neighborhoods rose too: in 1972, 6.4 percent in renewal neighborhoods compared to 14.5 percent in the total population; in 1983, 9.5 percent in renewal neighborhoods compared to 23.1 percent in the total population. It is likely that most of the youngsters who finished high school and those who obtained their academic degree left the renewal neighborhoods in search of better job opportunities.

According to King, Hacohen, Frisch, and Elazar (1987, 28), the performance of children in Project Renewal neighborhoods is characterized by a higher school dropout rate and low scholastic achievement as compared to the general population. A high illiteracy rate in Hebrew also exists among the adult population.

Employment

Participation in the labor force is decisive for the level of family income. Table 5.6 shows that the percentage of employed males decreased compared to the percentage of employed females in renewal neighborhoods: in 1972, 93.2 percent males, ages 30–44, were employed, compared to 27.4 percent females; in 1983, 88.4 percent males, ages 30–44, were employed, compared to 49.3 percent females. Another outstanding factor is the high percentage of young working women (54.9 percent in 1983), even though most of them are raising children. It is likely that in search of jobs, women have had better job opportunities than males.

Because of the decisive influence of employment on family income, the causes of unemployment or underemployment are important. Old age and disability are the main causes. The employment of females is influenced by their educational level, the number of children, and the husband's income (Ginor 1979, 154).

The rate of unemployment in renewal neighborhoods is significantly higher than the national average and is particularly severe in many neighborhoods in the development towns. Moreover, the problem of underemployment is particularly prevalent in development towns. A high proportion of those who work in the towns are employed in unskilled jobs; only a small number of job opportunities exist for skilled or semiskilled workers (King et al. 1987, 27).

To conclude, the socioeconomic gap between renewal neighborhoods and the overall society still exists. Factors of age, household size and composition, quality of housing, education, and employment are of importance in the creation of income differentials between renewal neighborhoods and the entire society. Income differences between groups may be of important social significance when a considerable part of the old are poor as is the case in Israel. Education also varies with age. It is likely that among younger ones more have completed at least elementary school due to compulsory education laws.

VALUES, CLASS, AND HOUSING

A society of immigrants from many countries—who bring with them the mentalities, traditions, customs, and cultural backgrounds of those countries—is more likely to develop social disparities. In Israel, clear disparities exist between two main ethnic groups of Jewish immigrants. Those from Europe and America, Ashkenazim, and those from Asia and Africa, Oriental Jews or Sephardim.[7] The most important change in the structure of Israeli society after independence was the tremendous rise in the share of the Orientals in the Jewish population—from about 22 percent in 1948 to 53 percent in 1976. This increased the importance of the economic and social differences between the two ethnic groups (Ginor 1979, 107).

More than half of the first wave of immigration in 1955–57, and later in 1965–66 came to Israel from North Africa and the Middle East. When Israel gained its independence in 1948, the Jews of North Africa formed only a small proportion of its population. Fifteen years later they formed the largest and the most cohesive community in the country. Besides being the largest community, the North African group was also the youngest, with a median age of 25, as against 31 for immigrants from Asia and 45 for immigrants from Europe. The average size of their household was five persons and many families numbered eight, ten, and even more children. In fact, arrangements for the absorption of the new immigrants had been made with the needs of European Jews in mind. Housing, for instance, was perfectly adequate for a family that had no more than three children. But for the large families from Moslem countries, the resultant overcrowding caused great unhappiness.

The immigrants were housed on the outskirts of cities, in tenements lacking an infrastructure of public services. The result of this policy was that many groups in this population remained on the fringe of society, feeling estranged and deprived. The immigrants brought with them cultures and traditions which differed markedly from those prevailing in Israel at that time. In most cases, Oriental families were large and dominated by strict hierarchy. Roles were clearly defined, with the responsibility for raising the family and caring for the home assigned to the women and the responsibility for financial support of the family to the men. Family life and family gatherings were, and remain today, very important, centered around the home. Extended, close-knit families of several generations living together have been the norm. The tiny apartments in multistoried buildings were a far cry from the courtyard family homes of their native lands. For families from rural areas housed in city neighborhoods, the adjustment was even more difficult. Immigration had a negative effect on traditional community and interpersonal relations. Family roles were eroded, and past experience could not be a model for present needs. Community cooperative activity became problematic, and traditional ethnic leadership, which had rested on old societal frameworks, became ineffective in the new situations.

An important characteristic that distinguished the North African immigration from that of other countries was that it arrived in Israel lacking its social and economic elite. The well-educated, the affluent, the trained technicians, the intellectuals, and the businessmen among them, had chosen to make their homes in the West. Israel had drawn those who lacked possessions or resources. Few of the men from these countries had been prepared, either through education or through experience, for the skilled or professional jobs available in Israel at that time. The immigrants' education levels were often low, and many, particularly the women, had no formal education at all. Lack of skills created serious employment handicaps for the immigrants and condemned them to low income levels (Chouraqui 1971, 285–315).

The lack of communication between immigrants of vastly different geographical, social, and historical backgrounds did nothing to relieve the disillusionment of the new arrivals. They lacked a common language, and there was a feeling of distress that resulted from the breakup of the customary social order into which the Jews of North Africa had been born and under which they had lived.

Oriental Jews have become a feature of the Israeli scene. They are dispersed in the north and the south, in towns, moshavim, and in renewal neighborhoods. Table 5.7 shows that in 1983 the percentage of residents in renewal neighborhoods whose continent of origin was Africa or Asia was much higher than those whose continent of origin was Europe or America; thus the overwhelming majority of the renewal neighborhoods' residents are Orientals.

The mass immigration which followed the establishment of Israel profoundly changed the face of the Jewish community. Producing a socially mixed population, this immigration suddenly created an enormous heterogeneity in a society that had formerly been rather selective and homogeneous. There were two other ways in which this change was expressed: unlike the old settlers, the new immigrants were not grounded in an ideology; and, again unlike the old settlers, the majority of these immigrants came from Moslem countries, and brought with them their cultural elements. The Orientals found themselves suddenly plunged into a different technology, new kinds of social and political relations, and a novel system of sociocultural values. The shock and the estrangement between this type of new immigrants and the European old settlers were mutual.

The main source of frustration for Oriental Jews was the prevalent stratification and ranking of ethnic groups. Weingrod (1966) discussed this pattern of ethnic stratification. He argued that Europeans (Ashkenazim), are ranked higher than Middle Easterners (Orientals). To come from Poland or Britain is more prestigious than to have one's origin in Morocco or Iraq. Middle Easterners are firmly convinced that they are discriminated against. A brief consideration of the longterm trends in these immigrants' social, economic, and political mobility shows how concertedly the prevalent pattern of social stratification and ranking has affected the actual status of the Middle Easterners. Weingrod (1966) reveals that a comparison of income according to occupation shows this rank order: European veterans,

Table 5.7. The Population of Selected Renewal Neighborhoods by Continent of Origin,[a] 1983

Neighborhood[b] (Settlement)	Israel[c]	Asia[d]	Africa[e]	Europe/ America[f]
Whole settlement (Ofakim)	4.9	12.2	76.8	6.1
Amidar (Or Yehuda)	10.3	59.1	21.4	9.2
Yeelim (Eilat)	11.0	15.5	52.5	21.0
A Quarter (Ashdod)	6.0	11.6	56.4	25.9
B Quarter (Ashdod)	4.2	10.9	61.9	23.0
D Neighborhood North (Beersheba)	4.1	10.8	65.3	19.9
Eliyahu (Beit Shean)	4.3	11.6	81.1	2.9
Haarava (Dimona)	1.9	11.8	78.3	8.1
Shaviv (Herzliya)	9.7	31.6	31.9	26.7
Tel Giborim (Holon)	17.2	36.1	16.4	30.3
Neve Yosef (Haifa)	15.6	10.7	40.7	32.9
Ramat Weizman (Yavneh)	4.9	33.7	57.3	4.1
Center (Yehud)	12.0	56.7	15.4	15.9
Morasha (Jerusalem)	7.8	17.9	62.6	11.6
Yad Eliezer (Nes Ziona)	10.6	51.6	19.0	18.9
Whole settlement (Netivot)	5.1	3.6	87.1	4.2
Dora (Netanya)	7.1	27.3	45.2	20.4
Amishav (Petah-Tikva)	5.0	40.2	36.5	18.3
Neviim Quarter (Kiryat Gat)	5.7	10.7	59.1	24.5
Shikun Mizrach (Rishon Lezion)	10.7	64.0	16.5	8.9
Kfar Gvirol (Rehovot)	9.4	46.2	19.4	25.0
Ramat Hashikma (Ramat Gan)	12.3	58.8	12.1	16.8
Morasha (Ramat Hasharon)	10.2	56.7	14.2	18.9
Whole settlement (Sderot)	5.1	8.4	71.2	15.3
Neve Eliezer (Tel-Aviv)	20.1	49.8	23.3	6.8

Source: Central Bureau of Statistics 1985b.

a. Continent of origin—percentage born abroad, by their continent of birth, together with Israel-born by their father's continent of birth.

b. The list is a sample of 26 renewal neighborhoods.

c. Israel-born—percentage of Israel-born whose father was also born in Israel.

d. Asia—percentage born in Asia and Israel-born whose father was born in Asia.

e. Africa—percentage born in Africa and Israel-born whose father was born in Africa.

f. Europe/America—percentage born in Europe/America and Israel-born whose father was born in Europe/America.

European immigrants, Middle Eastern veterans, and Middle Eastern immigrants. Thus, the incomes of European immigrants have risen far more quickly than those of Middle Eastern immigrants. They rank even higher than the income of Middle Eastern veterans. The conclusion is clear: ethnic affiliation is more important than the length of time spent in the country.

By the time Project Renewal came on the scene, Israeli society had changed considerably from the severe polarization and despair of the 1950s and 1960s. Among the Jewish population in the 1980s, the structure of ethnic inequality had at least three tiers. At the top were the Ashkenazim, still maintaining a predominant but not an exclusive hold on the top positions in business, politics, academic and cultural life, and other key areas such as the military. In the middle, there was growing equality between Ashkenazim and Orientals in living standards, educational and job attainments, housing, and overall opportunities. However, at the bottom, a large Oriental underclass still existed and lacked access to decent opportunities and conditions, and was increasingly bitter at being shut out from the improved conditions. The overall renewal strategy was to improve the physical conditions and level of services to these people and to bring the low-income residents to the point where they would be able to support and maintain the improvements beyond the stage of formal intervention by the project.

A recent illustration of the social conflict between the Oriental residents of project renewal neighborhoods and the Ashkenazic society is the mass Soviet immigration to Israel since 1990. The Oriental immigrants of the 1950s are increasingly bitter over their limited prospects in contrast to the Ashkenazic Soviet immigrants. In July 1990, a housing crisis protest movement sprung up at thirty locations around the country. This broad-based protest movement expressed the conflict between the distressed renewal neighborhoods and the overall society. Three groups were represented in the protest movement, also called "Tent City": (1) the original housing protestors who were employed but were put out of their apartments because they could not afford to pay the current rent; (2) welfare cases who simply could not make it on their own and who had a housing problem even before the recent wave of immigration; and (3) those who were unable to keep up their mortgage payments, and therefore lost their right to government housing. All the "Tent City" protestors were the children of immigrants from Oriental countries who arrived in the early 1950s. Bitter memories of their transit camps (ma'abarot) and ethnic discrimination, which had been dormant among those who had not managed to break through into mainstream Israeli society, were now beginning to emerge anew as the contrast between their own prospects and those of the Soviet immigrants raised some questions. The "Tent City" settlers were of the lower or lower-middle socioeconomic strata and most of them were from renewal neighborhoods. Knesset members, such as Ben-Menachem, Bitton, Peretz, and Shetreet expressed deep concern about their housing and employment conditions.

The differences between the sector of distressed renewal neighborhoods and the overall society are also reflected in the political arena. Dissatisfaction with bad housing conditions and social deprivation as well as value and cultural conflicts are expressed in political attitudes and political behavior.

Community creation in terms of cultural underpinnings is merely the framework for the pursuit of interests, the allocation of resources, and the advancement of careers in the name of community. This is also the arena where residents and bureaucrats alike are entangled in a battle to define areas of influence and to shape the power structure of the neighborhood (Hazan 1990).

POLITICAL IMPLICATIONS

In 1977, for the first time in Israel's history, voter loyalties began to shift away from the traditionally dominant Labor party. From then on the two major parties—the Labor Alignment and the Likud—split their followers, now differentiated along ethnic demarcation lines (Shamir and Arian, 1983). In 1977, the Israeli government led by the Likud initiated Project Renewal. Urban renewal became one of the highest government priorities. Renewal activities had begun earlier, in 1965, under the Labor party rule with the establishment of the Authority for Construction and Clearance of Renewal Areas by the Minister of Housing. This authority implemented only a few of its many programs during the ten years of its existence. However, in the mid-1970s, the Housing Ministry revived its interest in urban renewal. While the initial neighborhood renewal was carried out during the Labor party administration, it received a strong impetus with the political turnover of 1977. Some observers contend that the Likud owed its rise to power to the support of the "Second Israel," the residents of development towns and distressed urban neighborhoods, and therefore it felt compelled to fulfill their expectations. In early

1978, a Social Policy Team was set up by the government. Its emphasis was on the social aspects of Project Renewal. In late 1979 the first Neighborhood Steering Committees were set up. It became possible to discern the central principles established by the Social Policy Team for the new Project Renewal.

Already in the 1973 elections the Likud, the main opposition to Labor, had an advantage with Oriental voters since the latter's views on security issues were close to those of Likud (Torgovnik 1982). The persistent political hostility to Labor among the Orientals may have been fueled by a sense of being finally "liberated" from dependence on the jobs and other services doled out in an earlier day by the Labor establishment to the new immigrants. Thus, paradoxically, ethnic polarization grew in the political arena, while it was waning in terms of objective socioeconomic indicators.

Likud's political success in 1977, and its continuing achievements in the 1981, 1984, and 1988 elections, gradually shifted Israel to the right of the political spectrum in both the security and the socioeconomic domains. In 1973, 23 percent of voters carried conservative views. That percentage rose in 1981 to 32 percent; and in 1984 to 39 percent (Torgovnik 1986). Shamir and Arian (1983) argue that this shift does not necessarily mean an ideological change but rather an indirect anti-Labor and anti-establishment vote. By 1977 the Labor party was no longer able to attract the Oriental population, which traditionally supported the party. Labor was identified as a middle-class-based party, leading to a marked lower- and working-class voter preference for the Likud in 1977, 1981, 1984, and 1988. In the 1988 Knesset elections the dominance of the Likud was obvious as was the importance of the religious parties.

The majority of Israelis tend to cluster around the center of the political spectrum, especially since ideology, so prominent in the pre-state period, has yielded to pragmatism. This centrist trend was reflected in the 1984 elections and 1988 elections results. The shift to the right has been moderate in the 1988 elections. The electorate gave its support to the two largest and more moderate political blocs. Ethnic-class positions and views on security remain the two factors that have polarized the country since 1967. These two factors influenced the choice of the electorate and affected the shape of the government coalition that resulted from the 1984 elections (Arian 1986), and later from the 1988 elections.

The 1981 and 1984 elections results showed the importance of the ethnic issue (Arian 1986, 7). The social and economic gaps which

Table 5.8. Results of the 1988 Knesset Elections in 14 Renewal Settlements (%)

Renewal Settlement	Labor Alignment	Likud	NRP	Degel HaTorah	Shas
Ofakim	15.7	36.3	5.7	4.9	22.2
Or-Akiva	13.2	53.0	10.3	2.6	11.2
Beit Dagan	10.0	47.5	5.1	8.5	6.5
Beit Shean	14.5	46.4	8.1	5.6	13.7
Beit Shemesh	20.1	45.9	4.9	3.2	14.7
Gan Yavne	17.0	34.6	15.0	10.3	11.4
Yerucham	16.6	41.3	3.8	4.6	18.6
Kfar Yona	21.5	45.5	10.3	3.1	4.2
Netivot	3.5	35.4	10.4	13.3	23.7
Kadima	25.3	40.7	13.3	2.0	6.8
Kiryat Ekron	13.4	43.9	10.2	8.6	5.3
Sderot	29.3	39.4	4.8	5.4	14.3
Shlomi	11.7	39.7	15.1	3.4	4.5
Tel-Mond	24.0	41.2	5.2	5.3	9.8

Source: Labor Alignment Records 1988.

had been central to the Oriental support for the Likud remained, and the situation was repeated in the 1988 elections. The Likud provided Orientals with the political and psychological gratification of being the group which determined election outcomes. The 1984 elections marked the first time that Orientals attained majority status in the electorate, a trend that continued in the 1988 national and 1989 local elections as the Labor party failed to penetrate the growing ranks of Oriental voters. With regard to ethnic tensions, younger Orientals born in Israel have become more militant in pressing demands for equality. Table 5.8 shows that the clearest indication of the 1988 elections for the 12th Knesset is that among the sample of fourteen low-income settlements, which are wholly included in Project Renewal, the dominance of the Likud party is absolute. The Likud has been more acceptable on the ethnic issue than the Labor Alignment. The ethnic factor which dominated the 1988 Knesset elections also affected the religious parties. The elections results indicate a remarkable gain of political power of Shas in renewal settlements (especially in Netivot and Yerucham), and a loss of the National Religious Party (NRP) The role of religious parties has been greater in 1988 than it was in 1981 and 1984.

However, because ethnic identity is firmly associated with religious affiliation, the ethnic factor is submerged into and absorbed by the religious one. Most renewal neighborhood residents described themselves as being, to a greater or lesser extent, religious, and because the layout of local synagogues reflects the ethnic distribution in the neighborhood, the identification between the two seems to be fairly consistent.

Orientals have become dominant not only in the electorate. Achievements in promoting their equality are also notable in urban renewal and political appointments. Project Renewal, which was carried out and implemented under the Likud's rule in low-income, mainly Oriental neighborhoods, is perceived by the residents as Likud's achievement.

The Labor party was trounced by Likud in mayoral and town council elections on February 1989. Likud and religious party candidates prevailed in six major cities and many smaller localities previously held by Labor, in what appeared to be a reprise of the 1988 Knesset elections. Many Labor critics predicted that if the party cannot reverse its losses and block advances by Likud, it will remain out of power for decades to come.

The voting turnout in renewal neighborhoods is high. In settlements which are wholly included in Project Renewal the voting turnout in the 1989 mayoral elections was as follows: Ofakim (49%), Or Akiva (58%), Beit Dagan (75%), Beit Shean (52%), Beit Shemesh (52%), Gan Yavne (55%), Yerucham (56%), Kadima (57%), Kfar Yonah (50%), Kiryat Ekron (64%), Netivot (65%), Sderot (70%), Shelomi (54%), and Tel-Mond (54%).

The support for the Likud is obvious in these settlements. Table 5.9 shows that in the 1989 elections the Likud mayoral candidates prevailed in ten of these settlements. Labor candidates prevailed in four of the settlements. The voting results of the 1989 mayoral elections indicate the importance of the religious bloc, which includes three major parties: Shas, NRP, and Degel HaTorah. The 1989 mayoral elections in renewal settlements were a reflection of the 1988 Knesset elections. Socioeconomic differences are related to political affiliation on the national and the local level. Such differences are also pronounced between cities or neighborhoods and provide an additional impedient to the political integration of low-income settlements. The examination of the local results shows that the intensity of competition and the degree of voter interest continue to be influenced by the national level.

Table 5.9. Results of the 1989 Mayoral Elections in 14 Renewal Settlements (%)

Renewal Settlement	Labor Alignment	Likud	NRP	Degel HaTorah	Shas
Ofakim	0.2	25.6	13.0		16.3
Or Akiva	6.7	29.9	15.0		
Beit Dagan	7.4	33.1	7.0	4.7	5.1
Beit Shean	8.9	33.2	8.3		4.3
Beit Shemesh	26.4	25.1	14.2		9.2
Gan Yavne	33.7	15.4	18.2	10.1	17.9
Yerucham	5.8	19.8	6.4	18.2	
Kfar Yona	11.7	58.6	9.2		
Netivot	5.1	26.9	8.2	22.4	24.7
Kadima	43.3	14.0	25.5		
Kiryat Ekron	21.6	25.6	16.5		2.3
Sderot	45.7	16.6	6.6	6.2	14.3
Shlomi	7.1	20.9	17.0		7.3
Tel-Mond	17.8	27.2	6.1	9.7	12.6

Source: Labor Alignment Records 1989.

Despite the Oriental's support for the Likud on the local and national level, the representation of Project Renewal neighborhoods in the Knesset also included Knesset members from the Labor Alignment. One of them, Eli Ben-Menachem, has headed a low-income neighborhood lobby since December 1989. As a renewal neighborhood resident himself, he attempted to mobilize a number of Knesset members to speak up for the neighborhoods, and to set up a political body to defend their rights. Another Labor Knesset member, Shimon Shetreet, headed an interparliamentary lobby for housing the homeless.

THE DECISION-MAKING PROCESS
IN PROJECT RENEWAL NEIGHBORHOODS

Figure 5.1 provides the organizational chart of Project Renewal. The project is operating on the national level (a and b below), and on the local level (c and d below), as follows:

a. The Joint Policy Committee headed by the Deputy Prime Minister of Construction and Housing in participation with

the Jewish Agency for Israel. It determines the policy of renewal and budgetary frameworks.
b. The Interorganizational Committee composed of representatives of all the ministries concerned and the Jewish Agency
and centered in the Ministry of Construction and Housing. It
discusses specific programs and implementation of policies.
c. The Local Government and the Local Steering Committee
(LSC). The LSC is headed by the local government, with the
participation of representatives of the neighborhoods' residents and government ministries. It prepares and operates a
plan of action after approval by the interorganizational team.
d. An overall project manager is appointed in every neighborhood who is responsible for promoting and implementing the
social and physical programs in the neighborhood.

Goals, priorities, and programs began to develop incrementally
and unsystematically on the local level (Hoffman 1986, 90). In retro-
spect, this laissez-faire approach may have given more de facto power
in the initial phase of the project to government officials, who tended
to be the dominant force at the local level, and only later to the LSCs.
There were some shifts in the allocation of project resources in the
social and physical spheres over the years. Goals and priorities were
influenced by an ongoing debate, since the inception of the project,
between the perspectives of community workers, who tended to stress
programs for the entire community, and social workers, who were
more oriented towards dealing with individual deprivation and distress. It was recognized, though, that both professional orientations
address different aspects of the problems of disadvantaged neighborhoods that may not always be neatly matched with specific programs
and objectives.
A major shift of emphasis in the planning and budgeting process
occurred when Hagit Hovav took over as government coordinator in
1982. With the encouragement of the deputy housing minister, Moshe
Katsav, who had the political responsibility then for the project administration, Hovav began to introduce more central policy guidelines
and to set up a more detailed monitoring system of local programs,
implementation rates, and priorities. This has enabled the planning
and budgeting process to develop a more formal system of mutual
feedback between the national and local levels (Hoffman 1986, 91).
The aim of this system is to preserve the autonomy of the LSCs, while

Figure 5.1
The Organizational Chart of Project Renewal

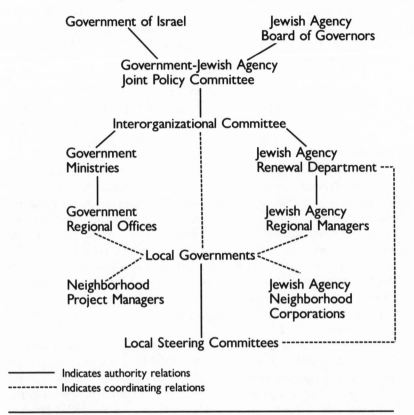

——————— Indicates authority relations
------------ Indicates coordinating relations

Source: Hoffman, 1986, 89.

encouraging them to be more aware and responsive to areas of need that are not receiving adequate attention.[8]

The Joint Policy Committee determines the goals of the project and the substantive areas in which it will operate, coordinates sources of funding for programs at the national and local level, and issues guidelines for the LSCs. These guidelines define procedures for the local planning and budgeting process, set the budgetary framework for each neighborhood, and set out the major areas of programming for the neighborhood. The latter are presented as recommendations to the LSCs but are not accompanied by any formal sanctions for noncompliance.

Work at the grassroots level was launched in the early years of the project in an atmosphere that combined vague overall goals and aspirations at the national level with an unclear picture of the precise needs of each neighborhood at the local level. Two of the principles behind the operation of Project Renewal was decentralization of decision-making, and neighborhood resident participation in the planning and implementation of renewal. It has been suggested since the project's inception that a considerable portion of decisions should be made at the local neighborhood level. The intent was to involve neighborhood residents in the problem-solving process, to increase cooperation with governmental authorities, and in the long-run to reduce the dependence of the distressed neighborhoods on the project. Project Renewal introduced a significant change in Israel's predominantly centralized modes of decision-making: "An important achievement of Project Renewal was the creation of a process unique in the State of Israel: public decision making in which rank-and-file residents were involved by virtue of right, and in a proportion that afforded them some influence. Although the residents did not succeed in realizing all of this potential, the very existence of such a possibility represents a revolutionary change and a considerable achievement" (Churchman 1987, 292).

Resident involvement was manifested in three ways: participation in public forums which were part of the planning and implementation process; participation in self-help programs ranging from educational tutoring services and para-professional work to build-your-own-home projects; and increased use of newly introduced or expanded services and programs in the health, educational, social, and cultural fields (King et al. 1987, 37).

The decentralization policy was implemented by creating a central element in the local organizational structure—the Local Steering Committee which exists in each renewal neighborhood. It consists of local residents who represent 50 percent of the membership, professionals, representatives of the municipal authority, local representatives of the government agencies at the regional level, and a representative of the Jewish Agency. The committee's tasks are: to weigh programs and project recommendations; to set priorities in view of available funds and the financial framework; to approve the annual proposed program and budget; and to approve the comprehensive plan. Every LSC appoints several professional subcommittees (such as Housing, Elderly, Adult Education, etc.), composed of local residents and related professionals. They collect data to define problems and goals and to develop ideas for programs which are then submitted to the Local Steering Committee.

The process of drawing residents into decision-making process begins with bringing to the residents' awareness both problems and the possibility of change. It continues with their involvement in the various committees which plan and implement neighborhood activities and policies. It means that opportunities for real sharing of decision-making powers by the residents through Project Renewal were to be found not only in the LSCs, but also in their numerous subcommittees that dealt with specific areas such as early childhood education, youth programs, the aged, and so forth.

In evaluating the LSCs' effectiveness in 1983, four years after their creation, three interrelated issues were addressed:

1. Decentralization—the actual power and influence of the LSC vis-à-vis other bodies in the planning and management of local renewal plans.
2. The influence of resident representatives within the committees, as compared to the influence exercised by the chairman (usually the mayor or his deputy), the staff, and the representatives of other bureaucratic organizations.
3. Representation—the extent to which neighborhood "representatives" actually represent their constituents (International Committee for the Evaluation of Project Renewal 1984, 32).

At present, the residents tend to view committees as having influence, although still not as much as governmental bodies. The extent of influence of the LSCs varies among communities. It has been recently argued that LSCs are not necessarily the most appropriate structure for continuity. Alternative types of structure should be examined for different types of communities, such as strengthened local government, borough councils, or community councils. However, the involvement in LSCs, in general, enabled the residents to experience the decision-making process on the local level as a way to improve the physical and social conditions in their neighborhood.

The Israeli government is ambivalent, however, about resident participation. Those who support involvement believe that it will improve the interaction and trust between service giver and receiver and ultimately enhance the level of service. The government recoils, however, from the involvement of residents, claiming that they are unqualified to be involved in the decision-making process. The inevitable result of this ambivalence is a double message, regarding resident participation, from the establishment.

A unique way to solve this problem, and this source of tension, has been the experiment with neighborhood self-management in Jerusalem. The Jerusalem Association for Neighborhood Self-Management was founded in 1980 by the Jerusalem municipality. The purpose was to develop, on an experimental basis, a novel approach to municipal government: to place at the center of the decision-making process for a neighborhood, a group of concerned residents, democratically elected by the neighborhood population. Upon completion of five years, the Jerusalem municipality, after careful examination of the cost-benefit of the accumulated experience, decided to embark on a process of integrating this new pattern. The decision was taken following a vigorous public debate.

CONCLUDING REMARKS

Two aspects of Project Renewal make it a unique chapter in the history of Israel's social and political development (King et al. 1987). The project provided a constructive outlet for the energy and frustration aroused by the protest movements of Oriental Jews in the 1970s. It also channeled efforts into social advancement and rehabilitation through local territorial units—disadvantaged neighborhoods— instead of focusing them on needy individuals.

Project Renewal, like its predecessors in the United States and elsewhere, is based on a "neighborhood" strategy. Unlike national programs of income maintenance, housing, or social services that are directed to people in need, Project Renewal's approach has been to improve an entire neighborhood both physically and socially. This area-based strategy was expected to eventually help people who live in these neighborhoods and bridge the gap between the distressed neighborhoods and the entire society.

However, the justification for area-based intervention is difficult: some policies are best served by universal provision and others more effectively aimed at specific deprived groups rather than areas. Area-based programs are a necessary but not sufficient condition for effective urban renewal.

In comparing the socioeconomic characteristics before the initiation of Project Renewal in Israel in 1972, and after it had been in operation in 1983, we conclude that Project Renewal was effective in narrowing the disparities between low-income neighborhoods and Israeli society as a whole. In different surveys, a sizeable proportion of the residents also reported improvements in the general quality of life and in specific service areas. For example, in a twenty neighborhood survey (International Committee for the Evaluation of Project Renewal 1984, 22) a majority (71 percent) of the respondents aware of Project Renewal thought it had changed their neighborhood for the better. Respondents saw the main contribution of the project in the fields of education, culture, and health. In another attitude survey (Hovav and Ben-Itzhak 1988, 7) 56.4 percent were satisfied with their neighborhood. Project Renewal created conditions which encouraged residents' involvement in their community activities. In a seven low-income neighborhood study (Ofek 1986), 76.4 percent of those who were very concerned about their neighborhood, were willing to be active at the local level. There was an almost even split between those willing to be involved in local community activity (47.9 percent) and those who stated that they did not wish to be involved (43 percent).

According to Spiro (1988), Project Renewal, as a directed change, aimed to assist populations in distressed neighborhoods. The government intended a new approach to community renewal that would include social and community rehabilitation through citizen participation. Project Renewal was accompanied by political commitment, an elaborate administrative structure, procedures of resource allocation, and identifiable self-correcting mechanisms. Project Renewal had an interorganizational decision structure and a degree of institutionalized citizen participation.

Project Renewal has contributed significantly to changes in resident participation in the planning and decision-making process. These, together with physical, social, cultural, and political changes, have narrowed the gap between low-income neighborhoods and the entire society. The relationship of local representatives with government representatives through different local communities enabled the access of renewal neighborhoods residents to the national level and encouraged them to take an active role in society.

The desired emphasis on people, social features, and the community was, at first, unsuccessful. Emphasis instead was placed on physical housing and environmental renewal. This occurred for a number of reasons. Project Renewal had raised high expectations. It was necessary to begin with programs that produced immediate results. The complex organizational structure was such that quick feedback was necessary to mobilize further resources. Physical renewal gave the whole policy, including the social community aspects, its necessary momentum (Torgovnik 1990, 54).

However, disparities still remain. Although the project provided a constructive outlet for the frustration aroused by the protest movement of the 1970s, the "Tent City" movement of 1990 illustrates that the differences between the distressed renewal neighborhoods and the larger society remain. In fact, the decreasing socioeconomic gaps, primarily in education, intertwined with increasing resident participation and awareness, might even improve and reinforce the negotiating position of deprived groups versus the larger society. Thus, the conflict might further increase around housing and employment issues, the very issues which ultimately express the feelings of neglect and deprivation among Oriental Jews living on the margins of the city. Several Knesset members predict the emergence of new, and perhaps violent, protest groups as the gap between the left-behind Orientals and newly arrived Soviet immigrants grows.

Thus, Project Renewal's agenda should continue in order to narrow the gap between Israel's poor neighborhoods and the rest of society. Central and local governments, the project's administration, and the residents of the neighborhoods ought to continue to plan and implement this unique Israeli experiment.

Notes

1. Urban renewal has also been closely linked with housing reform for the urban poor in Great Britain since the late nineteenth century (Gibson and Langstaff 1982). Urban renewal has been viewed as a means of improving housing and environmental conditions. Renewal policies eventually got entangled in the issue of housing standards and debate about the scale and nature of state intervention. According to Gibson and Langstaff (1982, 12) "the origins and continued development of urban renewal are primarily a function of state's response to the effect of inequality on the standard of mass housing provision."

2. The 1983 Census of Population and Housing publications contain basic demographic data from the complete enumeration and data on socioeconomic, housing, and education characteristics from the sample enumeration,

tabulated at various levels of geographical aggregation. These data, although derived from the individual or household record, represent characteristics of the population living in a specific geographical unit, and therefore can be used as indicators of that geographical unit (Ben-Tuvia 1987).

3. The rate of unemployment has risen gradually between 1980 and 1983. The International Committee for the Evaluation of Project Renewal suggested in its annual report for 1983 (1984, 62) that "a high priority should be assigned to issues of economic development and employment in the planning of future programs."

4. According to the 1983 Census of Population and Housing publications, housing density is the average number of persons per room. It is calculated by dividing the total number of persons living in households in a given geographical unit by the total number of rooms used for residential purposes by all households in that geographical unit.

5. This improvement can be found all over the world: "A century of urban renewal has transformed the housing conditions of the mass of the population. There is no longer an acute danger to public health from insanitary housing. The shoddily built, often overcrowded slums which characterized great swathes of the cities in the 1930s have mostly been cleared" (Gibson and Langstaff 1982, 287). By conventional housing standards much has been achieved but much remains to be done, and social inequalities persist.

6. To grade families by their economic situation, it is preferable to classify them by their income per person rather than by the total family income.

7. The major distinction among Jews is between Ashkenazim and Oriental Jews or Sephardim. There is a very high correlation between the European-American born and Ashkenazim, and the Asian-African born and Orientals (Shamir and Arian 1983, 93–94). Although the terms are commonly used in contemporary Israeli politics, they obscure as much as they reveal, as they are borrowed from other spheres. More appropriately, three divisions should be used consisting of an Oriental (eastern) community of Jews who never left the countries of Asia and Africa, the Sephardim whose language (Ladino) and ethnic culture originated in Spain before the expulsion of 1492, and the Ashkenazim (referring to Germany) whose hybrid language was Yiddish (Torgovnik 1986, 58–59).

8. The budget for 1990–91 for physical infrastructure is approximately 26 million dollars, and for social programs is approximately 20 million dollars.

References

Arian, Asher. 1986. "Introduction." In *The Elections in Israel, 1984*, ed. A. Arian, and M. Shamir, 1–11. Tel Aviv: Ramot.

152   HANA OFEK

Ben-Tuvia, Sheila. 1987. "Classification of Geographical Units According to the Socio-Economic Characteristics of the Population." The 1983 Census of Population and Housing. Publication no. 15. Jerusalem: Central Bureau of Statistics.

Carmon, Naomi. 1988. "Affordable Housing Renovation." A paper presented at the International Housing, Policy, and Innovations Conference of the Ad Hoc Committee on Housing and Built Environment of the International Sociological Association, Amsterdam.

Central Bureau of Statistics. 1973. Population and Housing Census, 1972. Jerusalem: Central Bureau of Statistics.

———. 1985a. Population and Housing Census, 1983. Jerusalem: Central Bureau of Statistics.

———. 1985b. Localities and Statistical Areas Population and Households, 1983 Census. Publication no. 4. Jerusalem: Central Bureau of Statistics.

Chouraqui, Andre N. 1971. "Between East and West." In Israel through the Eyes of Its Leaders, ed. I. T. Naamani, D. Rudavsky, and A. I. Katsh, 272–87. Tel Aviv: Meorot.

Churchman, Arza. 1987. "Issues in Resident Participation: Lessons from the Israeli Experience." Policy Studies Journal 16:290–99.

Gibson, Michael S., and Michael J. Langstaff. 1982. An Introduction to Urban Renewal. London: Hutchinson & Co.

Ginor, Fanny. 1979. Socio-Economic Disparities in Israel. Tel Aviv: University Publishing Project.

Hazan, Haim. 1990. A Paradoxical Community: The Emergence of a Social World in an Urban Renewal Setting. Greenwich: JAI Press Inc.

Hoffman, Charles. 1986. Project Renewal: Community and Change in Israel. Jerusalem: Renewal Department, Jewish Agency for Israel.

Hovav, Hagit, and Jehuda Ben-Itzhak, 1988. "The Community and Its Services: Attitudes of Renewal Neighborhoods' Residents." Jerusalem: the Ministry of Housing and Construction and the Social Policy Team. (Hebrew)

International Committee for the Evaluation of Project Renewal. 1984. Annual Report for 1983. Jerusalem: The Ministry of Housing and the Jewish Agency.

Jewish Agency for Israel. 1986. Guide to Project Renewal. Jerusalem: Renewal Department, Jewish Agency for Israel.

King, Paul, Orli Hacohen, Hillel Frisch, and Daniel J. Elazar. 1987. Project Renewal in Israel: Urban Revitalization through Partnership. Lanham, Md.: University Press of America and the Jerusalem Centre for Public Affairs.

Labor Alignment Records. 1988 Knesset Elections. Tel Aviv.

———. 1989 Municipal Elections. Tel Aviv.

Lerman, Robert, Eliahu Borukhov, and Dan Evron. 1985. "Project Renewal Housing Initiatives: Their Impact on Housing Conditions and Housing Values." Jerusalem: Brookdale Institute.

Ministry of Education. 1983. "Analysis of the 1983 Budget for Educational Welfare and Project Renewal." Jerusalem: Ministry of Education.

Ofek, Hana. 1986. "Patterns of Community Mobilization and Organizing in Slums Over Public Housing Issue." Ph.D. dissertation, Tel Aviv University. (Hebrew)

Shamir, Michal, and Asher Arian. 1983. "The Ethnic Vote in Israel's 1981 Elections." In *The Elections in Israel, 1981.* ed. A. Arian. 91–112. Tel Aviv: Ramot.

Spiro, Shimon, 1988. "Issues in the Evaluation of Neighborhood Rehabilitation Programs: Lessons from Israel's Project Renewal." *Megamot* 31: 269–85. (Hebrew)

Torgovnik, Efraim. 1982. "Likud 1977–81: The Consolidation of Power." In *Israel in the Begin Era,* ed. R. O. Freedman, 7–27. New York: Praeger.

———. 1986. "Ethnicity and Organizational Catchall Politics." In *The Elections in Israel, 1984,* ed. A. Arian and M. Shamir, 57–77. Tel Aviv: Ramot.

———. 1990. *The Politics of Urban Planning Policy.* Lanham, Md.: University Press of America.

Weingrod, Alex. 1966. *Israel: Group Relations in a New Society.* New York: Praeger.

PART III
- The Religious-Secular Cleavage

6 ■ The Emergence of Ultra-Orthodox Neighborhoods in Israeli Urban Centers

Yosseph Shilhav

HAREDI SOCIETY

The ultra-Orthodox Jewish community (referred to as Haredi; the individual within it is a Haredi, pl. Haredim) is a society whose religious conception rests on fundamentalist bases. Together with other cultural and religious traits, this community displays a complex attitude towards the modern world. The fundamentalist elements espouse the rejection of this world. However, this rejection, evoked in defense of the community's culture, values, and *Weltanschauung,* is by no means total. The Haredi community indiscriminately idealizes traditional patterns of organization and management only when cultural and religious patterns are involved. Therefore, the Haredi rejection of modernism is a differentiated one. The Haredi community is fully willing to accept and exploit all components of modernity that it perceives as neutral instruments, while rejecting those likely to serve as socializing agents for modern Western culture and society, which are considered a threat to the community's religious and sociocultural integrity. With such an approach, the Haredim can justify the use of computers, which are value-neutral, but reject television, which introduces an undesirable culture (Shilhav and Friedman 1985).

The following example, relating to the education system, sharply emphasizes this distinction. Paragraph 2 of the State Education Law, 5713/1953, defines the purposes of public education in Israel and stipulates, inter alia, that education is to be based on "the achievements of science." The Haredi community maintains separate education net-

---

This paper is based on studies that were carried out at the Jerusalem Institute for Israel studies.

works, some financially supported by the state. These have to maintain a modicum of consonance with the basic principles of the public education network. Therein lies their problem: how can they display support for values to which they cannot accede, such as the attitude of state education toward the "achievements of science?" In a textbook entitled *The Theory of Teaching,* intended for female students in Haredi teachers' colleges, a leading figure in the branch of Haredi education that enjoys state support (*Hahinuch Ha'Atzmai,* "independent education," a recognized but unofficial education system), enunciates the attitude toward science. "The achievements of science are most important to us," he writes, "but we cannot accept transient ideological conclusions of science as long as they are not consistent with the spirit of the Torah" (Oierbach 1958, 93). This sentence encompasses the entire attitude. The "achievements of science" are the applied, practical results of scientific research. These are the tools that science places at the disposal of humanity to improve life quality and expectancy. In contrast, what the Haredi educator terms the "ideological conclusions" of science are scientific theory and the research paradigm. The Haredim accept the "achievements of science" because the quality of their lives, and at times life itself, depend on them. However, they reject scientific theory because it belongs to a wider cultural and ethical system that may endanger the insular ethical world of the Haredi community.

This expresses the attitude of differentiation manifested by the Haredi population towards modernity. It is a community that dissociates itself from the social, cultural, and value aspects of Israeli society while maintaining instrumental and functional relations with that society. Thus, in various areas of activity, the Haredi community cultivates a dualistic mode of behavior. On the one hand, the Israeli cultural milieu and its values are anathema to the Haredim. On the other hand, they compete for the resources of that society. In this manner Haredi society carves out a distinct, separate space. The population residing in that space concurrently fights the secular Western foundations of the values and culture of Israeli society and competes for the same society's economic resources. One of the most important means of competition for resources is participation in Israeli political life. However, as shown below, this involvement, insofar as it affects the Haredi community, is merely instrumental and technical; it implies no acquiescence whatsoever to any particular values. This type of involvement is especially salient in the election campaign behavior of the Haredi political parties and their ambition to install functionaries in key positions affecting economic allocations.

The political processes accepted in modern Western society give expression to the social values by which this society orients its life. Freedom of expression, freedom of debate, and the freedom to persuade others find expression in the general political processes, including, of course, election campaigns. The Haredi community do not share these social values because Haredi society is a traditional one, totally controlled by its religious leaders (Flusser 1958). Obviously it is not a democratic society; it has no freedom of expression or debate, and, of course, accords no legitimacy to the pluralism of views. It is totally inconceivable that members of this community would ever be permitted to advocate opinions that do not conform with accepted viewpoints. This is not to say that the Haredi community is characterized by ideological homogeneity or a monolithic point of view. On the contrary, it is internally fractious and factionalized. However, the schisms and factions emanate not from the Haredi rank-and-file but from its leaders. These leaders also dictate modes of life, customs, and viewpoints, totally anchored in the Haredi worldview, which appears monolithic to the uninitiated observer but displays many varieties to the insider. Thus, a functionary of a Haredi political party, interviewed by a Haredi newspaper, stated that in the public controversy surrounding the passage of an amendment to the Law of Return, including the definition of "who is a Jew," he espouses the views of the Lubavitcher Rebbe, while on the Greater Israel issue he sides with Rabbi Eliezer Shach (two religious leaders with sharply antagonistic views). When the interviewer remarked on the seeming dichotomy, the functionary replied in amazement, "Can't I have my own view?" (Sheinfeld, 1987). It would seem that the maximum "own view" permissible to a Haredi Jew is a selection from the set of opinions held by reliable rabbinic leaders.

The parameters of individual freedom in the Haredi community are delimited by the significance this community attaches to two concepts. The first is *da'at Torah*, the primacy of rabbinic opinion, which acquired a meaning in the twentieth century that it had not known before. The term attests to the special status of learned rabbis, whose opinion is considered decisive not only in religious questions, but also on economic, social, and political issues, on which they are deemed infallible (Bacon 1983).

The second concept is *emunat ḥakhamim*, literally "faith in the sages." It, too, in its new connotation, refers to the obligation of every individual to obey, fully and unquestioningly, the instructions of learned rabbis in every sphere of life.

These limitations have the effect of obliterating individual freedom in the Ḥaredi community. Indeed, the community rejects the
concept of individual freedom in its essentially modern, Western connotation. This fact is of decisive importance in the shaping of Ḥaredi
voting patterns. In a much broader context, these two Ḥaredi concepts—the distinction between the instrumental and the ethical-
cultural components of modernity, and the duty to obey the religious
leaders—are the decisive factors in shaping the political behavior and,
in turn, the political geography of the Ḥaredi community.

THE ḤAREDIM AND THE STATE OF ISRAEL

This is not the place for a detailed discussion of the connection of
Ḥaredi religiosity and its cultural outlook with the Ḥaredi attitude toward the modern Jewish state. In order to understand our subject,
however, several basic principles on which this behavior is based
should be mentioned.

Judaism, as a code of laws, injunctions, and ordinances (i.e., everything embraced by the concept of *halakha*) that dictate the day-to-
day behavior of the observant Jew, developed as a system of
precedents. Thus construed, *halakha* developed when concrete questions, which developed organically within the community and
concerned themselves with the problematics of applying *halakhic*
principles under changing circumstances, were presented to the *halakhic* authorities (Goldman, n.d.). One of the characteristics of Ḥaredi
Jewry is its aspiration to avoid, to the extent possible, any confrontation between the terms of reality and those of *halakha*. By doing so,
the Ḥaredim avoid the need to resolve cases in which disparities
between the two worlds exist. This avoidance of confrontation is
achieved primarily by the avoidance of modernization; this is one of
the reasons for the insularity of Ḥaredi religiosity and its distinctiveness from modern orthodoxy.

The concepts of nationalism and the theories of modern sovereignty arose in the fifteenth and sixteenth centuries, but these subjects
were totally irrelevant for *halakha*. After the destruction of the Second
Temple and the loss of Jewish political independence in 70 C.E., and
until the restoration of Jewish political independence in 1948, *halakha* developed without reference to the subjects of kingship, government, or sovereignty, as it was clear that these matters were reserved
for the Gentiles. The Jews retained a nostalgic affinity for the Davidic

dynasty, both as a distant historical memory and as an expectation of the apocalyptic advent of the Messiah. In the here-and-now, however, the Jews were deprived of all these components of statehood. Upon the loss of political independence, responsibility for national leadership in all spheres of life was assumed by the religious leaders of that generation. The leadership confronted the difficult task of preventing national despair and assimilation among the Gentiles on the one hand, and thwarting the acceptance of hallucinations and illusions regarding false messiahs and imminent redemption on the other hand. Laws, *aggadot* (sing. *aggadah*, homiletic legends), and customs emanated from the need to secure these goals. One of the most famous *aggadot* concerns the three vows to which God swore the Jewish people, namely, that they would (1) not attempt to "storm the wall," that is, not organize as a unified body in an attempt to reclaim Eretz Israel by force; (2) not rebel against the nations that ruled over them; and (3) not attempt to hasten the end of days, that is, not to strive to achieve redemption before its due time. In recompense for these vows, God adjured the nations of the world not to enslave the Jewish people too harshly (Urbach 1969, 610).

Nevertheless, Jews continued to immigrate to Eretz Israel throughout their 1,878 years without national political independence. A Jewish community existed in Eretz Israel, and *halakhic* questions arose about everything connected with it. All these questions and deliberations, however, dealt with matters of personal obligations and conduct. National obligations or their practical significance were not dealt with since these were considered irrelevant to the situation faced by the Jewish people.

In recent times, with the awakening of Jewish national aspirations, and especially with the development of political Zionism as the national liberation movement of the Jewish people since the nineteenth century, growing segments of the Jewish public underwent a process of secularization and no longer viewed themselves as obligated by the principles of *halakha*. The arbiters of *halakha* were faced with a fundamental question: Was such a mobilization permissible or prohibited? The answer oscillated between the proponents and opponents of the Zionist movement.

Those voicing approval explained their positions in various ways. One school of thought advocated a compartmentalized attitude separating religion from politics. According to this view, the processes leading to the Jewish national rebirth in Eretz Israel were irrelevant from the religious standpoint. Territory, sovereignty, language, and culture are secular components which, for all their importance in sustaining the Jewish people, are not religious values and should not be depicted as such. Therefore, questions of religious prescription or proscription are inapplicable to these issues.

A totally different attitude, an "appropriationist" view, also regarded Zionism favorably but for a diametrically opposite reason. In this conception, even the ostensibly secular component of political Zionism is endowed with religious significance, dormant at times but fated to manifest itself in the future (Liebman and Don-Yehiya 1983). Metaphorically, one might say that the proponents of this approach appropriate secular Zionism, immerse it in a ritual bath, clothe it in prayer shawl and phylacteries, and transform it into part—sometimes the major part—of the faith.

Our concern, however, is with the opponents of the Zionist movement, because the hard core of contemporary Haredi religiosity is the successor to the attitude rejecting and negating Zionism. This rejection rests on two pillars. One is the "three vows" concept as a binding behavioral principle, valid in all generations and tantamount to a religious commandment for our generation as well. The second is the secular character of the Zionist movement and its impact on the nature of the future state, as well as the implicit threat such a state poses to a society committed to observance of the religious commandments and the maintenance of its unique social order. The Haredi opposition to the Zionist movement and to the state to which this movement aspired, therefore, was composed of two elements from the very outset. First, the Jewish people was fundamentally prohibited from taking its fate into its own hands, liberating itself of the gentile yoke, and becoming sovereign unto itself. At the same time, were the Jews to come upon political independence by "chance," or if the matter were confined to mere discussion of a hypothetical Jewish state, such a state would have to be guided by the principles of *halakha* rather than by the "laws of the Gentiles." As noted, this attitude of Haredi religiosity exists solely with regard to the Jewish state, and not with regard to any other state in the world (Teitelbaum 1961).

Political developments connected with the Zionist movement and its national aspirations undermined, to some degree, the first of these two components of Haredi opposition. The Balfour Declaration, asserting the British commitment to the establishment of a national home for the Jewish people in Palestine (2 November 1917), the confirmation of this declaration at the San Remo Conference (24 April 1920), and its incorporation into the League of Nations Mandate for

Palestine (22 July 1922) had repercussions that transcended the political and social spheres and penetrated the theological domain as well (Friedman 1977). This was a consequence of the international legitimacy bestowed on the Zionist cause, which could no longer be viewed as a "rebellion against the nations" since it was supported by Britain, then considered the dominant world power.

This situation caused consternation in anti-Zionist Haredi circles, a consternation that only increased after so many of the Jewish communities and Torah centers of Europe were annihilated in the Holocaust. In the aftermath of UN Resolution 181 (29 November 1947) favoring the partitioning of Palestine into Jewish and Arab states, and after the establishment of the Jewish state (15 May 1948), the internal Jewish debate moved from the theoretical onto the concrete level. The Jewish state was an internationally recognized fact, and Haredi religious thought had to relate to it not from the viewpoint of *ab initio* but *post factum*, as a fait accompli.

THE DISPERSION OF HAREDIM IN ISRAEL

Any discussion of the dispersion of the Haredi population in Israel, whether the community is being studied in a particular city or on a national scale, meets with a fundamental methodological problem: that of identification. There is no statistical source that identifies the Haredi population as such. There is no central registry of members of the Haredi community with a breakdown by factions and variations. Furthermore, the very definition of a Haredi is problematic. Any definition, including ours as presented above, suffers from overgeneralization and leaves a wide margin of groups whose inclusion within the Haredi sector is susceptible to challenge. In other words, there are groups that fit the definition of "Haredi" in certain aspects of behavior or religious outlook but differ from it in other respects. In order to discuss the political and geographic implications of the Haredi concentrations in Israel's cities, we can relate only to those groups that can be identified as Haredi under the criteria we have set, even if we know that we thereby exclude some of the Haredim or include some groups that do not truly belong to that community. Be that as it may, this problem affects neither the basic content of the study nor its analysis.

The difficulty that arises in precisely defining and identifying the Haredi community is, as stated, not merely technical; it is chiefly one of substance. This difficulty, however, places significant constraints on anyone dealing with this subject with respect to quantitative data on the Haredim as the objects of positivistic research.

Because there are no official statistics concerning the Haredi population, the only way to arrive at quantitative—albeit inexact—estimates is to use indirect indicators for which reliable statistics exist. Clearly, however, these alternate indicators elicit only close approximations rather than precise data. To illustrate the problem, we consider the question of the size of the Haredi population. As stated, Israel keeps no official records of individuals' community affiliations. To attempt an estimate of the size of this population group, we must therefore consult a known statistic representing that population. Several types of statistics meet this criterion, although none is a full substitute for an actual figure representing the number of Haredim in Israel.

The statistic most frequently used as an indicator of the size of the Haredi community is the share of votes accruing to Haredi political parties in the elections. In the twelfth Knesset elections in November 1988, the Haredi parties acquired 13 of the 120 seats in Israel's legislature. Using this statistic as the criterion, we find that about 11 percent of Israelis are Haredim. Examining enrollment in the Haredi school system as a proportion of total national school enrollment, we arrive at a figure of 10 percent for the 1989/90 school year. Importantly, however, neither of these two statistics represents the true size of the Haredi population. We know that many persons who voted for Haredi parties in the 1988 elections, especially supporters of the Sephardi-Haredi party Shas, were not Haredim and may not have been religiously observant at all. In other words, the political representation of the Haredim far exceeds their actual numbers and inflates the estimate of population size when this criterion is used. Neither are data on enrollment in Haredi schools exact, since quantitative data exist only for those institutions that maintain relations with municipal or governmental authorities. There are no statistical data on Haredi education networks that avoid such relations and eschew direct government support. Thus the data on Haredi school enrollment tend to lower the estimate of population size. However, it must be borne in mind that this downward bias is "corrected" by the large number of pupils from non-Haredi Oriental Jewish homes who attend Haredi schools. Furthermore, the Haredi population's birth rate is as much as twice as high than that of the Israeli population at large. Therefore, the proportion of Haredi children among all Israeli children exceeds the proportion of Ḥaredi adults among Israeli adults. This finding gives the estimate an upward bias. It also suggests that if the trend continues, the proportion of Ḥaredim in Israel's population will increase.

None of these indicators leads to a clear, unequivocal conclusion. A critical, topical approach to the aforementioned elicits an estimate placing the Ḥaredi population as approximately 8 percent of the population of Israel. This estimate has recently been validated from an unexpected source. In late 1990, all residents of Israel were issued chemical-warfare protection kits in view of Iraqi threats against the country. These kits included gas masks that were unsuited to the protection of bearded men. Therefore, the Ḥaredim asked for 100,000 masks of a special design. That is, there are 100,000 Ḥaredi men old enough to have beards. The Ḥaredim presumably overestimated slightly the number of special masks they needed. In any case, the number they chose corroborates the estimate mentioned above.

One convenient method of acquiring information about the Ḥaredi population is to identify and demarcate statistical areas populated exclusively by them. For these areas, statistics culled from Israeli censuses are tantamount to statistics on Ḥaredim, for only Ḥaredim live there. For this very reason, however, the statistical data on these areas are incomplete and imprecise, since the Ḥaredim tend to refrain from cooperating with the census takers and refuse to fill out the questionnaires, contending that this constitutes a violation of a *halakhic* proscription against counting Jews. Fear of the "evil eye," too, seems to contribute to this behavior.

Various institutions specialize in Ḥaredi affairs. Insofar as they possess confirmed, reliable compilations of data, they constitute another source of information. These sources taken together lead us to several admittedly imprecise conclusions. For our purposes, it suffices to mention here that Ḥaredim marry at a substantially younger age than the Israeli average. Their rate of natural increase is much higher than the national average, and their rate of labor-force participation is low, since most of the men engage in devotional studies well into adulthood. Their employment distribution suggests extremely low rates of employment in occupations requiring extensive training. By implication, the community has a relatively low level of income, and correspondingly, standard of living. Data relating to Ḥaredi areas corroborate these assumptions. Even these data, however, must be treated cautiously and skeptically. Not only are we unable to rely on the extent of Ḥaredi response to census questionnaires, but disclosures by Haredim of sources of income and employment are especially suspicious. The Haredim have two prima facie reasons to falsify these disclosures: fear of the tax authorities, and the fact that the deferral of military service is granted to Haredim who study in *yeshivot* (talmudic and theological colleges) on condition that they pledge all their time to devotional studies, eschewing employment of any kind. Data on the standard of living of the Haredim indicate little, since the Haredim disdain or proscribe some of the variables used as indicators of standards of living in modern Western societies. This is especially true with regard to use of leisure time and ownership of appliances such as television sets and VCRs.

At hand, then, is a special society that competes for resources that will secure convenient conditions for its way of life, while fundamentally opposing the values of the general society upon which it relies for the assurance of these resources. A serious attempt to assess the characteristics of Haredi society on the basis of accepted Western criteria indicates that these criteria are not effective for this society, and that any comparison made on such a basis is incorrect.

A previous study (Shilhav 1984a) already explored the reasons for the grouping tendencies of Haredim and the spatial and social effects of this process in the large Haredi concentrations of Jerusalem and Bnei Brak (the latter in metropolitan Tel Aviv).

These large concentrations were caused by sociohistorical urban developments. At present, growing Haredi communities exist in many Israeli towns and, in fact, throughout the country, from the Galilee to the Negev. This raises several issues. The first two must be presented almost simultaneously, and if we deal with one before the other, it is only because we cannot present them in the same breath.

First, in view of the foregoing, we must clarify for ourselves the way in which we shall identify the Haredi groups in the cities and towns of Israel. Next, again in view of all we have learned about the geographic groupings and social separatism of the community, we must assess the reasons for the geographic dispersion of members of this community in the small peripheral towns. After dealing with these two questions, we shall gauge the results of this process and try to understand the directions in which it is heading.

It was once conventional to identify large Haredi concentrations by indirect indicators, such as voting patterns and enrollment in Haredi schools. Other means of identification were the territorial markers that the Haredi community sets at its boundaries, such as the closing of streets to traffic on the Sabbath and the encircling of contiguous Ḥaredi area with '*eruv*—a special Sabbath perimeter within which one is allowed to carry objects (Shilhav and Friedman 1985; Shilhav 1983). These methods lose much of their effectiveness when applied in localities other than those with large Ḥaredi concentrations.

We begin with the Ḥaredi community's territorial markers. These signs can be applied and endowed with spatial significance only when the community is large, influential, and dominant within a distinct area. In contrast, when the Ḥaredi community is concentrated in two or three apartment blocks, the '*eruv* is meaningless. That is because the members of the community will not limit the area in which they carry objects on Sabbath to the space of a city block; in these cases they rely on the larger municipal '*eruv*. Even the closing or nonclosing of the area to traffic on the Sabbath indicates very little. The area may be too small or the community's political clout too meager to achieve a formal closing of the area. However, empirical observations in Ḥaredi neighborhoods of various cities indicate that the predisposition to territorial dominance and to cultural and social insularity exists even in places where the Ḥaredi community is not large.

These indirect indicators are harder to use outside the large Ḥaredi concentrations. Indeed, in past years up to and including the 1988 Knesset elections, one could assume that the Ḥaredi population might be identified by votes for Ḥaredi parties. After all, the relevant voting patterns were rigid; Ḥaredim would not vote for nonreligious parties, and non-Ḥaredim would not vote for Ḥaredi parties (Shilhav 1984b). Therefore, we may identify cities with large concentrations of Ḥaredim by examining the election returns of Ḥaredi parties by region. Adding statistics on enrollment in Ḥaredi schools, we may pinpoint the Ḥaredi concentrations in Israel's cities. Such a study was conducted. Its results are presented below.

The first set of statistics relates to voting patterns for Ḥaredi parties in Israel's cities for the Knesset elections of 1984. Importantly, most voters for Ḥaredi parties have been concentrated in Jerusalem and Bnei Brak in all years. In other words, most of the voters for these parties came from these concentrations. By computing a "concentration coefficient" for Ḥaredi voters, we may point at their major places of residence. The "concentration coefficient" is arrived at by calculating the percentage of votes for Ḥaredi parties in a given locale and dividing it by the percentage of votes for these parties nationwide. When the coefficient is greater than one, the percentage of votes for Ḥaredi parties in that locality exceeds the percentage nationwide, indicating that this locality is home to a relatively large concentration of voters for Ḥaredi parties. Calculating the concentration coefficient for the 1984 election returns, we find that the coefficient is highest (8.63) in Bnei Brak. That is, the percentage of votes for Ḥaredi parties in Bnei Brak was almost nine times the percentage nationwide. Indeed, Bnei Brak ranks highest also in the Ḥaredi concentration indices of other elections.

Ranking Israeli towns and cities in descending order by their concentration coefficients of Ḥaredi voters, we find that nineteen localities had coefficients greater than one in 1984, including five with coefficients greater than two. That is, in these five localities, the percentage of votes for Ḥaredi parties was more than double the percentage nationwide. The leader, as mentioned, was Bnei Brak. The others are Netivot, with more than four times the national percentage; Rosh ha-ʾAyin, with nearly four times; Jerusalem, with slightly more than three times; and Yeroham, with more than twice the percentage. Of interest here is not the cities' geographic location but their type. Three of the five localities are development towns, populated mostly by Oriental Jews. Two of them, Netivot and Yeroham, are in the Negev. The third, Rosh ha-ʾAyin, is in the center of the country, within commuting distance of Tel Aviv. This, of course, is a result of the participation of an Oriental Ḥaredi party in the 1984 elections, as we discuss at greater length below.

Repeating this study for the 1988 elections, we find an interesting development. The national percentage of votes for Ḥaredi parties doubled to 10.7 percent. (All data are quoted from or calculated on the basis of Central Bureau of Statistics publications on the results of the eleventh and twelfth Knesset elections.) The number of urban centers in which the concentration coefficient exceeded the national percentage grew from 19 to 22, and the number of localities with coefficients greater than two grew from five in 1984 to twelve in 1988. In other words, the centralization of these voters decreased, they were distributed in all parts of the country, and their numbers increased greatly. Most localities in the group of twelve are relatively new development towns; even the oldest of them, Safed, is not a major city.

However, an examination of Ḥaredi voting patterns in many of Israel's urban localities does not seem to reveal major growth of the Ḥaredi communities of these towns. A comparison of enrollment figures in the Ḥaredi school system in these development towns (according to 1990 statistics of the Ministry of Education and Culture Data Processing Office) with the percentage of votes for Ḥaredi parties in the same town shows a large disparity in favor of the percentage of voters. Since the schools chosen by families for their children's education are better indicators than voting patterns of the community to which the family affiliated itself, the Haredi population in these towns is presumably much smaller than the electoral statistics suggest.

Another question of concern here is why small Haredi concentrations come into being in development towns. Earlier studies show that the Haredim aspire to separatism within the modern Western city, for two reasons: (1) to attain cultural dominance and to gain economies of agglomeration and scale in the provision of goods and services unique to members of the group, and (2) in response to their profound fear of permissive, secular urban society, which they perceive as endangering the very existence of Haredi community culture. Stepping out of the large, protected Haredi enclave is ostensibly viewed as a venture into all the dangers and disadvantages that Haredi concentration is meant to prevent.

The Haredi concentrations in small and middle-sized urban localities in Israel came into being partly as a result of out-migration from the large concentrations, partly as a historical development, and partly by chance. An example of the latter is Kiryat Sanz in Natanya. A *hasidic* rebbe brought his community to Israel, and the group, after consultations with the relevant governmental agencies, was allocated a neighborhood in Natanya. It would have been equally possible to locate this *hasidic* enclave in any other city. The place of residence of a religious leader—usually a *hasidic* rebbe, but sometimes also a "Lithuanian" (*mitnaggedic*) rabbi—affects the choice of domicile of his community. So it was in Natanya, Rehovot, and other places.

An example of the historical Haredi community is that of Safed. Safed, as a holy city in the Galilee, always attracted diverse groups of religious Jews. Even if some of the town's Haredi residents migrated there only recently, the existence of the Haredi community there is historical.

Unlike enclaves of these two types, which are few in number, most Haredi communities in small and middle-sized Israeli localities are new, caused by out-migration from the large Haredi concentrations. This migration is a consequence of the high density of the Haredi concentrations in Jerusalem and Bnei Brak and the competition for residential space, which in turn causes housing prices in these Haredi areas to reach astronomical levels. It is the Haredi marriage tradition to impose upon the father of the bride the major financial burden of the new couple's needs, especially if the groom is regarded as a promising Torah scholar. This only intensifies the economic pressure and the sense of urgency of the problem. The foremost cause of out-migration from the large communities is, then, the need to expand outward—a choice made under duress. These Haredim prefer to stay in Jerusalem or Bnei Brak and would do so if it were only possible. The effect of these pro-expansion factors is complemented by general processes of suburbanization and remote suburbanization. The locational elasticity of the Haredi population is very high. This is a population group that can settle almost anywhere, since the nature of its employment is not place-dependent. The men engage in religious studies until they have been married at least several years. This occupation can be practiced anywhere and entails no specific locational characteristics. Nor are the other occupations of community members and its satellites place-dependent, since these do not require a high level of scientific or technological training.

However, the Haredi population has specific and characteristic needs with respect to its day-to-day consumer basket, its cultural attributes, and its social norms. More specifically, this population group demands kosher food under specific Haredi supervision. Its cultural needs manifest themselves, inter alia, in special Haredi education and scholastic institutions because the study of Torah, in one form or another, embraces all members of the community. The Haredim have special needs in matters of dress. Finally, they utterly reject the leisure culture of the modern Western city. At first glance we might assume that these special needs would increase the concentration of Haredim in precisely the large communities, for the greater the concentration, the easier it is to meet these special needs and create the cultural dominance that is so important to the community. Indeed, this was once a factor that magnified the propensity to density and separatism.

Today, however, the circumstances have changed. The factors causing out-migration are very strong, and they are coupled with modern facilities that make it possible to respond to the pressures of density without significant adverse effects. In view of the technological conditions of a modern society and the small scale of Israeli territory, geographic distance is not a real obstacle. When people, goods, amenities, and information are highly mobile, one may enjoy all the advantages of the large city without living there. From the Haredi viewpoint, this means that Haredim may live outside the large Haredi concentration while benefiting from all the services and advantages that this concentration can provide, by having them sent over distances. Modern society's liberation from place-dependence in the attainment of a certain standard of living creates a sense of loss of place (Meyrowitz 1985), or, more correctly, a broadened feeling of home. That is, the individual feels at home anywhere. From the instrumental viewpoint, the Ḥaredim are exposed to this development and know how to exploit it well in order to solve their housing problem. Therefore, when the forces of destiny clash with the special needs of the community, the potency of these forces, together with the dissolution of the sense of place, trigger a migration to localities outside the large concentrations. This "exodus" also solves the problem of the fear of secular urban influences, because these effects are especially prevalent in the major large cities and are less intense or nonexistent in small urban localities.

Nevertheless, out-migration to the small urban localities comes with a disadvantage, especially if we recall that the migrants are young couples, families just getting started. The disadvantage is the loss of first-hand, continuous contact with the spiritual leader: the *ḥasidic* rebbe, the community rabbi, or the *rosh yeshiva* (yeshiva head or dean). Even this contact, however, can be maintained at a distance, notwithstanding the great importance of the day-to-day patronage, and perhaps the supervision, of the leader in a traditional community such as this.

Thus we have seen that the spin-off of small Ḥaredi communities from the large concentrations has advantages and disadvantages from the Ḥaredi point of view. These observations permit us to explain the fact that most of the new Ḥaredi concentrations are turning toward development towns rather than the older and more established urban localities. The reasons for this are both economic and sociocultural. Of course, apartments in development towns are less expensive than those in the older cities. The development towns suffer from a negative migration balance, severe employment problems, a lower level of services, and a general stigma. The leaders of those towns have searched for ways to improve their situation and their image. The entry of a Ḥaredi population is seen as a possible way to enhance the towns' attributes. The needs of this community with respect to employment and levels of services seem to be modest (because of their aforementioned characteristics). The Ḥaredim are a stabilizing force in the community because they do not migrate in search of employment and are not interested in consumption fads. Therefore, it would seem possible to improve a town's demographic structure with relative ease by facilitating the entrance of Ḥaredi groups, which would, first of all, stabilize the migration balance.

It was this combination of inexpensive housing and the wishes of local leaders that attracted Ḥaredi groups to the development towns. However, we must not ignore the effects of the sociocultural factor on this development. The demographic and sociocultural differences between the development towns and the older, more established cities are well known. In the development towns, there is a large concentration of working-class Oriental Jews to which the Ḥaredim relate differently than they do to the affluent, secular, Ashkenazi population that characterizes the older cities.

The secular Ashkenazic population is very different in its cultural and social characteristics from the Ḥaredi population. This disparity evokes hostility, alienation, and suspicion among the Ḥaredim. The affluent, secular Ashkenazic population opposes the Ḥaredi way of life, engages it in struggle, and endeavors to prevent its spread. The Ḥaredim therefore view it as a hostile and dangerous population group. As a result Ḥaredim, especially young families, avoid spatial and social contact with members of this group and take great care not to become assimilated into a city that is largely secular in character. Ḥaredim also view such a locality as an impediment to their future development.

In contrast, the Ḥaredim regard members of the Oriental communities as traditional, if religiously unschooled. Since the Oriental communities have a basic affinity for tradition, the attitude toward those among them who are not religiously observant is more forgiving. The general attitude of the Ḥaredim toward the Oriental communities is slightly paternalistic and condescending. Because the Oriental communities are therefore not perceived as a threat to the Ḥaredim, the Ḥaredim find it easier to migrate to towns in which these communities predominate. Furthermore, since Ḥaredim regard their religious path as an absolute truth and the sole legitimate path of Judaism, they strive to promote this way of life among others. They believe that this mission—which is not a major one in their worldview—will be more successful among the Oriental communities than among the secular Ashkenazim, with whom it may fail altogether.

Thus far we have explored the model of distant dispersion. A second paradigm of dispersion comes about as the Ḥaredi population expands slowly within the Tel Aviv conurbation, as overcrowding in Bnei Brak catalyzes out-migration to other parts of the metropolitan area. The most notable destination is Petaḥ Tikva, where a Ḥaredi buildup is taking place in the midst of a long-established city. Petaḥ Tikva cannot be defined as a religious town, despite its long history as the so-called mother of settlements, founded by Torah-observant Jews. The rather significant Ḥaredi concentration in this veteran city is the result of two factors: the historical image of Petaḥ Tikva, in contrast with the more secular image of other parts of metropolitan Tel Aviv, and the relatively low cost of housing in this city in the past.

Petaḥ Tikva illustrates another principle. A "modern Orthodox" population preceded the Ḥaredim population in Petaḥ Tikva and unintentionally set the stage for them. This process has been noted in other localities. With the spreading Ḥaredization of all parts of Bnei Brak in the 1960s and 1970s, the modern Orthodox were crowded out of the city and moved eastward toward Petaḥ Tikva.

Thus we have seen various models of Ḥaredi concentrations in Israeli towns outside the large, traditional concentrations. These dispersion models create different types of interaction between the Ḥaredi community and its surroundings. Any analysis of these types of interaction are by necessity limited by our inability to define the identifying features of this population group with precision, and by the simple fact that not all of these concentrations were studied. Some of the analyses mentioned below are based on the conclusions of studies by the author of this chapter and are published here for the first time. Therefore, the discussion to follow is composed of ideas deduced from examples, although experience shows that the principle governing them is uniform and unchanging.

The Ḥaredi community in the small and middle-sized Israeli urban locality is discussed from two points of view: a community within a long-established city and a community within a new city.

A ḤAREDI COMMUNITY
IN A LONG-ESTABLISHED CITY

A Ḥaredi community may develop in a long-established, affluent city when one of two processes is at work. The first is Ḥaredi urban migration as a part of more general urbanization processes. The second is a planned, formal decision. The spontaneous migration of Ḥaredim to long-established, affluent urban areas is, in essence, part of the general urbanization trend and shows that even among the Ḥaredim not all members of the community behave alike. Some Ḥaredim display spatial behavior, in terms of residential choice, that resembles conventional spatial behavior of the population at large. These Ḥaredim choose their place of residence on the basis of their needs, their means, and the state of the market.

The second process is the outcome of a formal decision. That is, the local authority, usually in cooperation with the Ḥaredi leadership, decides to allocate land for the construction of a specific Ḥaredi neighborhood. Thus the territorial identity of the Ḥaredi residential space is created immediately. At times, the two processes converge and complement each other: Ḥaredi migration to a given urban locality creates an initial Ḥaredi nucleus, to which an area designated from the outset by the authorities is later "attached," into which an organized Ḥaredi community enters, thus expanding the Ḥaredi zone. The urban areas into which spontaneous Ḥaredi migration spreads are, of course, the metropolitan areas. The largest such area in Israel is greater Tel Aviv. Indeed, Ḥaredi concentrations are observable in the city and on its outskirts, from a nucleus in Tel Aviv itself to Petaḥ Tikva, located on the eastern side of the conurbation, and as far as the outer fringes on the north and south (Natanya and Reḥovot, respectively).

The interaction of the Ḥaredi community with its urban environment is a function of the nature of the city and the size and strength of the community. In principle, Ḥaredi communities everywhere aspire to establish a cultural dominance that will permit them to lead their social and religio-cultural lives in order to avoid threats by any way of life that conflicts with their community values. When the community is very small, and its demographic weight and political power within the city's population slight, it focuses on developing its residential area as a "protected neighborhood," maintaining only functional or instrumental interaction with the urban surroundings. The community imports its material needs—especially food with Ḥaredi *kashrut* certification—from a large Ḥaredi concentration outside the area. The community endeavors to establish the services it needs, such as a synagogue attuned to its tastes and special schools for its children, within or adjacent to its boundaries. As the community grows, and certainly if it becomes large enough to gain representation on the city council, it continues striving to adapt its immediate environment to its needs and way of life. As stated, the nature of the city also determines, in part, the community's strength. The power of the community is measured not as a stand-alone attribute but rather against the background of the characteristics of the city in which it functions. This is best illustrated by two differing examples: Tel Aviv and Petaḥ Tikva.

In an old section of Tel Aviv, part of the core of the metropolitan area, there is a concentration of several dozen (perhaps more) Haredi families. This connection—the heart of Tel Aviv and a Haredi community—sounds implausible, but it exists. Only someone who knows the Haredi community well may comprehend the intrinsic paradox of this geographic combination. For Israel's Haredim, Tel Aviv, especially its entertainment and amusement districts, symbolizes the repulsive, threatening, degenerate nature of modern Western urban culture, a culture of hedonistic, brutish permissiveness and moral perversion. Yet Haredi families have penetrated the very heart of this area. This penetration is part of a general revival process in downtown Tel Aviv, an area whose quality of residence deteriorated as it aged and as the move to the suburbs gained strength. At present, the district is reconsolidating itself as a residential neighborhood with a young population composed of yuppies, bohemians, artists, students, and others— people who tend to live in an urban center in the process of renewal. Among all these are some Haredim.

Some of these Haredi families have lived there for some time and are, in fact, the vestiges of the veteran population of the "Little Tel Aviv" that preceded the tremendous growth of the last three decades. As for the other Haredim, there remains the interesting question of why they chose to live in such an area. Interviews with members of the Haredi community in the area indicate that some of them work nearby and selected their places of residence for the same reasons that inform the decisions of any other population group. Their willingness to live in an area whose ambiance clashes with their own set of values may be explained by their ability to distinguish between the functional-instrumental level of their urban lives and their cultural and value milieu. Apparently they relate only to the practical aspects of the city, which provides them with employment, health services, and the like, disregarding all the rest. Thus, as the Sabbath enters late Friday afternoon, one may find a Haredi Jew dressed in *kapota* and *streiml* stepping into an upper-story synagogue for Sabbath prayers while, on the ground floor of the same building, other Jews sit in a café desecrating the Sabbath. The sight of Haredim, in their traditional Sabbath dress, sharing a sidewalk with the secular young people of Tel Aviv, whose appearance is so different, as they maneuver around the café tables, evokes idyllic images. We shall see, however, that the matter is not so simple.

Some of these Haredi families have no functional connection with the area. They might be men who devote all their time to devotional studies and whose wives, too, are not employed nearby. The explanation that some of them offered for having chosen to live here sheds light on an important aspect of the Ḥaredi attitude toward the city, even if we cannot verify whether the explanation is true. They claimed to have chosen this area not *despite* its secular character but *because* of it. One interviewee reports having moved there "in order to bring the Jews back to their Father in Heaven." Any intelligent person will understand that the intention is not to save the souls of the people sitting in the cafés. The meaning of this attitude is more profound.

The Ḥaredi rejects the secular urban landscape, refuses to make peace with it, and certainly denies it legitimacy. If so, why does he enter it? The answer we have heard shows that this is a demonstrative incursion. The Ḥaredi ideology rebels against the possibility of an urban area in Eretz Israel that obliterates its Jewish culture, with all its identifying marks, becoming instead a "universal" urban space undistinguished from any gentile city in the world in any respect. Here the Ḥaredi operates in compliance with the very principle that would cause him to expel any alien elements from the Ḥaredi space, but in reverse. Just as the Ḥaredi totality in his space is liable to be harmed by any manifestation of "desanctifying" secularism, so too in a space the very nature of which is the antithesis of sanctity. By introducing his religious symbols in that space, this Jew negates the totality of its secularism and establishes Judaism in the very face of secularism. This is not a reconciliation but an act of opposition and protest. The picture of the Jew dressed in *kapota* and *streiml* in the midst of the urban milieu of Shenkin or Dizengoff Street in Tel Aviv is a picture not of utopia but of conflict and protest—an example not of coexistence but of demonstrative juxtaposition of two opposing cultures. In the Ḥaredi mindset, the secular Tel Aviv culture is invalid and dangerous. The individual Ḥaredi therefore opposes it by setting up his own "counterculture," which, in his opinion, represents true Judaism. This is a cultural-ideological explanation that coexists with the functional one, neither contradicting the other. It is the extremist attitude of a very small Ḥaredi community in the midst of an urban environment the cultural context of which is fundamentally dissonant.

A second example of a Ḥaredi community in a long-established city is that of Petaḥ Tikva. Again, this community has historical roots in the city. The veteran Ḥaredi core of Petaḥ Tikva has been augmented with a new Ḥaredi influx through a process of intrametro-politan migration, especially from Bnei Brak, and in-migration from other parts of the country.

As noted above, the Ḥaredi penetration of Petaḥ Tikva was preceded by a concentration of young modern Orthodox families, many of whom left Bnei Brak when it underwent extreme Ḥaredization. The existence of a non-Ḥaredi but Orthodox group facilitates the influx of Ḥaredim, since the ways of life of the Ḥaredim and the modern Orthodox do not clash markedly. A large Orthodox community means, for the Ḥaredim, a space endowed with Jewish cultural components such as synagogues, Sabbath observance, and (relatively) modest dress. All these facilitate the Ḥaredi penetration of an area without the creation of acute conflicts.

It is precisely these factors, however, that make the modern Orthodox anathema in Ḥaredi eyes. This would seem quite surprising only to those who fail to understand Ḥaredi attitudes. The more proximate or similar a group is to the Ḥaredim, the more they avoid it because it endangers their sociocultural structure. The danger is that their youth may be attracted to the other group and may even wish to "intermarry." The protective ramparts built by the leadership to safeguard the community from all outside influences would thus be breached. Therefore, the Ḥaredim may view the modern Orthodox favorably at the time they move in. Later, however, this convenience gives way to a perception of menace and hostility.

In Petaḥ Tikva, the attitude of the Ḥaredim toward the non-Ḥaredi Orthodox is ambivalent. The community is not yet large enough to dispense with them, and therefore they are even willing to share a candidates' list in elections for the municipal council. At the same time, the Ḥaredim are making all the preparations for separation and segregation. They are establishing separate institutions and developing their leaders separately, without any coordination with their political partners. In other words, the municipal political partnership has an instrumental rather than an ideological basis. Be this as it may, this alliance, even if not a true partnership, gives the Ḥaredi community a sense of power that transcends its size and specific gravity among the population of Petaḥ Tikva.

An example of the modus operandi of a Ḥaredi community that regards itself as powerful was provided when a movie theater opened its doors on the Sabbath in Petaḥ Tikva. The municipal bylaws of most Israeli cities proscribe the operation of places of entertainment on Friday night. With the spread of Western forms of amusement in Israeli society and the embracing of leisure culture by Israeli society, there has been an increased demand for entertainment on the "weekend" (an expression that itself conveys a

Western-secular rather than a Jewish concept). Thus social pressure mounted for permission to open places of entertainment on Friday nights, as well. Tel Aviv was the first city to accede; there the matter passed without controversy.

In the wake of Tel Aviv and other cities, Petaḥ Tikva experimented with the opening of movie theaters on Friday nights. This attempt, however, met with ferocious opposition from the Ḥaredi community, as expressed in fierce, even violent demonstrations coupled with another method quite accepted among Ḥaredim. Since Ḥaredi society rejects the possibility of open, free debate because it is so dangerous, it delegitimates dissent from any source. In the present case, the embodiment of dissent was the mayor of Petaḥ Tikva (a member of the Labor party), who favored opening the movie theaters on the Sabbath. For his troubles he was not only opposed by the Ḥaredim but veritably demonized. This, again, is a normal phenomenon among a population group that has no tradition of debate—the ostracism and trampling of the opponent, coupled with character assassination so sweeping that he is depicted as totally unfit for association.

In the struggle over the movie theaters in Petaḥ Tikva, however, a coalition of the strangest kind developed, which seems to have had no parallel since the 1950s: modern Orthodox joined the Ḥaredi demonstrations and elevated the struggle to the level of Orthodoxy at large. The evident reason for this escalation was that Sabbath movies in localities outside Tel Aviv was a far-reaching innovation, and Petaḥ Tikva had thus far maintained a traditional public face. Therefore the Orthodox of all hues regarded the novelty as a radical change in the historical image of the city. For a long time to come, then, one could witness every Friday night young Ḥaredi men demonstrating together with the modern Orthodox youth of Bnei Akiva, both regarding their Laborite mayor as their common foe.

Despite this wall-to-wall cooperation among the Orthodox, the struggle failed; the theaters stayed open on the Sabbath. It seems that the Orthodox public, including its leadership, underestimated the secular powers' fixity of purpose. What the secularists had once viewed as a minor sacrifice for the sake of the "traditional character" of the city and for the cause of coexistence with the town's Orthodox residents, had now become a fundamental issue concerning the freedom to choose one's leisure pursuits without dictates from anyone associated with the side of religion.

At that time, various (non-Haredi) rabbis and religious circles began to take exception to the struggle and its character, since it had caused more desecration of the Sabbath than the screening of films on the Sabbath had. The modern Orthodox quit the struggle. When the Haredim found themselves without allies, they realized there was no longer point in further struggle, and they, too, abandoned the fray. The price was paid by the mayor of Petah Tikva, who had acquired a blatantly antireligious image in the eyes of the city's Orthodox residents. In the mayoral elections of 1989, the religious residents of Petah Tikva opted for the Likud candidate, tipping the balance in the latter's favor and unseating the object of their opprobrium.

Summing up, we see that the Haredi community in a long-established city is not demarcated by a protected space in the manner of the large concentrations; such a community is too small and powerless to expel all the functions and residences of different character. A Haredi concentration in a long-established city is therefore a mixed community, unless it is built as a Haredi neighborhood from the outset. The community's ability to affect the character of its urban surroundings is usually limited to the provision of goods and services and the introduction of its territorial symbols to the space it occupies.

A HAREDI COMMUNITY IN A NEW CITY

The expression "new city" refers here to a planned city, in the sense that both the location and the very existence of the city are not a result of orthogenetic processes, but in external, institutional decisions. Such a city's internal layout, too, is planned before any building on the site is begun. One expects a Haredi concentration in this kind of city to be part of the town plan. This is not the case. Israel's affluent new cities, such as Arad in the Negev, Carmiel in the Galilee, or Ashdod on the southern coastal plain, neither planned any Haredi residential area nor set aside any function that could be called Haredi. Furthermore, Arad and Carmiel were established with no religious schools of any kind; even state-religious schools (for the modern Orthodox) were founded there only after a struggle (Gonen and Shilhav 1979). In Ashdod, the situation was different. There the education system was originally designed as a two-track one, with an equal number of state and state-religious schools.

Nevertheless, there is a large Ḥaredi concentration in Ashdod, a significant concentration in Carmiel, and a small community even in Arad. How did Ḥaredim migrate to these cities? Clearly their arrival was not part of the town plan; it developed later on.

We have already discussed the reasons for migration of Ḥaredim to new cities, some of which are known in Israel as development towns. Indeed, differences in nomenclature are significant; we distinguish between cities that are perceived as successful and those regarded as less so. Ḥaredim settled in cities of both types, but the characteristics of their spatial organization differ somewhat with the type of city.

We illustrate the growth of a Ḥaredi community in this type of city, as exemplified by Ashdod, a town on Israel's southern coastal plain. We choose Ashdod because it has the attributes of a "successful" city along with some characteristics of a development town that has not yet reached the "take-off" point, as we shall see.

Ashdod had a population of about 80,000 as of 1990 (as reported by the Municipality of Ashdod), with 22,000 dwelling units in sixteen residential neighborhoods. The 1,500 Ḥaredi families in Ashdod form a distinct community within a defined area: the Gimmel quarter, which is of interest to us only for the processes that led to this agglomeration there. Study of these processes may inform us about other Ḥaredi concentrations.

As a new city, Ashdod was planned in detail before its construction began. The residential neighborhoods were built in sequence, each designed as an autonmous urban spatial unit that would meet its population's retail, commercial, and service needs. The Gimmel quarter was tenanted in the early 1960s by immigrants, mostly Oriental Jews. It is relatively far from the developed centers in the Aleph and Bet quarters. The major source of employment for its residents was an industrial building plant in the neighborhood itself. In the late 1960s, in view of the neighborhood's poverty and the social stigma it had acquired, residents embarked on protest activities. It took nearly a decade for these activities to show first results; renovation work including the construction of housing for young couples began in the late 1970s. Some of these dwelling units were purchased by *ḥasidic* Ḥaredim, marking the first Ḥaredi penetration of Ashdod. We have explored the motives under which Ḥaredim act when entering a city in this fashion. However, the great momentum that led to the creation of a large Ḥaredi agglomeration in Ashdod should be credited to the activities of the Gerrer (Gur) Rebbe. A Gerrer activist argues that

Ashdod's Ḥaredi area is the third-largest in Israel, following the communities in Jerusalem and Bnei Brak. This claim cannot be verified with precision, but Ashdod's Ḥaredi area is undoubtedly very large and well developed in relation to other such areas. When the large Ḥaredi concentrations were filled and housing prices skyrocketed, the Gerrer Rebbe ordered his *ḥasidim* not to attempt to find flats in the large, expensive communities, but rather to relocate to development towns and other areas where inexpensive housing was available. The *ḥasidim,* accustomed to all-embracing guidance by the rebbe, responded in typical fashion by requesting more detailed geographic instructions.

The Gerrer Rebbe visited Ashdod in 1978 and selected, among all parts of town, the Gimmel quarter. Today his adherents explain the choice in a way that corresponds to what we already know about the locational considerations of the Ḥaredim. The rebbe found a forlorn neighborhood, beset with poverty and crime that drove residential conditions, and accordingly, housing prices to rock-bottom levels. The ministry of construction and housing had built numerous apartments in the neighborhood, for which demand tended to zero in view of the area's nature. The ministry offered these vacant flats to the Gerrer *ḥasidim,* who responded by tenanting about 200 of them. They were followed by Belzer *ḥasidim,* who claimed another 150 flats. Thus a Ḥaredi community began to flourish in the area. In 1990 the community numbered approximately 1,500 families in five cohesive enclaves, three *ḥasidic* and two "Lithuanian" *(mitnaggedic).* The neighborhood had a total population of 11,500 persons, of whom 4,050, or about 30 percent, were Ḥaredim.

Thus the Ḥaredi agglomeration in Ashdod was instigated by the institutional initiative of the Ḥaredim, who sought to utilize a source of badly run-down and very inexpensive housing, helped by a governmental establishment that wished to solve the same problem in its inverse aspect, that is, to dispose of surplus housing and, perhaps, to modify the image of the neighborhood by tenanting it with Ḥaredim.

When the Ḥaredi concentration came into being, it began to interrelate with its surroundings in a manner totally different than that observed in the established cities. In Ashdod the Ḥaredi community has a defined space, known and recognized as such. Moreover, the Ḥaredi communities congregate in subneighborhoods or enclaves. (The Hebrew term used is *qirya,* literally "village.") Each enclave bears the name of its specific Ḥaredi group: Gur, Belz, and Pittsburgh (ḥasidic); Ponevezh and Avramski ("Lithuanian").

The internal spatial organization of the Ḥaredi area embraces all manifestations of cultural dominance: the nature of commerce and services, religious institutions, and Ḥaredi schools. The quarter has only two state schools—one state-religious and the other general/secular—as against eight Ḥaredi schools for less than one-third of the quarter's population. The quarter's many synagogues are also used as centers of devotional study.

The territorial manifestations of the Ḥaredi boundaries are also of interest. The problematics of territorial symbols such as the ʾeruv and the closure of streets to vehicular traffic on the Sabbath were mentioned above. One would not expect to find these symbols in the established cities, but they do exist in a town such as Ashdod, for two reasons: the Ḥaredi area in Ashdod is large and well-defined, and the residents of the area, a majority of whom belong to Oriental communities that view tradition favorably, expressed no opposition to such symbols. Another matter of interest is the difference between ḥasidic and mitnaggedic attitudes as manifested by these symbols. The Gerrer enclave installed its own ʾeruv; as expected, these ḥasidim do not rely on the municipal ʾeruv that encircles the entire town limits. The "Lithuanian" Avramski community did the same. However, the Gerrer ʾeruv encases the entire quarter, not only the Gerrer enclave, whereas the Avramski ʾeruv encircles only the small Avramski area. This behavior does more than hint at the spatial orientation of the members of these two communities.

Indeed, the Gerrer ḥasidim treat the surrounding population with what may be described as cultural patronage. They offer religious studies, lectures, and activity groups for their non-Orthodox neighbors, even admitting non-Ḥaredi children to their schools. Non-Ḥaredi children in the neighborhood, including some who are not even religiously observant, do attend the Ḥaredi schools. Such an influence is possible only among a population that has a profound affinity for tradition but lacks knowledge and ideological background in the intricacies of the faith. That the Ḥaredim chose to establish their community within such a population is not only of economic significance but also has social, cultural, and political consequences. Thus, in the 1988 Knesset elections, quite a few voters cast their ballots for blatantly Ḥaredi parties even in polling precincts in which no Ḥaredim live. The city leaders contend that this is an external impact of the Ḥaredi area on its surroundings. Such an impact is unique in the nature of Israel's development towns and similar neighborhoods in the large established cities.

CONCLUSION

Thus we see that the Haredi community as a sector of Israeli society constitutes a socially, politically, and spatially singular behavioral model. Despite all the methodological and statistical difficulties that arise in presenting clear-cut quantitative data on this community, its significance in Israeli society and the Israeli urban landscape is self-evident and conspicuous. It is a community whose main concern is the promotion of its own particularistic interests. The nature of its political activity in the wider contexts of Israeli society is tailored to this principal aim. The parameters of Haredi involvement in Israeli politics and other realms of life in the country are limited to matters connected with the welfare of community members and the preservation of the Haredi leadership's ability to foster community life while maintaining maximum supervision of the cultural and educational content of this life. Consonant with this doctrine, the political representatives of Haredi Orthodoxy do not trouble themselves with Israel's foreign affairs and defense problems, but are concerned that the obligation of military service not apply to the young men of their community who study in *yeshivot*. Education policy is of no concern to them as long as their own school systems, divorced from those of the state, receive the financial allocations they need. There are many similar examples.

The point of departure for this behavior is the Haredi community's selective rejection of modernity. The word to emphasize here is selectivity: Haredi Orthodoxy distinguishes, as we have seen, between the instrumental elements of modernity, which it accepts, and its values, which it rejects. The Haredi community's great error, one that thrusts it into a state of existential paradox, is the assumption that such a distinction can be sustained on the practical level. Such a differentiation between these dimensions is theoretically correct, but the thought that the diverse elements of modernity may be isolated and dichotomized into instrumental and value categories is untenable in practice. Elements of modernity that seem culture- and value-neutral may serve as agents for the transmission of the values and culture in which they were created. The same is true with regard to the nature of Haredi political activity. Haredi politics in Israel originated in the sending of representatives to safeguard the community's interests and resource allocations. The political processes of Israeli society have not penetrated the Haredi community, and the community's political representatives are simply liaisons with the surrounding world for the fulfillment of its defined functional needs. The definitive feature of this political activity at present, however, is the gravitation of Haredim to power centers and positions and an overstepping of the limited parameters of representation of Haredi concerns. Furthermore, some young Haredim are insisting on the adoption by Haredi society of the political norms of democratic Israeli society. This, of course, refers more to the technical transference of such patterns as majority decision-making than to the internalization of Western democratic social values. Nevertheless, it is certainly a major change. Some believe that the gravitation to politics, positions, and various power centers in Israeli society at large will compel Haredi politicians to deal with decision-making processes in general Israeli concerns not specifically connected with the particularistic interests of the Haredi community. These observers argue that this development will cause greater openness among Haredim toward Israeli society and will, by nature, mitigate the community's hostility, which originated in its insularity.

The political realm is not the only example of this process; another may be the employment of Haredi women. Haredi society treats the employment of women as nothing more than a way to sustain a family in a manner permitting the husband to free himself of all obligations and duties. Thus he may dedicate himself to his true calling, the one that resides on the value level: full dedication to Torah study. From the Haredi viewpoint, the dichotomy in this case is absolutely clear. The wife's function is instrumental, the husband's is on the level of values. However, major changes are taking place in this simple structure. The conventional occupations of Haredi women—teaching, clerical work, and petty trade—no longer generate enough jobs to meet the demand. This is especially true of occupations requiring vocational training, such as teaching. The curriculum most typically pursued by Haredi girls is pedagogical training in Haredi teachers' colleges. Again, however, the supply of Haredi teaching jobs fails to keep up with demand, meaning that many girls, unable to find work in the occupation for which they have been trained, seek training in other vocations. These include a very wide range of occupations requiring technological, administrative, paramedical, or other training. One consequence of this is that the vocational qualifications of Haredi women—as a generalization, of course—are continuing to develop, and the occupational and intellectual credentials of this group, measured by the customary Western criteria, often exceed those of their husbands and may therefore threaten the latter's supremacy. How will this development affect Haredi society? The women's vocational training, and *a fortiori* their employment, exposes them to various influences of the modern world.

These influences are not confined to the instrumental level only, as community leaders assume. Rather, they include cultural and social values which, over time, seep into the Ḥaredi women's world. As long as these women accept the aforementioned functional dichotomy between themselves and their husbands, the community will be able to continue undisturbed. If a man succeeds in his devotional studies successfully and is accepted as an outstanding scholar, his wife will find it easier to accept the dichotomy of functions between them. However, in a society that treats complete devotion to Torah study as the norm rather than the domain of a select elite, it is only natural that not all those who study will achieve erudition. Of course, one does not presume the existence of a correlation between a man's attainments and those of his wife. Thus, a woman may find opportunities for study, advancement, and development, while her husband reaches a "dead end." In such a situation, the possibility—or, from the Ḥaredi point of view, the danger—arises that these women will begin to have second thoughts about the structure foisted upon them by the community's values. Such a development would threaten the foundations of the Ḥaredi community's existence, for these women would be challenging the cornerstone of that community: the family unit, in whose cultivation and preservation the community has invested tremendous effort.

In the spatial dimension, too, several questions arise as to the future nature of the community and its relations with Israeli society. The tremendous advancements in communications and transportation, coupled with globalization processes, have made it possible for the Ḥaredim to select the geographic advantages of developing small, scattered concentrations in various urban localities throughout Israel without sacrificing the advantages of large-group life in terms of the provision of services unique to the community. However, a small Ḥaredi apartment complex or neighborhood does not permit the same degree of insularity that a large Ḥaredi area provides. The residents of a small Ḥaredi neighborhood in an outlying city are more closely related to their general urban system than their counterparts who reside in a large Ḥaredi urban area. Furthermore, the intimate relations among various subgroups within the Ḥaredi community, coupled with geographic dispersion, are triggering a process of increase in individual members' spatial mobility. As we know, an increase in components of mobility in one domain may spread to other domains as well.

The Haredim of Israel, as a community that strives assiduously to preserve the cultural and religious traditions that typified the Jewish communities of eighteenth-century Eastern Europe, station themselves squarely against the religious, cultural, and value norms of Israeli society. At the same time, the Haredi community depends on Israeli society for its sustenance, and is consequently prone, unwittingly by itself, to processes of change, the results of which are difficult to predict at present. When discussing the processes at work in the Haredi community, one should also bear in mind that Israeli society's attitudes toward religion and tradition, too, are changing. These changes lead to polarization between the secular leisure and consumption culture and the Haredi world. How Israeli society will develop as a Jewish society is a question that touches upon the very roots of the relationships discussed here. To answer the question, however, would require inquiry and deliberation exceeding the parameters of the present discussion.

References

Bacon, Gershon C. 1983. "*Da'at Torah* and the Birthpangs of the Messiah." *Tarbiz: A Quarterly for Jewish Studies* 52, 3: 497–508. (Hebrew)

Flusser, David. 1958. "The New Dogmatism." *De'ot* 6: 10–13. (Hebrew)

Friedman, Menachem. 1977. *Society and Religion*, 33–34. Jerusalem: Yad Izhak Ben Zvi. (Hebrew)

Goldman, Eliezer. (n.d.). *Halacha and the State*. Publication of the Kibbutz Hadati. (Hebrew)

Gonen, Amiram, and Yosseph Shilhav. 1979. "Spatial Competition between School Systems: The Case of State-Religious Education in Israel." *Geoforum* 10: 203–8.

Liebman, Charles S., and Eliezer Don-Yehiya. 1983. *Civil Religion in Israel*. Berkeley: University of California Press.

Meyrowitz, Joshua. 1985. *No Sense of Place*. Oxford: Oxford University Press.

Oierbach, Moshe. 1958. *The Theory of Education: A Handbook for Education and Instruction in Religious Schools*. Jerusalem: The Center for Haredi Literature in Israel. (Hebrew)

Sheinfeld, Moshe C. 1987. An interview with the newspaper *Erev Shabbat*, issue no. 181, 3 July. (Hebrew)

Shilhav, Yosseph. 1983. "Communal Conflict in Jerusalem: The Spread of Ultra-Orthodox Jewish Neighborhoods." In *People, Territory, and State:*

Pluralism and Political Geography, ed. S. Waterman and N. Kliot, 100–13. London: Croom Helm.

———. 1984a. "Spatial Strategies of the Haredi Population in Jerusalem." *Socio-Economic Planning Science* 18, 6: 411–18.

———. 1984b. "The Conflict between Religious and Non-Religious Communities in Israel as an Issue in Political Geography." *Horizons: Studies in Geography* 9–10: 143–56. (Hebrew)

———, and Menachem Friedman. 1985. *Growth and Segregation: The Ultra-Orthodox Community of Jerusalem*. Jerusalem: Jerusalem Institute for Israel Studies. (Hebrew)

Teitelbaum, Rabbi Joel. 1961. "The Decree of the Three Oaths." In *Va-Yoel Moshe*, 2nd ed. New York: Jerusalem Press. (Hebrew)

Urbach, Ephraim E. 1969. *The Sages: Beliefs and Opinions*. Jerusalem: Magnes Press. (Hebrew)

7 ■ Gush Emunim New Settlements in the West Bank: From Social Movement to Regional Interest Group

Giora Goldberg

Since its inception in 1974, Gush Emunim ("Bloc of the Faithful") has been a fascinating sociopolitical phenomenon. No political group of such small size has ever attracted so much attention in Israel's academia or public debate. Several factors have contributed to the Gush's attractiveness from the perspective of social science, the mass media, and the general public. First, the Gush has demonstrated an enormous amount of sociopolitical uniqueness. It represents a mixture of extremist ideology with a very efficient and effective political practice. In most cases, ideological zealots are politically impotent. High levels of political efficiency and effectiveness are typically tied to pragmatism and moderation. Another unique component of the Gush's innovative orientation is the integration of religious and nonobservant Jews into one political framework. The basic political strategy of the Gush is also unique. In an extremely politicized state such as Israel, where party politics is almost everything, it is unusual for political entrepreneurs to stand outside of the party system and to exert political influence through an interest group. Gush Emunim as a powerful interest group symbolizes the antithesis of a political system dominated by centralized political parties. Another distinct characteristic is the revival of the pioneering spirit of Israeli society by the Gush. The heritage of the founding period in the Zionist history is so crucial that a political group which is identified with the pioneering spirit is still considered a leading force in society.

Another reason why Gush Emunim has become so attractive is because it has had a major impact on Israeli society. The ideological

189

principles of the Gush have been the most important challenge to the existing political ideologies. Furthermore, Gush Emunim's influence on major public policies has been crucial. In its heroic years between 1974 and 1977, the Gush managed to fulfill policies opposed by the Israeli government. In 1977, the new Likud government adopted the settlement policy of Gush Emunim, which was considered illegal in the period of the Labor government. The main success of the Gush was the building of Jewish settlements in the Samaria mountains. In its "expansion era" of 1977–81, thousands of Gush supporters joined a few dozen settlements in this area. Gush Emunim is now (1992) the leading force of the 100,000 Jewish settlers in the West Bank and any future peace arrangement that concerns the status of the West Bank will have to take the Gush into account.

It is important to understand that Gush Emunim of the 1970s changed dramatically during the 1980s. In the 1970s, the Gush was a social movement; in the 1980s, it became primarily a regional interest group. This is the central thesis of this chapter.

A social movement is an unconventional group that has different degrees of formal organization and that attempts to produce or prevent radical or reformist type of change (Wood and Jackson 1982, 3). As a social movement, Gush Emunim attempted to transform the secular values of Israeli society into fundamentalist Jewish values. The fulfillment of such values, for the Gush, was primarily through settlement in the old biblical land of Judea and Samaria, also known as the West Bank.[1] The fundamentalist normative changes and the settlement policy requested by the Gush, placed it on a collision course with the secular Israeli society.

The loud voices of Gush protesters in the 1970s, however, weakened in the 1980s. In the last decade the Gush shifted its focus from the national to the regional level. Specifically, it began to operate as a regional interest group. A regional interest group is organized by its members to represent regional interests to other organizations in the political system. As such a group, the Gush attempted to accelerate settlement in the West Bank through pragmatic economic demands. Yet, unlike most regional interest groups that tend to be policy-oriented only, the Gush also had an ideological platform. The conflict of interests between the Gush and the Israeli government deepened over the Gush's budget requests and its goal of massive housing construction in the West Bank. The conflict gradually centered on the economic and political interests of the region, the West Bank.

SIGNS OF FAILURE

Over time, it has become apparent that the Gush is far from achieving a complete political victory. Its failure to prevent the Israeli government from signing the Camp David Accords (1978), including the Autonomy Plan for the West Bank Palestinians, was the first indication of the limited political power of the Gush. In spite of the fact that the Autonomy Plan has not been yet implemented, it stands as a permanent threat to Gush Emunim. The Gush could not prevent the final Israeli withdrawal in 1982 from the Sinai Peninsula, which included the evacuation of Jewish settlers from the Yamit district of northern Sinai. Moreover, the annexation of the West Bank by the state of Israel has no chance to be realized in the near future. The expectation of the Gush that hundreds of thousands of Jewish settlers would move to the east and fill the West Bank with massive Jewish population is also not coming true. The Palestinian uprising, Intifada, which erupted in December 1987, has been a further strike against the Jewish settlements in the West Bank. In fact, it turned into a guerrilla war in which the Israeli army failed to guarantee a reasonable defense to the Jewish settlers in the West Bank.

The attempt of Gush Emunim to become a dominant factor in Israeli society has broken down. Its main goal, transforming the Israeli belief system into a fundamentalist religious-messianic set of values, has not been achieved. Furthermore, the Gush is no longer the most dynamic force in the religious community. If the 1970s were characterized by an attempt on the part of Gush Emunim to become the leading political force in the religious community, the 1980s demonstrated that the Gush is merely one phenomenon among several other religious-political developments which appeared during the decade. Three of these religious political developments are described below.

In 1983, a new religious party, Shas, was founded. This is an ethnic party which represents Oriental Jews. Because most Gush Emunim supporters are Ashkenazim, Shas does not threaten Gush Emunim directly. However, the intersection between religiosity and ethnicity is an important development among religious Jews. This new political formula is gaining more electoral support from one election to another. The second development was the success of Kach, Meir Kahane's party, in the elections of 1984. It was the first time that a fascist-racist political party entered the Knesset. Kach's popularity rose between 1984 and 1988. But on the eve of the 1988 elections the party was outlawed by the Supreme Court. Although Kach did not identify itself as an exclusive religious party, it became a meaningful force in the religious sector. Kach was a typical antisystem party. Its uniqueness was expressed in an overt hostility towards Arabs. The impact of Kach in the West Bank was marginal, but its success among the Jewish population west of the Green Line was striking.[2] The third development was Memad, a moderate religious party with a dovish orientation, which emerged towards the 1988 elections. Memad represented an antithesis to Gush Emunim's principles. In spite of the electoral defeat of Memad, its very existence poses a significant challenge to Gush Emunim in the context of the religious camp.

These internal developments suggest that Gush Emunim is merely one phenomenon in the religious community. This conclusion challenges the substance of "the iceberg model of political extremism" portrayed by Sprinzak (1981). The model assumes that the Gush has never been an isolated group of religious fanatics which emerged from nowhere. Gush Emunim is the tip of a giant iceberg. The Gush represents the religious-nationalist subculture, the iceberg, which has strong organizational, financial, and legal bases and is supported by large circles in the political establishment. The Gush, as the spearhead of this religious-nationalist subculture, is dependent to a large extent on the base of this subculture. The central force in this subculture is the National Religious Party (NRP).

Using this model one may assume that as long as the NRP becomes stronger the Gush would gain power and influence; if the NRP becomes weaker the Gush is supposed to lose some of its impact. Indeed, in the "golden age" of Gush Emunim (1974–77) the NRP was relatively strong. NRP's drastic decline in the elections of 1981 and 1984 (four parliamentary seats in 1984 compared to twelve in 1977) could be cited as an explanation of the slowdown of the Gush in the 1980s.

A contrasting alternative explanation is that the NRP is dependent on Gush Emunim more than vice versa. Accordingly, the fact that the NRP became strongly identified with the Gush was harmful for the NRP. Most of the Oriental supporters of the NRP were not ready to accept the leadership of Gush Emunim in the religious community. They preferred the Likud and Tami in 1981. Tami was a new Oriental party which rejected the ideological principles of the Gush. Later, after 1983, Shas became the main alternative for religious Oriental voters.

The argument concerning the feeding of Gush Emunim by the iceberg is misleading. At an earlier stage, when the Gush was mainly perceived as a protesting social movement, it was heavily supported by large portions of the religious public. However, since Gush Emunim's transformation from a social movement into an interest group whose main activities are settling the West Bank, its mobilization capability among the religious public has decreased. Those tens of thousands of young religious protesters who joined the mass demonstrations of the Gush in the 1970s have not fulfilled its ideology of settling in the West Bank. In the 1970s most of the members of Bnei Akiva, the youth movement of the NRP, were easily mobilized for the Gush protest activities. In the 1980s most of Bnei Akiva members did not support Gush Emunim. A new trend has developed among the members of this youth movement. In religious circles it was called "blackization" which means becoming ultra-Orthodox without adhering to nationalist orientation.[3]

Thus, the iceberg seems to have separated from its tip—Gush Emunim. The iceberg model was appropriate for analyzing the success of Gush Emunim in the 1970s. Yet the model became irrelevant in the 1980s. This might explain the difference between the two decades. In other words, the fact that Gush Emunim, the tip of the iceberg, has been separated from its base, the religious nationalist subculture, could explain why the Gush became weaker in the 1980s. Another speculation is that Gush Emunim's enfeeblement might be explained by arguing that the base of the iceberg has diminished and therefore the Gush has begun showing signs of failure. There is no sufficient evidence for consolidating these two arguments.

GUSH EMUNIM AS A REGIONAL INTEREST GROUP

The Gush moved from the national to the regional level. Here lies the clue for understanding the new Gush Emunim of the 1980s. The conventional wisdom, which argues that the Gush has been severely weakened, or has virtually disappeared from the public agenda, ignores that basic change. It is unjustified to analyze Gush Emunim in the 1980s as a social movement. In fact, one would find that the Gush has been extremely weakened on the national level. It might be argued that the transformation itself, from the national to the regional level, is a result of Gush Emunim's weakening. According to this argument, the failure to attain major goals necessitated the design of a new set of goals; goals that had a better chance of being accomplished. However, a better interpretation is that in a highly centralized political system, as Israel was until the 1970s, an effective penetration of a new political force into the political arena could be accomplished only from the center. After its founding period Gush Emunim began to express regional interests.

One of the reasons why the regional character of Gush Emunim has been ignored in the literature is because of the ideological image of this group. Traditionally, a political group whose ideological salience is so high, will be perceived within a national context. Regional interest groups tend to be policy-oriented rather than ideology-oriented. But there are examples, Gush Emunim being one of them, in which regional interest groups are ideology-oriented. The regional-territorial nature of Gush Emunim means that "the iceberg model of political extremism" is inappropriate for the analysis of the Gush in the 1980s. An iceberg which is clearly national should have a national tip, not a regional one as Gush Emunim. As long as the Gush emphasized mainly its national character in the years 1974–77, it was possible to use this model. Most academic literature on Gush Emunim still concentrates on its national dimension. While Sprinzak (1981) and Lustick (1988) are typical representatives of this school, which is still the mainstream of the social science literature on Gush Emunim, the studies by Newman (1985) as well as Goldberg and Ben-Zadok (1986), introduce a regional approach to Gush Emunim. Goldberg and Ben-Zadok (1986) argue that a "territorial cleavage" is being formed between the larger Israeli society and the Gush settlement in the West Bank. Accordingly, this regional settlement has various elements of distinctiveness: political-geographical, socioeconomic, ideological, and electoral.

A deep conflict of values exists between Gush Emunim and the larger society. While doves consider the West Bank as an occupied area which is primarily a Palestinian territory, most hawks emphasize the strategic importance of this area for Israel's security. For Gush Emunim this is the original biblical land which had been consecrated by God. Gush Emunim also totally rejects Western culture and its growing impact on the larger society (Raanan 1980, 117). According to the Gush ideology, the decline of the secular Israeli society is a stage in the coming of the Messiah (Rubinstein 1982, 114).

One of the components in the conflict of interests concerning Gush Emunim is the issue of budget allocations. The opponents of the Gush argue that the funds that are allocated to the Gush should be earmarked for the poor Oriental population, and especially to the residents of the development towns. In spite of the decentralization process which Israel had undergone during the 1980s, financing of the West Bank settlement is still administered through the political center. The Gush settlement did not develop an independent economic infrastructure and thus it is heavily dependent on the government and the Israeli economy. The government and the Jewish Agency are the main financial providers of the settlement in the West Bank. It is estimated that about 2 billion dollars were invested in the West Bank during the period 1968 to 1986. In the years 1968–76, 750 million dollars were invested there—an average of 83.3 million dollars a year. After 1977, the Likud governments increased the sums to an average of about 143 million dollars per year. But the National Unity Government, which was established in 1984 and included both Likud and Labor, dropped the annual average to about 125 million dollars. Most of the funds were allocated for building the infrastructure (Benvenisti 1987, 51).

Since the early 1980s, the territorial cleavage has widened. A new element in this process is the Palestinian uprising, Intifada, which started in December 1987. It has drastically widened the "territorial cleavage" between Israel and the Gush settlement in the West Bank. As mentioned earlier, this violent uprising is actually a guerrilla war. That is, in the beginning, it was a guerrilla war against the Israeli army. Later, especially since the spring of 1989, it evolved into a limited civil war between Arabs and Jews in the West Bank. Gush Emunim is leading the Jewish population in this civil war. The Israeli political establishment has largely ignored the urgent security needs of the West Bank Jewish settlers, who feel more isolated than ever. The Intifada has heightened the feelings of alienation between Gush Emunim and the larger society, especially the doves.

The Intifada has important implications for the hopes of Gush Emunim to enlarge the number of Jewish settlers in the West Bank. The motivation of potential nonideological migrants to move to the West Bank has declined. This kind of settler was the typical newcomer to the West Bank in the 1980s. In contrast, in the 1970s the ideologically driven Gush supporters constituted a vast majority of the West Bank Jewish population. The nonideological settlers of the 1980s were motivated by economic reasons. Because the government subsidized building in the West Bank, the area attracted tens of thousands of Israelis who were not Gush Emunim believers. Most of them preferred to live near the Green Line. Namely, within the metropolitan areas of

Tel Aviv and Jerusalem. Gush Emunim settlements are mainly located along the Samaria mountains, outside of the metropolitan areas.

SOCIAL-DEMOGRAPHIC CHARACTERISTICS

The Jewish population in the West Bank included only 1,182 residents in 1972 and more than 70,000 towards the end of the 1980s (Benvenisti 1987, 43). In June 1988 the Gush's population in the West Bank numbered 10,672 people (World Zionist Organization 1988). That means that the Gush accounts for only 15 percent of the Jewish population in the West Bank. Thirty-nine settlements in the West Bank were established by Gush Emunim. The average population per settlement is 267 people, much less than the average population in other Jewish settlements in the West Bank. That means that most Gush Emunim settlements are small communities.[4] Only 3,029 residents live in the Gush Emunim settlements which were established in the 1980s. This is much less even than the population of one of the new West Bank towns unaffiliated with Gush Emunim. Immanuel, for example, an ultra-Orthodox town founded in 1983, has 4,700 residents.

In the 1980s a few thousand new settlers joined the Gush Emunim settlements which had been established in the 1970s. Therefore, the total number of Gush settlers who joined in the 1980s is much higher than the 3,029 mentioned above. However, in general, the mobilization power of the Gush in the 1980s was small and it did not fulfil the expectation of its leaders. Moreover, it is noteworthy that not all the settlers who joined the Gush communities in the 1980s were fully identified with the Gush ideological principles. Families and individuals who desire to settle in a nonurban community in the West Bank have to apply for candidacy through one of the settlement movements. Most of the movements are controlled by the major political parties. Only Gush Emunim and the Agricultural Union (Ha-Ichud Ha-Chaklahi), a very small settlement movement, are not affiliated with political parties. The formal duty to join the West Bank nonurban settlement through these movements artificially increases their mobilization power. It is impossible to estimate how many of the newcomers of Gush Emunim do not fully accept its ideology. In any case, this phenomenon actually means that the ideological attractiveness of the Gush is even lower than the limited numbers indicated above.

There are no systematic reports on trends of migration in and out of the West Bank settlements. However, data on the population size in each of the settlements in the first and second quarters of 1988 enable us to discover the net migration. The growth of the Gush Emunim settlements was 3.7 percent, while that of the other settlements in the West Bank was much higher—6.6 percent (World Zionist Organization 1988). The growth tendency is quite surprising because the relevant period was the first stage of the Intifada. No new settlements were founded during this period (1988). It can be argued that initially the Intifada was not perceived as a war but rather as riots assumed to end soon.

Most of the population in Gush Emunim settlements, 61.3 percent, consists of children. Out of the 10,672 Gush Emunim total West Bank population, only 4,126 are adults. The percentage of children in other West Bank settlements is lower and stands at 53.4 percent. This difference is explained by the higher number of religious people in Gush Emunim settlements as compared to other West Bank settlements. The fertility rate of Jewish religious couples is clearly higher than that of nonreligious couples.

The Gush Emunim settlements are divided into three types: twenty-six religious settlements (average population, 293), seven secular settlements (average population, 136), and six mixed settlements (average population, 301). Mixed settlements are those in which observant and nonobservant Jews dwell together. This form of social integration is one of the Gush's important principles. The number of residents in the secular settlements is 950 which is 8.9 percent of the total Gush Emunim population in the West Bank. The mixed settlements constitute 16.9 percent of that total. It is impossible to estimate the exact proportions of secular and religious settlers in these two types of settlement. The general share of secular settlers in the Gush's West Bank population, however, is roughly estimated at 15 percent. The relatively high proportion of secular settlers probably reflects the phenomenon mentioned above, that is, some people join the Gush settlements because settling in a nonurban community in the West Bank is administered only through settlement organizations.

The ethnic composition of Gush Emunim communities does not reflect the proportions of Oriental and Ashkenazim in the society at large. The data from the census conducted by the World Zionist Organization (1986) reveal that the proportion of Oriental Jews in thirty-six of the Gush communities in the West Bank is 30.2 percent as compared to approximately 55 percent in the general population.

Although Orientals are underrepresented in the Gush settlements, their share is much higher than commonly believed. The proportion of Orientals in the settlements which had been founded in the 1970s is 27.2 percent, while in those established in the 1980s the proportion stands at 35.8 percent. That means that over time the ethnic domination of the Ashkenazim has declined. Despite these numbers, it is important to understand that the Gush leadership is mainly Ashkenazic.

The percentage of white-collar workers in Gush Emunim settlements, 62 percent, is very high when compared to the general Israeli population (World Zionist Organization 1986). The proportion of white-collar workers is higher in the old Gush settlements, those founded in the 1970s, than in its new settlements of the 1980s: 64.6 percent to 56.5 percent respectively. This tendency might reflect the changes in the ethnic composition of the Gush, as an increase in the proportion of Orientals is related to a decline in the proportion of white-collar workers.

Data on education in the Gush Emunim communities are incomplete. It is limited to males in thirty-six settlements and is not measured by years of school, but by level of education. The percentage of those who received academic degrees is 19 and that of high school diploma graduates is 31.4 (World Zionist Organization 1986). Because most Gush Emunim settlers are religious, the percentage of academic degree does not fully reflect educational achievements. A large portion of religious people graduate from *yeshivot*, special nonacademic Orthodox schools, rather than universities.

Income levels were not measured in studies on the West Bank population. Some data about housing conditions might shed light on the economic welfare of Gush Emunim settlers. Some of the Gush's political opponents argue that the settlers are upper-middle class. This argument weakens the pioneering image which Gush Emunim tries to project. Due to their isolation, as well as heavy military threats, it is clear that Gush Emunim settlements are poorly located in pure economic terms of financial value. The Intifada has even strengthened this trend. An analysis of housing unit sizes in the Gush settlements in the West Bank reveals that most of them live in modest, some even in poor, housing conditions.[5]

Considering the size of their families, their housing conditions, and their wealth, it cannot be argued that the general population of the Gush settlers belongs to the upper-middle class. Only a minority of them belongs to the upper-middle class. In general, the largest group is middle-class and a significant number is lower-middle class.

THE IMPACT OF AMANA

Gush Emunim was a highly unified movement until 1976. There was no separation between the political arm and the settlement movement. The prominent figures of the Gush led the political action and the settlement effort. In 1976 the Gush formed a settlement movement which was named Amana ("Covenant"). Later, Amana was recognized by the Israeli establishment as a settlement movement. The leaders of the Gush represent a national orientation with respect to its aims and targets, while the Amana leaders represent the new localistic orientation which emphasizes the interests of the Gush Emunim settlements and their inhabitants. In other words, Amana is one of the major indicators of the regionalization process of the Gush.

Over time, signs of tension between Gush Emunim and Amana have emerged. Amana has been strengthening politically while the power of the Gush leaders has been weakening. The strengthening of Amana is the result of several factors. In 1977, when the Gush concentrated on building the infrastructure of the West Bank, Amana became its main financial arm. A large share of settlement funds passed through the Jewish Agency. The funds granted by the Jewish Agency were allotted to Amana and not to Gush Emunim. Furthermore, Amana became superior to Gush Emunim in organizational terms. The Gush has been traditionally weak at the organizational-bureaucratic level. As a protest group, it developed a sense of contempt toward bureaucratic procedures. Most settlement movements are controlled and directed by political parties. In Israel, where political parties are so influential, their dominance over the affiliated settlement movements is salient. Amana is the most autonomous settlement movement in Israel in terms of the relations between political parties and their settling organizations. It is much easier for a settlement movement, affiliated with an interest group rather than a political party, to maintain its independence and to fully control its own resources. Gush Emunim's financial resources are scarce, mainly because it is not a political party funded by the state. This gives an advantage to Amana vis-à-vis the Gush. Amana is more acceptable than the Gush to Israeli society. The Gush, in contrast, is experiencing a great deal of hostility and opposition from large sectors, mainly from urban, secular, and leftist circles. This proves an important advantage to Amana over Gush Emunim.

The struggle between Gush Emunim and Amana is mostly latent. Three informal groups participate in this struggle: the ideology-oriented Gush Emunim leaders, the implementation-oriented Amana activists, and the largest group, which is committed to neither of the two groups. The original Gush faction tried to nominate its loyalists to key posts in Amana. There were periods when these efforts were fruitful, but from time to time the Amana activists succeeded in gaining temporary independence. The dominance over Amana itself has fluctuated. It all means that politically, Gush Emunim is no more a highly unified movement.

Amana is not the sole regional organization which constitutes a threat to Gush Emunim. During its founding era in the mid-1970s, Gush Emunim was actually the only organization which led the West Bank settlers. Later, two additional types of regional political organization were created in the West Bank. One of them was the Council of Judea, Samaria, and Gaza (Mohezet Yesha). This was a semiformal forum consisting of most of the settlement leaders, whose main task was to represent the Jewish population in the West Bank and Gaza. Gush Emunim dominated this organization in spite of efforts made by other settlement sectors, primarily by secular circles, to weaken its hold. This might be explained by the common background and high social cohesiveness of the Gush settlers. In addition, the Gush was the largest organized ideological group in the West Bank and Gaza.

The other type of regional organization which emerged in the West Bank was a form of local government known as the regional council. Most of the regional councils were controlled by Gush Emunim administrators with a strong orientation towards regional interests.

ELECTORAL BEHAVIOR

Table 7.1 describes the results of the 1988 Knesset elections in Gush Emunim settlements in the West Bank as compared to the general electorate.[6]

Three political parties are clearly overrepresented in the votes of the Gush settlements when compared to the general electorate. The NRP is the leading force in the Gush communities. Tehiya, a mixed

Table 7.1. Results of the 1988 Knesset Elections (%)

Party	Gush Emunim Settlements	General Electorate
NRP	33.5	3.9
Tehiya	26.3	3.1
Likud	16.1	31.1
Moledet	10.6	1.9
Agudat Israel	5.4	4.5
Shas	3.8	4.7
Tzomet	1.8	2.0
Degel HaTorah	0.7	1.5
Labor	0.4	30.0
Ratz	0.1	4.3
Mapam	0.1	2.5
Others	1.1	10.5[a]
Total	100.0	100.0

a. The gap between the percentage of "Others" in the two categories is mainly a result of the inclusion of Arabs in the general electorate.

party of religious and nonreligious elements, and Moledet, a new nonreligious party which emphasizes the idea of transferring the Palestinians to Arab states, were also extremely successful in the Gush communities.

At first glance the slight overrepresentation of Agudat Israel might be viewed as an unusual finding because Agudat Israel is a non-Zionist political party. However, the explanation lies in the inclusion of Poalei Agudat Israel, an ultra hawkish party, in the Agudat Israel list to the 1988 elections. Seven political parties are underrepresented in the Gush West Bank settlements when compared to the general electorate. These are Likud, Shas, Tzomet, Degel HaTorah, Labor, and Ratz and Mapam (two left-wing parties).

Despite the fact that the NRP is the leading force, it is noteworthy that the total gains of the religious parties—44.5 percent—are much less than the proportion of religious voters in the Gush communities. The extreme right-wing parties—Tehiya, Moledet, and Tzomet— gained together 38.7 percent, although they are not identified with religious viewpoints.

When the Gush's religious settlements are compared to its other communities, interesting trends are observed. The NRP achieved 40.1 percent in the religious settlements but only 17.7 percent in the secular and mixed settlements. The Likud captured just 11.9 percent of the religious votes but 26.2 percent in the secular and mixed settlements. Tehiya had similar success: 27 percent in the religious settlements and 24.6 percent in the other settlements. The relative weakness of the religious component in electoral decisions is especially reflected by the success of secular parties such as Moledet and Tzomet in the religious communities; both parties gained 10.4 percent of the votes. Tehiya, a mixed party, together with Moledet and Tzomet, achieved 37.4 percent in the religious settlements, which is quite close to the achievement of the NRP in this sector—40.1 percent.

A longitudinal analysis is also required to understand the main electoral trends in the Gush communities. Three Knesset elections were analyzed for this purpose: 1981, 1984, and 1988 (Central Bureau of Statistics 1981, 1984, 1989). The results show that the Likud has declined over time and lost during this decade about half of its supporters among the Gush West Bank settlers. Tehiya declined too, but to a lesser extent. The decline in the electoral strength of the Likud and Tehiya is partly related to the rise in strength of the NRP. The NRP first became the largest party in the Gush communities in 1988. Another major trend is the success of Moledet in the 1988 elections. Kach gained only 2.7 percent in 1984 as compared to 10.6 percent by Moledet in 1988. Moledet and Tzomet, both being secular parties, gained 12.4 percent in 1988. This was the most dramatic result of the 1988 elections in the Gush communities: the rise of the ultrahawkish secular parties such as Moledet and, to a lesser extent, Tzomet. When Tehiya was founded before the 1981 elections it was a revolutionary action for religious voters to support a mixed party. The current phase is direct support for secular parties. It reflects the superiority of national and security elements over religious elements.

It might be argued that the superiority of security considerations over religious ones expresses, to some extent, the regionalization process which characterized Gush Emunim during the 1980s. The religious parties represent the basic spirit and ideology of the Gush. Parties such as Tehiya, Tzomet, and Moledet represent mainly the concrete security interests of the settlers. The support for the NRP depends on the readiness of this party to promote the Gush's regional interests. The elections of 1984 clearly proved this point. The NRP was then perceived as a party which was not satisfying the regional interests of Gush Emunim. In contrast, Morasha (an electoral front of Matzad and Poalei Agudat Israel), representing a hawkish security platform, was perceived as the genuine supporter of Gush interests.

The results were strikingly in favor of Morasha, which received four and one-half times the number of votes that the NRP did. The success of the NRP in the 1988 Knesset elections came only after its merge with Matzad and after the Gush settlers were convinced that the renewed NRP was strictly devoted to promoting their regional interests. The Intifada reinforced the inclination of Gush settlers to defend their regional and local security interests. It also increased their tendency to vote for political parties that were strongly committed to these interests.

POLITICAL REPRESENTATION

Gush Emunim's hopes for a significant augmentation of its supporters in the Knesset were not fulfilled in the national elections of 1988. These hopes were based on an expected increase in the strength of the Tehiya party. Predictions based on election polls gave Tehiya seven or even eight parliamentary seats as compared to the five gained in the 1984 Knesset elections. However, Tehiya was clearly defeated, winning only three seats. Only one of the three elected Knesset members of Tehiya is a Gush leader—Rabbi Eliezer Waldman, dean of a famous *yeshiva* in Kiryat Arba, near Hebron. The second representative of Gush Emunim in the Knesset is Hanan Porat, a member of the NRP. Both Waldman and Porat live in Judea. In addition, there is a third Knesset member who resides in the West Bank: Likud's Gideon Gadot lives in a settlement next to the Green Line.

The West Bank settlement as a whole is heavily overrepresented in the Knesset. The number of eligible voters in the West Bank in 1988 was 26,671. The voting turnout was 90.1 percent, which means that 24,000 settlers took part in the elections. This number is roughly sufficient for one parliamentary seat. Gush Emunim, with two of the three West Bank representatives among its leaders, is even more overrepresented. In spite of this, the Gush perceived the 1988 elections results as a failure, especially because of Tehiya's electoral fiasco. The Gush also lost in 1988 its sole representative in the cabinet: Yossef Shapira, one of the NRP leaders, who served in 1984–88 as a minister without portfolio. He was the chief spokesman of the West Bank settlers and particularly of Gush Emunim.

In terms of attitudes towards Gush Emunim, the Israeli political system is divided into four groups. The first group is the direct supporters of the Gush settlement policy, namely, four political parties:

Tehiya, Tzomet, Moledet, and Poalei Agudat Israel. A number of NRP and Likud leaders are also a part of this supporting group. Most Knesset members who support the Gush belong to a parliamentary forum which lobbies for assistance to the settlements.

Some of the leaders of NRP, Shas, and especially the Likud, constitute a second group which is indifferent to the promotion of Gush Emunim's interests. However, the Knesset members of this group occasionally support policies of Gush Emunim, especially if they are legal or establishment-oriented. In case of polarization between the right and the left on a Gush issue, they will join the supporting group.

A third group consists of the hawkish Labor members of the Knesset and some of the religious leaders affiliated with the ultra-Orthodox parties, such as Shas, Agudat Israel, and Degel HaTorah. The group does not support Gush Emunim, but also does not initiate anti-Gush proposals or policies. In some cases they might join a fourth group which is overtly opposed to anything related to the promotion of Gush's ideas or interests. This group consists of the leftist wing of Labor, three small parties left of Labor (Ratz, Mapam, and Shinui) and the Arab Knesset members.

It is estimated that the four groups are equal in size. Each of them includes approximately thirty Knesset members. The only group which is organized is the direct supporters, a fact which gives its members a significant advantage. Nevertheless, the balanced distribution of attitudes towards Gush Emunim in the Knesset frequently creates a parliamentary deadlock on Gush issues.

Both major parties, Likud and Labor, are inconsistent in their attitudes towards the Gush. The second and third groups, which express moderate views, are overrepresented in the cabinet, which, similar to the Knesset, comes to a deadlock when the Gush is on the agenda. Therefore, it is not surprising that Gush Emunim requested, following the 1988 Knesset elections, the formation of a right-wing governing coalition. The Likud's decision to form a National Unity Government with Labor, while Tehiya, Tzomet, and Moledet were left in the opposition, was a striking failure for the Gush leaders.

A National Unity Government is the worst cabinet from Gush Emunim perspective. The most desired situation is a right-wing coalition. A Labor-led government is an intermediate possibility, because in such a case the Likud automatically becomes highly supportive of Gush Emunim. In fact, the best period of the Gush in terms of political support was 1974–77 under a Labor-led government. Since the formation of a National Unity Government in 1984 and until its dismantling in 1990, Gush Emunim has had continuous difficulties. The support for establishing new settlements in the West Bank declined. Economic constraints became a crucial factor when decisions on the creation of new settlements were made. The leading ministers were seeking for a compromising "working formula" in which Gush Emunim was not included. Before 1984, when one of the two major parties was in power, the Gush became a focus for dispute between the government and the leading opposition party. Since 1984, Gush Emunim leaders felt that they were the main victims of the cooperation between the Likud and Labor. In their view the Likud prefers governmental benefits and payoffs over ideological fulfillment through Gush Emunim. In addition, they complain that the National Unity Government has not reached a consensus to act decisively in order to bring the Intifada to an end.

CONCLUSION

As a social movement Gush Emunim's uniqueness is more symbolic than political. The strength of the Gush is limited. In spite of the huge budgets allocated to the West Bank settlement by the political establishment, by the government and the Jewish Agency, it seems that the West Bank settlers were manipulated by the political establishment more than the establishment was manipulated by the settlers. Israeli governments, especially those led by the Likud, wished to keep the West Bank under Israeli control. Settling these territories clearly contributed toward achieving this target. The benefits allocated to the settlers were marginal in relation to their contribution to the national effort. The settlers were greatly disturbed by the surrounding Arab population, especially since the outburst of the Intifada. Their economic well-being is less than that of the average Israeli. They are isolated from the larger Israeli society and are considered extremists and narrow-minded nationalists.

The violence of the extreme wing of the Gush against Arabs and in some cases even against Israeli soldiers during the Intifada, has intensified the negative public image of the Gush. Most Gush Emunim activists who express extreme views and use violent means are those who consider Gush Emunim a social movement. The majority of Gush Emunim settlers emphasize concrete regional issues.

The "golden age" of Gush Emunim from 1974 to 1977 was an intermediate period. In 1973, in spite of its electoral victory, the Labor party lost its historic status as the dominant party. The Likud, as well as parts of the NRP, used Gush Emunim to break down the old Labor regime. The public protest which followed the grave consequences of the 1973 war helped Gush Emunim in its remarkable penetration of the political arena. These circumstances will not be repeated in the near future. The Gush failed to achieve its long-range ideological goals. The Gush will stagnate as a national social movement, yet its regional characteristics will be strengthened. The focus on regional issues saved the Gush from deterioration. The new regional emphasis was an adaptation effort in order to survive. Social movements which are unable to adopt such survival strategies are doomed to disappear.

The transformation of Gush Emunim into a regional interest group decreased the intensity of its conflict of values with Israeli society. The Gush's vocal demands in the 1970s for fundamentalist changes in the secular Western values of Israeli society, primarily those of materialism, consumption, and the absence of Jewish spiritualism, receded in the 1980s. The mass immigration of new pioneers returning to the old biblical land, a major goal of the Gush, did not materialize. Instead, small numbers came and, moreover, they were motivated by the lower housing costs. The conflict of values, still potentially deep, became less strident and more latent.

The conflict of interests with Israeli society and the government is growing, however. The main bone of contention is the issue of budgets. Considering its small size, the Gush is still successful in obtaining financial resources for its settlements. The Gush's budget share, however, is declining in comparison to the 1970s and is far from being sufficient for attaining the goal of mass settlement of the West Bank.

From Gush Emunim perspective, the implementation of settlement policy in the West Bank is unsatisfactory. Its expectation that this settlement would be considered as a most urgent national mission was not fulfilled. The Gush's heavy political clout as well as its direct and indirect political representation in the Knesset did not produce a massive accelerated settlement. In the 1980s, the Gush remained a small group, primarily regional, and, to a large extent, economically dependent on the political center and the metropolitan areas of Tel Aviv and Jerusalem. To conclude, the Gush has been transformed into a regional interest group.

Notes

1. The West Bank was captured by Israel from Jordan in 1967. It encompasses two natural geographic units: the mountains of Judea (south) and Samaria (north), and the western strip of the Jordan rift.

2. The Green Line is the 1949–67 Israel-Arab (Jordan) armistice line.

3. The ultra-Orthodox community is not committed to a nationalist ideology which emphasizes factors such as use of military power, territorial expansion, and statism. The most extreme part of that community rejects even the mere fact of Israel being a Jewish state. The term "blackization" relates to the traditional black clothing which ultra-Orthodox men use to wear.

4. In fourteen Gush Emunim settlements there are less than 200 residents. All these tiny communities were formed in the 1980s. The eleven settlements whose population exceed 300 residents had been formed in the 1970s. The average population in the seventeen settlements which had been formed in the 1970s is 450, while the average population in the twenty-two settlements which had been formed in the 1980s is only 132 (World Zionist Organization 1988).

5. Data from 1985 on thirty-three Gush Emunim settlements are the basis for this conclusion (World Zionist Organization 1986). Housing units were allocated to those under 60 sq. meters and those over 60 sq. meters. No less than 56.1 percent of the total units belong to the under 60 sq. meters category. Taking into account the relatively large size of the religious families indicates that many of them live in crowded conditions. It is true that many of the small housing units are located in the new settlements, in which many temporary housing units are built initially. Housing conditions are better in the old settlements in which permanent units have already been built. The percentage of the under 60 sq. meters category among the permanent housing units is only 31.2 percent. The units over 60 sq. meters are divided into those under 100 sq. meters units and those over 100 sq. meters. The percentage of units over 100 sq. meters out of the total permanent housing stock is 41.9 percent.

6. The Central Bureau of Statistics summarizes the elections results in Gush Emunim's settlements only by percentage for each settlement. Average percentages have a large potential of bias since the size of each settlement is not taken into account. After the 1988 Knesset elections, *Nekudah*, a settlers' magazine, published results in absolute numbers for twelve of Gush Emunim West Bank settlements (*Nekudah* 1988). These twelve include all the "old" settlements founded in the 1970s (except for Kochav Haschachar) and only one new settlement, Nili, founded in the 1980s. Because the old settlements are much larger than the new ones, these results relate to most of Gush Emunim voters. In any case, at least three-quarters of the voters are included in the following analysis. The total number of voters in these twelve settlements is 2,727.

References

Benvenisti, Meron. 1987. *The West Bank Handbook*. Jerusalem: Kaneh. (Hebrew)

Central Bureau of Statistics. 1981. *Results of Elections to the Tenth Knesset (30.6.1981)*. Special series No. 680. Jerusalem: Central Bureau of Statistics. (Hebrew)

———. 1984. *Results of Elections to the Eleventh Knesset (23.7.1984)*. Special series No. 775. Jerusalem: Central Bureau of Statistics. (Hebrew)

———. 1989. *Results of Elections to the Twelfth Knesset (1.11.1988)*. Special series No. 855. Jerusalem: Central Bureau of Statistics. (Hebrew)

Goldberg, Giora, and Efraim Ben-Zadok. 1986. "Gush Emunim in the West Bank." *Middle Eastern Studies* Vol. 22, No. 1: 52–73.

Lustick, Ian. 1988. *For the Land and the Lord*. New York: Council on Foreign Relations.

Nekudah. 1988. "Final Summary of Elections Results in Judea, Samaria and Gaza Settlements." No. 125. (Hebrew)

Newman, David. 1985. "Spatial Structures and Ideological Change in the West Bank." *The Impact of Gush Emunim: Politics and Settlement in the West Bank*, ed. D. Newman, 172–82. London: Croom Helm.

Raanan, Tsvi. 1980. *Gush Emunim*. Tel Aviv: Sifriat Poalim. (Hebrew)

Rubinstein, Danny. 1982. *On the Lord's Side: Gush Emunim*. Tel Aviv: Hakibbutz Hameuchad. (Hebrew)

Sprinzak, Ehud. 1981. "Gush Emunim: The Tip of the Iceberg." *The Jerusalem Quarterly* 21: 28–47.

Wood, James L., and Maurice Jackson. 1982. *Social Movements: Development, Participation and Dynamics*. Belmont, CA.: Wadsworth.

World Zionist Organization. 1986. *The Agricultural-Demographic Census in 1985*. Tel Aviv: Settlement Division, Department of Statistics. (Hebrew)

———. 1988. *Data on Israeli Population in Judea and Samaria*. Tel Aviv: Settlement Division, Department of Statistics. (Hebrew)

PART IV
- The Left-Right Cleavage

8 ■ Kibbutzim and Moshavim: From Ideological Symbol to Interest Group

Neal Sherman

The kibbutz and the moshav constitute an integral element of Labor Zionism, the dominant ideological-political movement within organized Zionism and within the state during the period 1933–77.[1] The kibbutzim and moshavim contributed directly to the advance of the overall Zionist endeavor, and to the achievement of Labor Zionist goals within the political system of the Yishuv.[2] In return, the Labor Zionist leadership guaranteed that the Zionist movement and the state would allocate the resources required for the expansion and institutionalization of the cooperative settlement sector. But the trends of change in Israeli society struck at the status of the kibbutzim and moshavim. Their collective and egalitarian values, which in the past enjoyed wide support in Israeli society, lost much of their appeal. Individualistic and materialistic values, as well as new consumption and class norms, became widespread. The eroding support for the values of Labor Zionism also reflected the protest against the hegemonic control of the parties that represent this movement. Consequently, the Likud came to power in the 1977 elections and headed the Israeli government until 1992.

The rise of the Likud to power within less than ten years led to a situation in which the basic, long-established ground rules governing

Author's note: The research projects on which this paper is based were financed by the Ford Foundation, the Settlement Department of the Jewish Agency, and the Board of Trustees of the Settlement Study Centre. I would like to express my gratitude for their support. I also wish to thank my colleague Levia Applebaum for her assistance in deciphering settlement statistics. I am also indebted to Yerahmiel Goldin, director of the Detailed Planning Branch of the national Rural Planning and Development Authority, for the valuable information and explanations that he provided. Finally, I owe a special word of appreciation to Moshe Schwartz, my partner and friend, for the ideas and insights that he has shared with me throughout the years.

relations between rural settlement cooperatives and the Zionist movement and the state were cast in doubt. The settlements and their regional and national organizations plunged into an economic crisis of staggering proportions, triggered by the Likud's management of the Israeli economy in general and its treatment of the agricultural sector in particular. This crisis called into question, in unfamiliar and unfavorable circumstances, the obligations of the general Zionist public and the Israeli public towards the kibbutzim and the moshavim. Moreover, within the kibbutzim and the moshavim themselves, economic difficulties generated great strain. Financial distress threatened to overwhelm the individual's sense of obligation to the community and the settlement's loyalty to the regional and national organizations with which it is affiliated.

Briefly, the settlement cooperative sector finds itself today in the midst of an acute economic and organizational crisis, as yet unresolved. The symptoms of the crisis are heavy debts and lack of financing. Its roots are to be found in the changes which have taken place in the relations between the kibbutz and the moshav and the rest of Israeli society since the achievement of independence and, more intensively, since the Likud's rise to power in the elections of 1977.

THE DOMINANT DEMOGRAPHIC AND ECONOMIC POSITION OF THE KIBBUTZIM AND THE MOSHAVIM IN THE ISRAELI RURAL SECTOR

The dominant demographic and economic role of cooperatives is one of the distinguishing features of the Israeli rural sector. The results of the last national census, conducted in 1983, show that the kibbutzim and moshavim together numbered 715 settlement points, constituting 81 percent of the total number of Jewish rural settlements and 76 percent of the grand total, which includes both Jewish and Arab villages. The rural settlement cooperatives' population totaled 265,435, equivalent to 81% of the Jewish rural population; 63% of the total rural population; and 6.6% of the total national population (Central Bureau of Statistics 1987, 51, 54, 65).

Within the cooperative settlement sector, the settlements which are members of movements associated with the Labor Alignment and its constituent parties are predominant. Movements tied to the Labor stream constituted 91 percent of the kibbutzim (table 8.1), and support for the Labor Zionist political parties among the members is overwhelming (table 8.2). Sixty percent of the moshavim belong to Tnuat HaMoshavim, the Labor associated movement, though here rank-and-file political support is less clear-cut, as the voting data show (tables 8.1 and 8.2). Defections from support are concentrated in the postindependence, "new immigrant" moshavim, in which Oriental Jews predominate. Nonetheless, Tnuat HaMoshavim is unmistakably part of the Labor establishment, with its top leaders sitting in party councils and being accorded places in the Knesset as movement representatives.

The relative weight of the cooperative settlement sector in agricultural production parallels its demographic significance. As shown in table 8.3, the kibbutzim and moshavim dispose of 72.1% of the manpower employed in agriculture, 70.6% of the cultivated area, and 77.4% of the capital invested. With these resources they account for 81.1% of the value of agricultural production and 80.9% of value added in the sector.

In addition to the leading role played by the settlement cooperatives in agriculture, individual kibbutzim and regional organizations of kibbutzim and moshavim have pioneered the development of industrial activities in the rural sector. The kibbutzim have undergone an "industrial revolution" since the late 1950s, so that today about a quarter of the kibbutz labor force is engaged in industrial or marketed service activities. No parallel industrialization of individual moshavim has taken place. But the moshav regional organizations, like those of the kibbutzim, have been active in establishing a network of agro-industrial undertakings, some producing inputs for agriculture, while others sort, pack, or process agricultural produce (Bar-El 1987, 21–55, 57–104; Lanir 1987, 29).

Another special feature of the Israeli rural sector is that though rural, it is not peripheral, in the usual sense of socioeconomic retardation (Wilkansky 1980). Data from the 1983 Census may serve to illustrate this point. As table 8.4 shows, the standard of housing in the moshav sector and the extent of ownership of a number of important consumer durables exceeds the overall average among Jews in Israel on most measures reported by the last national census. (The communal nature of the kibbutz economy makes comparisons of this sort impossible.) In the measures of formal education reported in the census, the kibbutzim have achieved a standard exceeding the urban Jewish norm. The moshavim tend to lag behind the city in the extent of postsecondary education, in all the subgroups defined by the census

Table 8.1. Kibbutzim, Moshavim Shitufi'im, and Moshavei Ovdim (Moshavim): Movement Affiliation and Political Party Association, 1983

Settlement Type	Movement	Political Party	Number	Pop.[a] ('000s)	% of Total	
Kibbutzim	HaKibbutz Ha'Artzi	Alignment: Mapam[b]	83	38.5	31	33
	HaTnuah HaKibbutzit HaMe'uhedet	Alignment: ILP	160	67.5	60	58
	HaKibbutz HaDati	NRP	16	6.5	6	6
	Kibbutzei HaNo'ar Hatzioni	Ind. Lib.	5	1.9	2	2
	Po'alei Agudat Yisra'el	PAI	2	1.2	1	1
	Halhud HaHakla'i	—	1	—	—	—
	Total		267	115.5	100	100
Moshavim Shitufi'im	Tnuat HaMoshavim	Alignment: ILP	5	1.3	11	14
	HaTnuah HaKibbutzit HaMe'uhedet	Alignment: ILP	6	1.3	14	14

Table 8.1 (continued). Kibbutzim, Moshavim Shitufiʾim, and Moshavei Ovdim (Moshavim): Movement Affiliation and Political Party Association, 1983

Settlement Type	Movement	Political Party	Number / Pop.[a] ('000s)	% of Total
	Igud HaMoshavim Shel HaPoʾel HaMizrahi	NRP	10 / 2.9	23 / 31
	Halhud HaHaklaʾi	—	3 / 0.7	7 / 8
	Moshvei HaOved Hatzioni	Ind. Lib.	8 / 1.2	18 / 13
	Moshvei Herut-Betar Hatzioni	Likud: Herut	4 / 0.8	9 / 9
	Poʾalei Agudat Yisraʾel	PAI	4 / 0.8	9 / 8
	Amana (Gush Emunim)	—	4 / 0.3	9 / 3
	Total		44 / 9.2	100 / 100
Moshvei Ovdim (Moshavim)	Tnuat HaMoshavim	Alignment: ILP	244 / 86.4	60 / 61
	Igud HaMoshavim Shel HaPoʾel HaMizrahi	NRP	66 / 26.8	16 / 19
	HaʾIhud HaHaklaʾi	—	46 / 13.4	11 / 10

Table 8.1 (continued). Kibbutzim, Moshavim Shituf²im, and Moshavei Ovdim (Moshavim): Movement Affiliation and Political Party Association, 1983

Settlement Type	Movement	Political Party	Number Pop.[a] ('000s)	% of Total
	Moshvei HaOved Hatzioni	Ind. Lib.	17	4
			5	4
	Moshvei Herut-Betar Hatzioni	Likud: Herut	13	3
			2.6	2
	Po²alei Agudat Yisra²el	PAI	6	1
			2.4	2
	Hitahdut Halcarim	Likud: Liberal	5	1
			1.5	1
	Unaffiliated	—	7	2
			2.5	2
	Total		404	100
			140.7	100

Sources: Central Bureau of Statistics 1985a, 169–74; 1987, 46, 65, 216; 1988, 52.

Abbreviations:

ILP = Israel Labor Party

NRP = National Religious Party (Mafdal)

PAI = Po²alei Agudat Yisrael

a. Jewish residents.

b. Mapam left the Labor Alignment and ran independently in the elections to the 12th Knesset.

Table 8.2. Support for the Party with which the Settlement Movement of the Labor Zionist Stream Is Associated, 1973–1988 (%)

Election	Kibbutzim[a]	Moshavim[b]	National Total
8th Knesset,		Veteran[c] = 71.4	
31.12.73—	89.7	New[d] = 57.5	39.6
Alignment		Total = 61.5	
9th Knesset,		Veteran = 50.3	
15.05.77—	80.3	New = 40.3	24.6
Alignment		Total = 43.0	
10th Knesset,		Veteran = 76.0	
30.06.81—	93.6	New = 49.4	36.6
Alignment		Total = 56.3	
11th Knesset,		Veteran = 73.5	
23.07.84—	83.6	New = 47.3	34.9
Alignment		Total = 53.8	
12th Knesset,		Veteran—	
01.11.88—		New—	
Alignment	Me'uhedet: 81.7	Total = 43.0	30.0
Mapam	Artzi: 75.8		2.5

Sources: Central Bureau of Statistics 1977, 5, 57–59; 1985b, xxv, 96–98; 1988, 101, 110–11.
a. 1973, 1977: Combined results of HaKibbutz HaMe'uhad, Ihud HaKvutzot V'HaKibbutzim, and HaKibbutz HaArtzi.
   1981, 1984: Combined results of HaTnuah HaKibbutzit HaMe'uhedet (formed by the union of HaKibbutz HaMe'uhad and Ihud) and HaKibbutz HaArtzi.
   1988: As detailed in the table.
b. All elections: Tnuat HaMoshavim, including the moshavim *shitufi'im* associated with the movement.
c. Veteran = founded before independence.
d. New = founded after independence.

Table 8.3. Agricultural Inputs and Outputs by Settlement Type, 1981 (%)

Settlement Type	Manpower	Cultivated Area	Capital Inventory	Value of Production	Value Added
Kibbutz	21.7	37.5	26.9	39.1	42.0
Moshav Shitufi	2.5	3.0	3.4	3.5	3.6
Moshav	47.9	30.1	47.1	38.5	35.3
Private Jewish	15.7	9.5	15.9	9.5	11.5
Private Non-Jewish	10.8	18.4	5.9	8.2	6.3
Institution	1.4	1.5	1.0	1.2	1.3
Total	100.0	100.0	100.0	100.0	100.0

Source: Maron 1987, 249, 253.

Table 8.4. Housing and Consumer Durables: Rural-Urban Comparisons for the Jewish Population, 1983 (%)

Housing Living Conditions	Total	Urban Localities	Moshâvim and Shitufi'im
Possessing			
Telephone	75.8	76.3	67.8
Two or more cars	5.5	5.3	10.2
One or more cars	46.4	45.5	61.1
Live in dwelling with			
Electric boiler	32.4	33.3	13.0
Solar heater	55.7	54.6	80.5
Two or more lavatories	19.3	18.5	34.9
Live in dwelling			
Owned	71.8	71.8	79.6
With 4 rooms or more	23.6	22.5	47.6
With 2 rooms or less	22.2	22.7	12.7
Persons per room			
Average (not %)	1.0	1.0	1.1
More than 2	3.8	3.7	5.8
Less than 1	39.8	40.2	34.9

Source: Central Bureau of Statistics 1986a, 102–5.

Table 8.5. Formal Education: Rural-Urban Comparisons for the Jewish Population, 1983 (%)

Settlement Type	Certificate		Years of Schooling		
	Academic Degree	Secondary and Higher	≥ 13	0–4	Median (years)
Jews—grand total	8.9	50.6	23.1	9.0	11.6
Urban Localities	9.0	49.9	22.9	9.2	11.5
Moshavim and Moshavim Shitufi'im	5.1	47.9	17.4	10.8	11.5
Kibbutzim	8.9	68.4	32.7	0.8	12.5

Source: Central Bureau of Statistics 1986b, 304–9.

according to ethnicity and nativity. However, the gaps are not large, and the median years of education prevailing in the moshavim are equal to the urban standard (table 8.5).

The absence of a pronounced urban-rural socioeconomic gap and the predominant role of the settlement cooperatives within the Jewish rural sector and within Israeli agriculture must be understood in terms of the close, supportive relations between the rural settlement cooperatives and the political center of the Zionist movement and Jewish society in Israel. The historical evolution of these relations will be discussed in the following sections of this chapter.

THE POLITICAL ORIGINS OF KIBBUTZ AND MOSHAV: DOMINANCE OF THE RURAL SECTOR

Cooperative predominance was achieved only after the establishment of the state in 1948. Through most of the Yishuv period, private farmers were the leading element in Jewish agriculture, producing almost all of the citrus fruit which was the Jewish economy's major export commodity. In parallel, the private village settlements (*moshavot*) were the leading demographic element in the Jewish rural sector (Bein and Perlmann 1982, 39). The rural settlement cooperatives were able to overtake the private sector, first of all, by virtue of the consistent support accorded to them by the Labor Zionist political leadership and by central non-Labor leadership elements within the political systems of the Zionist movement, the Yishuv, and the state. Secondly, the cooperatives were able to benefit from the economic consequences of major political events, which either did not benefit or actually harmed private farming interests.

The settlement cooperatives won the support of dominant political leaders because of their symbolic importance for Labor and general Zionist ideology and because of their practical contribution to the achievement of Zionist objectives (Sherman 1979; Sherman and Daniel 1979, 228–29). From the general Zionist ideological point of view, settling the land and working it constituted the most direct and literal realization of the idea of return to the Land of Israel. Agricultural settlement and agricultural labor also constituted a refutation of anti-Semitic accusations that the Jews were a rootless, parasitic nation, afraid of hard labor, and incapable of producing basic life-sustaining goods.

In the struggle over "Hebrew labor" during the Yishuv period, the private farmers' claim to a share in the symbolic value attributed to agricultural settlement was discredited, and a monopoly over this moral resource was established for the kibbutzim and moshavim. The Labor Zionists successfully attacked the private farmers for their habit of hiring Arab farmhands, accusing the farmers of selfishly preferring private profit to their national obligation to provide employment to a maximal number of Jewish workers. The kibbutzim and moshavim, by contrast, espoused the principle of "self-labor." Accepting the socialist contention that all wage labor entails exploitation of employee by employer, the kibbutzim and moshavim were committed to basing their agricultural production on the work of members only, hiring neither Arab nor Jewish wage labor.

In terms of the ideological concerns specific to the Labor stream within Zionism, the moshavim and even more so the kibbutzim represented a particularly high degree of realization of movement ideals. Within the framework of their settlements, moshav and kibbutz members took it upon themselves to build new communities based on the principles of socialism and cooperation. Thus, the moshavim and kibbutzim came to symbolize socialist ideals for Labor, just as they symbolized general nationalist ideals for the great majority of the supporters of the Zionist cause.

In practical terms, the kibbutzim and, to a lesser degree, the moshavim served as the organizational means by which the Zionist political leadership concretized the Jewish claim to the lands which the Zionist movement purchased and thus expanded the territorial base of the Yishuv. Whereas private land purchases and private agriculture were concentrated in the light sandy soils of the coastal plain which were best suited for citrus production, Zionist political and security objectives demanded land purchase and settlement in outlying areas, which were often characterized by difficult climatic conditions and limited economic potential, as well as being exposed to Arab attacks. The cooperative settlements, and particularly the kibbutzim, in which social and national ideals were assigned greater weight relative to considerations of economic profitability, could be directed to such settlement sites as required for the realization of national objectives.

In addition to the practical contribution inherent in the very act of settlement, the kibbutzim also served Labor Zionism in particular and the Yishuv in general by serving as a channel for the recruitment of high-quality individuals to leadership positions in Labor and Yishuv organizational frameworks. The symbolic and practical importance of the role fulfilled by the kibbutzim and the widespread public acknowledgment of the significance of this role brought to the ranks of the kibbutzim many of the most dedicated and capable members of the younger generations. Members whose talents were required for public service outside of the settlement sector would be seconded to fulfill such duties, with the communal economy of the kibbutz providing for the families of those who were married. In particular, members of the kibbutzim played a leading role in the development of the defense capabilities of the Jewish community. The kibbutzim served as a rural hinterland in which underground units could be organized and trained.

Just as the services provided by the kibbutz and the moshav to Labor Zionism and Zionism in general were both spiritual and concrete, so too both moral and practical support were offered to the cooperative settlements by Labor and the broader Zionist movement. Most basically, the founding of kibbutzim and moshavim was (and still is) dependent upon the public resources provided by Zionist agencies and later by state agencies as well. Settlement nuclei (*garinim*) sometimes brought a certain amount of capital generated by the members' wage work for investment in their new villages. However, land and, in general, the bulk of the investment capital required were provided by Zionist and state agencies. These agencies also provided a variety of supporting services crucial to the success of the settlements: initial planning and economic analysis, and agricultural research and extension. Settlement needs were assigned very high priority in the allocation of Zionists' budgets. During the period 1922–45, the Jewish National Fund almost invariably allocated over 80 percent of its annual expenditure to agricultural settlement needs. Similarly, in most of the years during the period 1921–46, agricultural settlement constituted the single largest item of expenditure of the Zionist Executive, later the Jewish Agency (Horowitz and Lissak 1977, 76, 79).

In addition to financial backing, the cooperative settlement sector was favored with regard to the recruitment of manpower. The Zionist and Labor leadership allocated a leading role in youth work in the Diaspora to youth movements based upon the kibbutz movements and instructors drawn from the ranks of the kibbutz settlements. During the period in which quotas were imposed upon Jewish immigration to Palestine by the British authorities, the Labor stream demanded, and the Zionist authorities accorded, priority to those who had passed through the stages of ideological formation and agricultural training which were intended to lead the new immigrant to join the cooperative settlement sector.

However, not only material resources of manpower, land, and capital were crucial in enabling the cooperative settlement sector to grow and to institutionalize its organizational forms, at both the individual settlement and suprasettlement levels. The high status accorded to the settler as "pioneer" by the Zionist and Yishuv leadership, and by world Jewish and Yishuv publics at large, constituted a vitally important status benefit and a reinforcement to the settlers' internal sense of the rightness of the way of life to which they had committed themselves. Those who went to the kibbutz, and to a lesser but still significant degree those who went to the moshav, took upon themselves to surrender personal freedom and accept cooperative discipline. The settlers could generally expect to pass through an extended period of hard work and material hardship before their labor would provide them with a comfortable living. In many instances the settlers also left the security of areas of dense Jewish settlement and exposed themselves to an increased danger of attacks by Arab forces. The high status attributed to the settlers by their ideological movement and by the general public, and the reinforced sense of purpose to which they contributed, thus constituted a major form of compensation offered to the settlers in return for the risks and hardships that they took upon themselves.

With the backing provided to them by the Labor Zionist movement and the broader Zionist public and institutions, the cooperative settlement sector was able to exploit the potential inherent in three crucial political events for the strengthening of its economic position within the rural sector. First, the boycott on sales of fresh produce to the Jewish population declared by the Arab leadership during the uprising of 1936–39 proved more effective than all previous rhetoric campaigns in strengthening the demand for the vegetables, fruit, and livestock products produced by the settlement cooperatives. Second, the boycott helped kibbutzim and moshavim which had for many years suffered losses in their farming activities to turn the corner to profitable agricultural operations. The outbreak of World War II strengthened even further the demand for the fresh produce of the kibbutzim and the moshavim, while it cut off private citrus production from its export markets. Finally, the War of Independence and the mass immigration which followed independence guaranteed the continued profitability of foodstuffs production.

The main significance of independence, however, lay in the extension of Labor hegemony from the Zionist and Yishuv institutions to the apparatus of the state. The vastly expanded land and the additional financial resources which assumption of state power made available were used, together with the Zionist settlement budget, to implement an intensive nationwide program of rural settlement, based upon workforce drawn from the waves of mass immigration. The extension of kibbutz and particularly of moshav settlement during the first years of independence completed the turnabout in the demographic and economic balance between cooperative and private rural settlement.

THREE DECADES OF LABOR DOMINANCE, 1948–1977

The data in table 8.6 on the growth in the number of rural settlements in each organizational category illustrate the priority accorded to settlement cooperatives in the postindependence settlement drive. Table 8.6 also shows that whereas the kibbutzim outnumbered the moshavim in the pre-independence period, the situation was reversed during the early fifties. Candidates for settlement drawn from the waves of mass immigration had not undergone ideological indoctrination to the values of kibbutz socialism, and could not accept the communal way of life of the kibbutz, in particular the system of communal child-rearing then in practice. Thus, meeting national settlement objectives and providing absorption opportunities for the new immigrants within the settlement program demanded that the moshav be assigned priority in the distribution of settlement sites.

Though the achievement of independence completed the process which led to the displacement of private by cooperative settlement as the dominant element within the rural sector, the realization of the central, consensual objective of the Zionist movement also set the stage for a process of loss of revolutionary elan in Israeli society (Sherman and Daniel 1979, 230–31; Sherman 1982, 56–58; and sources cited). The normalization of Jewish national life upon the conclusion of the heroic period of the struggle for independence brought with it the gradual decline in commitment to collectivistic ideals, both nationalist and socialist in character, and a parallel rise in the importance attributed to individualist and materialist values. This trend in Israeli society in general was felt in the settlement cooperatives as well, both as a result of the influence of the environment and as a result of the passing of generations in the veteran moshavim and kibbutzim. In the bulk of the new immigrant moshavim, relatively little success was achieved in bringing the settlers to internalize a commitment to socialist principles, whatever successes were achieved in imparting skills in agricultural and in the operation of cooperative organizational forms.

At the same time that the respect accorded to pioneering service to the public welfare tended to decline, the image of the kibbutzim

Table 8.6. Jewish Rural Settlements by Settlement Type, 1948–1987

Settlement Type	8.11 1948	31.12 1949	1958	1966	1977	1987
Kibbutz	177	211	228	232	245	268
Moshav Shitufi		25	20	22	45	47
Moshav	104	120	344	343	369	409
"Private Moshav"[a]		37	—	—	—	—
Noncooperative Village[b]	34	55	79	60	50	61
Intervillage Center[c]			7	15	18	24
"Community Settlement"[d]						95

Sources:
1948: Central Bureau of Statistics, *1958 Statistical Abstract*, 14.
1949: Central Bureau of Statistics, *1950 Statistical Abstract*, 14–15.
1958: Central Bureau of Statistics, *1959 Statistical Abstract*, 14–15.
1966: Central Bureau of Statistics, *1967 Statistical Abstract*, 28–29.
1977: Central Bureau of Statistics, *1978 Statistical Abstract*, 42–43; Central Bureau of Statistics 1978, 67–69, for settlements in the administered territories.
1987: Central Bureau of Statistics, *1988 Statistical Abstract*, 50–51.

a. Villages with a cooperative structure like that of the moshav, but founded by movements not espousing a socialist ideology; later reclassified as moshavim, together with the moshavim of the Labor Zionist stream.

b. The decline in the number of settlements is a result of population growth and reclassification as urban settlements.

c. A settlement planned to provide social and economic services for surrounding agricultural settlements.

d. A nonagricultural rural settlement, organized formally as a cooperative.

and moshavim as filling such a role tended to be weakened. The security situation in most of the country improved, as better roads and means of transportation together with the increasing number of Jewish villages brought the settlements out of isolation. Moreover, the settlements in dangerous border areas came to be defended by the army, rather than themselves constituting the front line, defending the rest of the Jewish community.

On the economic front, the relative importance of the agricultural sector's contribution to the national product and to foreign exchange earnings declined (table 8.7). At the same time that their unique, sectoral contribution to the national economy was becoming less significant, the settlers were coming to be seen less as sacrificing personal economic well-being in order to contribute to the achievement of national and social objectives. The kibbutzim and moshavim tended to turn inward and to concern themselves with members' welfare, and indeed many of the veteran settlements succeeded in achieving an ad-

Table 8.7. The Relative Weight of Agriculture in Gross National Product and Exports, 1949–87

	Agriculture[a] as a percentage of:	
Year	GNP	Exports
GNP—1952; Exp.—1949	9.1	73.3
1957	10.7	44.2
1967	7.1	23.8
1977	5.3	14.3
1987	3.8	9.4

Sources:
GNP
1952, 1957, 1967: Central Bureau of Statistics, *1971 Statistical Abstract*, 146–47, 164–65.
1977: Central Bureau of Statistics, *1984 Statistical Abstract*, 183.
1987: Central Bureau of Statistics, *1988 Statistical Abstract*, 191.
Exports
1949, 1957: Central Bureau of Statistics, *1958 Statistical Abstract*, 266–71.
1967: Central Bureau of Statistics, *1968 Statistical Abstract*, 205.
1977: Central Bureau of Statistics, *1978 Statistical Abstract*, 217.
1987: Central Bureau of Statistics, *1988 Statistical Abstract*, 241.
a. Agriculture, forestry, and fishing, as percentage of total GNP; food, live animals, beverages, tobacco, as percentage of exports.

mirable standard of living. The principle of self-labor tended to give way in both the kibbutzim and the moshavim before the demands of profitability. The economic distress which characterized many of the new-immigrant moshavim of the fifties was not viewed as an expression of a willingness to accept self-sacrifice in order to serve collective goals. Instead, the continuing difficulties which faced these villages were seen as a failure in immigrant absorption, which raised unpleasant questions regarding the fairness of the division of means of production between the veteran settlements and their postindependence counterparts.

The acquisition of new territories in the 1967 war brought a limited revival of new settlement efforts, which had almost come to a standstill during the decade 1957–67 (table 8.6). Once again the public saw scenes of small groups of youngsters setting up Jewish outposts in isolated rural locations. However, two major factors limited the positive overall effect of this revival of settlement upon the standing of the kibbutzim and moshavim in the public esteem. First, the pioneering image of the new settlements was soon balanced by the image of moshav members in the Rafiah Approaches area of Sinai, grown wealthy within a short time through export of vegetables and flowers. This economic success was based on hard work and efficient use of the means of production provided by state and Zionist agencies. But it was also based on extensive exploitation of cheap Arab wage labor. Indeed, when the 1967 war opened the border between Israel and the territories, employment of Arab labor in both the kibbutz and the moshav became more prevalent and more widely noted. The importance of adherence to the principles of self-labor and Hebrew labor in the settlement cooperatives' victory in the struggle to achieve ideological precedence over the private farmers will be recalled.

Secondly, the post-1967 settlement revival could not restore the erosion of the centrality of the settlement cooperatives as a national ideological symbol because in the post-1967 period new settlement rapidly became the focus of one of the most bitter political conflicts dividing Israeli society, namely the argument over the boundaries of the state and the future of the occupied territories. The Labor Alignment has contended that Israel should return those parts of the territories which are not necessary for reasons of national security and which might, in fact, constitute a security burden because of their large Arab populations. Settlements would, obviously, be directed only to those territories which Israel intends to retain within the framework of an ultimate peace settlement, based on the principle of territorial compromise. Right-wing opponents, in addition to challenging the validity of Labor's estimates of the security implications of relinquishing control over parts of the Land of Israel, have attacked the underlying ideological claim that the government of the state of Israel is at all entitled to make judgments of this sort. The Right claims that the whole Land of Israel belongs, not to today's flesh-and-blood citizens of the state of Israel, but rather to the historical Jewish people. Today's generation has no right to give up territories which belong not to it alone, but to all the generations of the Jewish people, past and future. Thus settlement in all parts of the Land of Israel is a moral obligation imposed on today's Jews by their membership in the historical Jewish people.

The gradual decline in the status of the settlement cooperative sector, brought about by the factors discussed in the preceding paragraphs, was paralleled by a decline in the overrepresentation which the settlements had long enjoyed in party institutions. Continuing overrepresentation in the Knesset and particularly the considerable overrepresentation in the government were explained largely by the fact, noted above, that kibbutz settlements served as a recruitment channel for political leadership positions. Thus, in addition to those movement members who held their positions as sectoral representatives, several kibbutz members sat in the Knesset and the government because of their personal standing as national leadership figures (Sherman 1980, 156–57; Ben-David 1978/79, 219–20).

However, despite their weakened public standing, until the end of the period under discussion, the kibbutzim and moshavim continued to enjoy the benefits of the public financial support afforded new settlements, as institutionalized during the pre-independence period, and the benefits of a series of measures enacted to help maintain the profitability of agricultural production. These measures included subsidization of imported feed grain; production planning for a wide range of crop and livestock products and guaranteed minimum prices and/or price subsidies for production within the framework of plan quotas; subsidized working capital for a wide range of crop and livestock products for both domestic and export markets; and grants and highly subsidized long-term loans for capital investments in agriculture. Though conflicts broke out periodically between the kibbutzim and moshavim over control of central political and administrative positions within the Ministry of Agriculture and over the distribution of resources, the basic premise that the settlement cooperatives were entitled to extensive public backing in order to help sustain their economic viability did not arouse serious controversy (Medding 1972, 24–27, 39–43).

THE 1977 ELECTORAL "UPHEAVAL" AND ITS AFTERMATH

The 1977 elections were the last conducted within the framework of general Labor dominance. More specifically, they were the last elections in which the Labor outlook regarding the role of the kibbutzim and moshavim within the rural sector and within the nation served as a generally accepted frame of reference for all involved in the election campaign. Critical comments regarding aspects of public support for the settlement cooperatives were included in the party platforms of Labor's major challengers, the Likud and the Democratic Movement for Change (DMC), but did not achieve any degree of prominence in the arguments waged before the general public. Instead, the symbolic value of association with kibbutz and moshav settlement was taken for granted, and parties associated with settlement movements presented their villages to the public as one of the party's accomplishments. The newly established DMC, lacking a settlement movement of its own, published lists of supporters from the kibbutzim and moshavim. The Alignment broadcasted a controversial television advertisement which presented what was described as the failure of a settlement of the Herut moshav movement, as a way of reminding the public of the successes of the Labor-associated rural settlement cooperatives (Sherman 1980, 157–61).

After the elections, the kibbutzim and moshavim found themselves in opposition, together with the Labor Alignment. Only five kibbutz and two moshav members were among the original thirty-two Alignment candidates elected to the 9th Knesset in 1977, whereas the Alignment faction at the opening of the 8th Knesset in 1973 had included eleven kibbutz and three moshav representatives among its fifty-one members. Of course, representation in the government declined even more radically. The government presented by Golda Meir after the 1973 elections included four ministers from the kibbutzim and one from the moshavim. Begin's government included only one minister who was a moshav resident, and he had long since ceased to be viewed as a movement representative, appearing before the public in his role as a private businessman instead (*HaAretz*, 28 December 1973; *Davar*, 7 January 1974; *HaAretz*, 11 March 1974; *Ma'ariv*, 15 April 1977; Kinerati 1977).[3]

The Right's political success brought in its wake both attacks on cooperative settlement's role as a central national symbol and changes in settlement and agricultural policy which hurt the material interests of the kibbutzim and moshavim. On the ideological front, victory in the elections emboldened the Likud to speak out in contradiction to Labor Zionism's version of the struggle for independence and the building of the state, including Labor's interpretation of the role of rural cooperative settlement within the Jewish national revival. Moreover, control of the government and the ability to make use of the material and symbolic resources of the state in presenting its ideology gave unprecedented public prominence to the views of the Right. The Right's thrust against the Labor-associated settlements was twofold. First, elements of a revisionist historiography were presented, downplaying the contribution of the rural settlement sector to the achievement of independence. Prime Minister Begin led the way in an attempt to equate the importance of the Revisionist military underground organization, which he had headed, to that of the Hagana and Palmach underground in which the rural settlement cooperatives, particularly the kibbutzim, had played a leading role. Secondly, the Right raised the claim that the rural settlement cooperatives of the Labor stream had lost touch with the national mission of settlement, as witnessed by their opposition to the program of settlement in Judea, Samaria, and Gaza undertaken by the Likud government. The true pioneering spirit of Zionism, according to the Right, was now to be found in Gush Emunim, a religiously inspired ultranationalist movement, which was conducting settlement activities in the West Bank. Thus, a Likud election advertisement from the 1981 campaign equated Karnei Shomron, a Gush Emunim settlement, with Hanita, a kibbutz and one of the most reknowned of the "stockade and tower" settlements established in the face of the Arab uprising of 1936–39 (*Ma'ariv,* 31 May 1981; Sherman 1982, 60–63).

Towards the elections of 1981, the Right's ideological offensive against the rural settlement sector took on a more virulent aspect. The Likud moved from reinterpretation of the Zionist past to a frontal attack on the kibbutzim, in the context of their relations to the neighboring development towns, many of whose predominantly Oriental residents are employed in kibbutzim and kibbutz regional enterprises. The Likud, and Herut in particular, had long based an important element of their electoral appeal upon their role as spokesman for the resentment of the postindependence Oriental immigrants against the Labor and Ashkenazic establishment of the veteran Yishuv and the Zionist movement. In the 1981 elections, the Likud placed strong emphasis on the ethnic issue. Within this framework, it presented the kibbutzim as a privileged elite, whose position was maintained through favoritism in the distribution of public resources. The kibbutzim were thus made into one of the prime symbols of the establishment's responsibility for the failures of absorption and the continuing socioeconomic gap; and at the local level, incitement against the kibbutzim reached a violent pitch (Weiss 1981; Rahat 1981). Even after his reelection, Prime Minister Begin made use of his New Year's address to the nation, usually reserved for conciliatory and consensual appeals, in order to attack the kibbutzim.

The two election campaigns since 1981 have been much calmer, and such vocal and concentrated attacks against the rural settlement cooperatives have not been repeated. However, the economic crisis, discussed below, into which both the kibbutzim and moshavim have plunged in the years since 1977, has kept the rural settlement cooperatives before the public in a negative light without the need for any special effort on the part of right-wing activists. Since 1984 the tremendous debts accumulated by the rural settlement cooperatives have not left the headlines. The cooperatives appeared before the general public as debtors, indeed as bankrupts, in dire need of emergency financial assistance in order to guarantee their continued existence. Kibbutz and moshav representatives have emphasized the role of national economic conditions and government policy in producing the settlements' debts. However, the cooperatives' reputation has been tarnished by critical reports which have stressed internal factors: weak cooperative discipline and unjustifiably high levels of consumption; mismanagement of cooperative economic affairs, either through simple incompetence or as a result of the influence of the internal politics of the settlements and their regional and national organizations; and, particularly in the case of kibbutzim, entanglement in unsavory speculative investments (Ben-Me'ir 1987; Sherman et al. 1984; Sherman et al. 1987; Schwartz, Marvid, and Arian 1988; Kapra 1986; *Hadashot*, 7 February 1985; Lifshitz 1985; Kartin and Horvitz 1985).

The roots of the economic crisis of the moshavim and the kibbutzim may indeed be seen to lie in the situation created by the economic liberalization policies of the Likud after its entry into the government in 1977. Runaway inflation, on the one hand, and a relatively stable exchange rate, on the other, created a situation in which the export earnings of the agricultural sector could not keep pace with the rising cost of inputs. In addition, inflation was soon accompanied by rising real interest rates, which rapidly compounded any losses incurred by farmers.

The impact of such unfavorable general conditions in the economy was intensified by the Likud's agricultural and settlement policies. In general, the Likud acted to reduce the priority accorded to agriculture relative to industry and tourism in government budgeting (table 8.8). From a high point of 0.76 fixed by Labor in the months preceding the 1977 election, the agriculture/industry and tourism ratio declined to levels which were prevalent before 1977 and then reached a low of 0.24 and 0.27 in 1984/85–1985/86. The apparent strengthening of agriculture's position in 1986/87–1987/88 in the wake of the establishment of the National Unity Government is misleading. The improved ratio is the result of emergency debt relief budgets necessary to prevent the collapse of the settlement cooperative sector rather than any new service and development initiatives.

Table 8.8. Government Budget Allocations to Agriculture as a Proportion of Government Budget Allocations to Industry and Tourism, 1972/73–1987/88

Year	Budget Allocated to Agriculture as a Proportion of the Budget Allocated to Industry and Tourism
1972/73	0.41
1973/74	0.44
1974/75	0.51
1975/76	0.46
1976/77	0.33
1977/78	0.76
1978/79	0.78
1979/80	0.45
1980/81	0.51
1981/82	0.43
1982/83	0.38
1983/84	0.33
1984/85	0.24
1985/86	0.27
1986/87	0.50
1987/88	0.38

Source: Comptroller-General, Ministry of the Treasury. Various years.

The thrust of the more detailed policy measures which reflected this downgrading of agriculture was to cut back government intervention and expose the farmer to the vicissitudes of the market. The Likud index-linked the development loans provided for investments in designated agricultural branches and reduced the percentage of the total investment covered by funds provided by the government. Subsidized working capital for production for the domestic market was almost completely eliminated. With less subsidized credit available, the cooperatives were forced to turn more to the banks and to the "gray market" for credit and to pay the rising real interest rates which had become prevalent. Moreover, unfavorable general conditions and unfavorable sectoral policy measures interacted: because of inflation, the nominal "keys" established for agricultural development loans during the budget authorization stage would be sadly out of date by the time the farmer actually carried out his investment, and even more out of date by the time the farmer actually received reimbursement of the funds expended from the Ministry of Agriculture. To cover the gap between the key and actual expenditure and to cover the time lag between expenditure and reimbursement, it was necessary to take expensive credit from commercial sources.

Other agricultural policy measures introduced by the Likud included the freeing of many crops from the framework of government production planning and quotas. The end of planning went hand in hand with the elimination of price subsidies and guaranteed minimum prices aimed at stabilizing farm income and guaranteeing profitability.

Finally, the Likud's settlement program during the period 1977–81 was focused on areas within the occupied territories whose settlement was opposed by the Labor Alignment. Therefore, priority in the establishment of new villages was automatically accorded to movements not associated with the Labor Zionist stream. Moreover, a growing proportion of new settlements, both within and without the pre-1967 war borders, did not adopt either the kibbutz or moshav organizational pattern. As the data in table 8.6 show, the majority of the villages founded after 1977 did not belong to the traditional settlement cooperative sector. Thus, there took place a sharp decline in the proportion of the government budget's new settlement allocation expended to establish kibbutzim and moshavim, in general, and in particular kibbutzim and moshavim of the movements of the Labor stream. If during the years of Labor government, 100 percent of the new settlement budget was devoted to areas in which the Labor settlement movements could operate, during the years 1979/80–1987/88 between 41 to 63 percent of the government new settlement budget was earmarked for areas within the territories which were considered out of bounds by the Labor stream (Comptroller-General, Annual Reports 1979/80–1987/88).

On the whole, the settlement cooperative sector reacted improperly to the general economic conditions and the new set of agricultural and settlement policy measures with which it was faced. A conservative policy of belt-tightening was called for, with limitation of both investments and consumption. However, belt-tightening is unpopular and cooperative officials are elected or appointed by those who are elected. It was easier to continue taking credit, even expensive credit, than to try to dampen members' expectations of growth and a higher standard of living (Sherman et al. 1987; Sherman and Schwartz 1989). Such an approach seemed plausible since the secondary cooperatives established by the settlements, the so-called purchasing organizations, had developed into regional agro-industrial complexes which were large and attractive clients for commercial lenders. Thus the organizations could obtain lending funds to the individual settlements. The purchasing organizations and their associated enterprises were attractive clients, among other reasons, because of their roots in the settlement cooperative sector. On the basis of decades of historical experience, lenders and cooperative members as well believed that in the end, the cooperatives would not be allowed to fall. The government and the Zionist authorities were assumed to be the implicit guarantors of the settlement cooperative sector's debts (Schwartz, Marvid, and Arian 1988, 10–11).

Thus, the cooperatives failed to link consumption levels closely to income and debt levels; and rather than cancel or postpone development, investments were undertaken despite the clear prospect that they would be based upon fatally expensive loans. In the case of the kibbutz movements, lack of prudence went even further. The managers of the movement central funds, responsible for maintenance of the real value of cash reserves in a period of hyperinflation, yielded to the temptations offered by the stock and financial bubble of the latter years of the second Likud government and indulged in large highly speculative financial operations. These led, when the bubble burst, to multimillion dollar losses, and to the loss of face mentioned above.

Ultimately, it was made clear that the general public's commitment to the cooperative settlement sector was not fully commensurate with the degree of financial support required to solve the problem which an unfavorable environment and unwise management responses had created. In 1985 the appeal of one of the smaller, moshav-based purchasing organizations to receive a supplement to emergency relief which had already been provided was denied. The organization went into receivership and ten out of the twelve moshav-based purchasing organizations collapsed in its wake (Schwartz, Marvid, and Arian 1988, 9–10). During the period since, the desperate need for special, sectorwide assistance of massive proportions has been continually on the public agenda.

CONCLUDING COMMENTS: THE CURRENT SITUATION

It is significant that the collapse of the purchasing organizations came in 1985 during the term of the National Unity Government, with a representative of the moshavim in office as minister of agriculture and Labor's Shimon Peres serving as prime minister. Given the proportions of the cooperatives' debt problems and the difficult situation facing the Israeli national economy, the partial revival of Labor's and the settlement cooperatives' political fortunes was not enough to guarantee the kibbutzim and the moshavim a quick and easy solution to their troubles. In fact, a comprehensive proposal for the moshavim was formulated only in 1987. The long- and short-term debts of 374 moshavim, and 49 moshavim and other settlements on the Golan Heights and in the Jordan Rift, were estimated at $1,114,000,000 as of 30 September 1986. The package proposed included payment of 10 percent of the debt by government and the Jewish Agency, cancellation of 10 percent of the debt by creditors, and rescheduling of the payment of 57 percent of the debt over a period of five to twenty years. The government would refinance 73 percent of the rescheduled debt at a below-market interest rate (Supreme Steering Committee for the Moshav Economy 1987, 6). After a period of debate, a moshav debt relief program was authorized, and an administrative apparatus established for its implementation. However, the terms of the settlement seem very difficult to many moshav members, and to some neutral observers as well, and the signing of agreements, moshav by moshav, has been proceeding very slowly (Freeman et al. 1988, 29–33). The kibbutz package presented in 1989 is based on similar principles. Debts totaling NIS 650,000,000 are to be paid by the government, and creditors are to cancel a further NIS 1,000,000,000. NIS 3,100,000,000 of debt are to be rescheduled at reduced interest (Deutsch 1989; Greenstein 1989).

When viewed on the background of the standing once enjoyed by the moshavim and kibbutzim in Israeli society, their success in obtaining emergency assistance must be seen as a Pyrrhic victory. Once public resources had been allocated to the rural settlement cooperatives because of a presumed identity between settlement and national interests. Medding's comments regarding one of the kibbutz movements may be taken as applying to the entire settlement cooperative sector:

> their direct and immediate economic interests . . . were regarded as central to Zionist and national concern. Consequently no special claims needed to be made, and no particular demands pressed, for their interests were supported as part of the national and Zionist effort. Thus the primacy of collective [read: cooperative] agriculture's needs was recognized and a major proportion of Zionist resources invested in it without typical pressure-group activity on its part. (1972, 24)

After the economic catastrophe of 1977–84, the kibbutz and the moshav were forced to appear before the political system and the general public vocally demanding public resources to relieve sectoral distress. Like any other interest group, they were forced to speak in terms of their needs, rather than their contribution, and to bargain with the government. They appeared, in short, as a sector like any other sector (Goren 1989; Binder 1989).

Today, despite the residual symbolic value attached to cooperative settlement, the kibbutzim and moshavim must adjust to a situation in which their basic status is that of an interest group of declining internal significance within a political bloc whose fortunes have been suffering a secular decline. Indeed, although the Labor stream's electoral fortunes recovered somewhat from their nadir of 1977, the settlement cooperative sector's political representation continued to decline. Whereas Labor Alignment had allocated 7 out of the 32 seats it won in 1977 to the kibbutzim (5) and moshavim (2); in 1988 the Labor Alignment and Mapam, which broke away and ran independently, gave the settlement cooperatives only 5 positions out of 42, allocating 4 to the kibbutzim and 1 to the moshavim (*Davar,* 3 November 1988). The kibbutzim were given two places in the 1988 government, the moshavim none, as opposed to four and one, respectively, in the Labor government which took office in January 1974 (*HaAretz,* 23 December 1988).

With their political influence thus reduced, the kibbutzim and moshavim must find ways of adjusting to circumstances in which they will be left to make their way by their own devices much more than in the past. Even those unsympathetic in principle to the kibbutzim and moshavim could not stand by and see the bulk of the Jewish rural sector collapse and cease to function, and thus the massive debt relief programs have been adopted. However, as noted, most moshav purchasing organizations, once considered the economic muscle of the moshav sector, did collapse and have ceased functioning, and together with them a number of associated regional agro-industrial enterprises. The fate of these organizations constitutes a precedent which will undoubtedly influence expectations and behavior in the settlement sector and in the sector's relations with government and the Zionist institutions. Furthermore, creditors have been forced to cancel large debts. As a result, it seems unlikely that credit availability will ever be restored to the level prevailing when the implicit public guarantee of settlement cooperative liabilities was still taken to be valid. Finally, the debt arrangements left the settlements with what are still painfully large sums to repay. Meeting debt repayment schedules will demand much hard and efficient effort on the part of the kibbutzim and moshavim and will undoubtedly impose considerable hardships in many settlements.

The kibbutz movements have thus far weathered the storm with relatively limited major losses. The regional organizations of the kibbutzim are plagued by heavy debts and are currently engaged in a process of extensive retrenchment, but they have not collapsed like those of the moshavim. Only a handful of small, relatively new kibbutzim have been disbanded during recent years, despite the economic and social problems of the period. This resilience is largely accounted for by the strength of national movement organizations, which have been able to mobilize considerable funds from stronger settlements in order to provide relief to those facing financial distress. Movement leadership is engaged today in an effort to avoid a situation in which the size of movement reserves and the strength of the strong settlements' commitment to mutual assistance and joint liability will once more be put to the test.

The moshav movement has suffered much severer institutional damage as a result of the ten year crisis. A generally lower degree of ideological commitment and much weaker national movement organization left the structures of moshav cooperation much more vulnerable to the influence of spiraling debt. The purchasing organizations collapsed; the national movements economic enterprises collapsed; and while settlements have not been abandoned, in a growing number of settlements economic cooperation among members has, in effect, been dissolved. It is no doubt indicative of future trends that the just-elected secretary of Tnuat HaMoshavim explained his decision to run for the post in a radio interview in terms of his desire to help guarantee the future of the family farm in Israel, and made no mention of the words moshav and cooperation.

Notes

1. In the kibbutz, the community owns and manages all means of production, and consumption is also controlled to a large degree by communal decisions. In the moshav *ovdim*, the family farm serves as the basic unit of both production and consumption. All farm holders are members of a single, comprehensive village cooperative which, in theory, should provide all necessary services to all the production branches found in the members' farms. The moshav *shitufi* is an intermediate form of settlement cooperative. The means

of production are owned and managed by the community, as in the kibbutz. However, in the moshav *shitufi* the member families are recognized as the basic decision-making units for consumption, as in the moshav. When the text refers to the kibbutz and the moshav, implying the entire settlement cooperative sector, the moshav *shitufi* should be seen as included. When the text discusses the moshav as a distinct topic, or when the moshav and the kibbutz are contrasted, the term "moshav" refers to the moshav *ovdim* only. Israeli settlement cooperatives of all types are unique in that in addition to their registration as agricultural cooperatives, they are also recognized as village municipal authorities within the framework of the local government system.

2. The Jewish community in Turkish and British Palestine is referred to in Hebrew as the "Yishuv."

3. All the data in this paper regarding kibbutz and moshav political representation refer to the Knesset and the government (cabinet) as first constituted immediately after each national election.

References

Bar-El, Raphael, and Ariela Nesher, eds. 1987. *Rural Industrialization in Israel*. Boulder: Westview.

Bein, Alex, and Ruth Perlmann 1982. *Immigration and Settlement in the State of Israel*. Tel Aviv: Am Oved. (Hebrew)

Ben-David, Yitzhak. 1978/79. "The Kibbutz Between 'Center' and 'Periphery'." *The Kibbutz* Vol. 6–7: 203–35. (Hebrew)

Ben-Me'ir, Me'ir. 1987. "The Moshav—Crisis and Solution." *Economic Quarterly* Vol. 38, No. 134: 244–48. (Hebrew)

Binder, Uri. 1989. "The Shalom District Farmers' Demonstration Turned into a Violent Battle with the Police." *Ma'ariv*, 6 March. (Hebrew)

Central Bureau of Statistics. 1977. Results of the Elections to the Ninth Knesset, 17.5.1977. Jerusalem: Central Bureau of Statistics.

———. 1978. *List of Localities: Their Population and Codes, 31.12.1977*. Jerusalem: Central Bureau of Statistics. (Hebrew)

———. 1985a. *1983 Census of Population and Housing. List of Localities*. Publication no. 6. Jerusalem: Central Bureau of Statistics.

———. 1985b. *Results of Elections to the Eleventh Knesset, 23.7.1984*. Jerusalem: Central Bureau of Statistics.

———. 1986a. *1983 Census of Population and Housing. Housing Conditions and Possession of Household Equipment*. Publication no. 9. Jerusalem: Central Bureau of Statistics.

———. 1986b. *1983 Census of Population and Housing. Educational Characteristics of the Population and Languages Spoken*. Publication no. 10. Jerusalem: Central Bureau of Statistics.

———. 1987. *1983 Census of Population and Housing. Population and Localities.* Publication no. 12. Jerusalem: Central Bureau of Statistics.

———. 1988. "Results of the Elections to the Twelfth Knesset, 1.11.1988—Preliminary Data." *Monthly Bulletin of Statistics,* Vol. 39, No. 12, supplement: 95–120. (Hebrew)

———. Various years. *Statistical Abstract of Israel . . . (1950; 1958; 1959; 1967; 1968; 1971; 1978; 1984; 1988)* Jerusalem: Central Bureau of Statistics.

Comptroller-General, Ministry of the Treasury. Various years. *Financial Report to the Date 31 March . . .* (1972/73–1987/88). Jerusalem: Comptroller-General.

Davar. 3 November 1988. "The 120 MKs of the 12th Knesset." (Hebrew)

Deutsch, Yitzhak. 1989. "The Price of a 'Rescue Mission'." *Ma'ariv.* 12 March 1989.

Freeman, Daniel, Nava Haruvi, Ya'ir Levi, and Pablo Mandler. 1988. *Consolidation of the Moshavim.* Research Report. Rehovot: Settlement Study Centre. (Hebrew)

Goren, Yehuda. 1989. "The Farmers of the North Sprayed the Acco-Safed Road with Eggs and Chickens." *Ma'ariv,* 6 March. (Hebrew)

Greenstein, Yossi. 1989. "Far Reaching Changes Expected in the Kibbutz [Debt Relief] Arrangement." *Ma'ariv,* 30 March. (Hebrew)

HaAretz. 28 December 1973; 11 March 1974; 23 December 1988. (Hebrew)

Hadashot. 7 February 1985. "The Treasurers are Concerned with Money and the Kibbutz Members are Concerned with Values."

Horowitz, Dan, and Moshe Lissak. 1977. *The Origins of the Israeli Polity.* Tel Aviv: Am Oved. (Hebrew)

Kapra, Michal. 1986. "Puncture in the Bika." *Ma'ariv,* 27 June. (Hebrew)

Kartin, Avi, and Menahem Horvitz. 1985. "The TAKAM [HaTnuah Hakibbutzit HaMe'uhedet] Secretariat: 'The Police will Investigate'." *HaAretz,* 22 July. (Hebrew)

Kinerati, A. 1977. "The Begin Government Presents itself to Receive the Confidence of the Knesset." *Davar,* 20 June. (Hebrew)

Lanir, Yosef. 1987. *The Kibbutz Movement: Review and Data.* Efal: Yad Tabenkin. (Hebrew)

Lifshitz, Oded. 1985. "Economists, not Speculators." *Al HaMishmar,* 4 February. (Hebrew)

Ma'ariv. 15 April 1977. "To Renew and To Continue"; 31 May 1981. "Zionism 1938—Hanita Zionism 1981—Karnei Shomron". (Hebrew)

Maron, Stanley. 1987. "Changes in Israeli Agriculture." *Economic Quarterly* Vol. 38, No. 134: 249–53. (Hebrew)

Medding, Peter. 1972. *Mapai in Israel: Political Organisation and Government in a New Society.* Cambridge: Cambridge University Press.

Rahat, Menahem. 1981. "The Quarrel Between Kiryat Shmona and the Surrounding Kibbutzim." *Ma'ariv,* 10 July. (Hebrew)

Schwartz, Moshe, Arie Marvid, and Ofer Arian. 1988. *The Organizations: Three Moshav Purchasing Organizations Before and After the Crisis.* Research report. Rehovot: Settlement Study Centre. (Hebrew)

Sherman, Neal. 1979. "The American and Israeli Models of Agricultural Development: A Comparative Analysis." In *The Role of U.S. Agriculture in Foreign Policy.* ed. R. M. Fraenkel et al., 181–220. New York: Praeger.

————. 1980. "The Agricultural Sector and the 1977 Knesset Elections." In *The Elections in Israel, 1977,* ed. Asher Arian, 149–70. Jerusalem: Jerusalem Academic Press.

————. 1982. "From Government to Opposition: The Rural Settlement Movements of the Israel Labour Party in the Wake of the Election of 1977." *International Journal of Middle East Studies* Vol. 14, No. 1: 53–69.

————, and Abraham Daniel. 1979. "The Concept of the 'Industrial Village' and the Israeli Cooperative Sector." *Sociologia Ruralis* Vol. 19, No. 4: 227–45.

————, and Moshe Schwartz. 1989. "The Effect of Public Financial Assistance on the Management of Moshav Economic Affairs." Working paper. Rehovot: Settlement Study Centre.

————, Johnnie Sternberg, Moshe Schwartz, and Ruth Perlmann. 1984. *Settlers and Settlement Agencies.* Rehovot: Settlement Study Centre. (Hebrew)

————, Johnnie Sternberg, Miriam Eger, and Tikva Cohen. 1987. *Special Financial Assistance to the Bikat HaYarden Moshavim.* Rehovot: Settlement Study Centre. (Hebrew)

Supreme Steering Committee for the Moshav Economy. 1987. Untitled [known as the "Ravid Report"]. No place. (Hebrew)

Weiss, Shimon. 1981. "Tension between the Kibbutzim of the Galilee and the Residents of Kiryat Shmona." *Davar,* 2 July. (Hebrew)

Wilkansky, Rachel. 1980. *Core and Periphery in the Development of Israel.* Ph.D. diss., The Technion, Israel Institute of Technology. (Hebrew)

PART V
■ Cleavages in the City

9 ■ Jerusalem: Central Authority and Local Autonomy

Ira Sharkansky

There is Jerusalem above and Jerusalem below. Jerusalem above refers to the Holy City. Religious Jews expect that the Messiah will come, perhaps today, and return the city to its biblical glory. When secular Jerusalemites use the same expression, they mean an ideal city that is far better than others both architecturally and socially. Jerusalem below refers to the earthly city, where the realities of daily life produce the sounds of traffic, the scurry of cats around the garbage, and the tensions of different communities.

This chapter focuses on Jerusalem below. Because of the images associated with Jerusalem above, however, the earthly city is not like other places. Jerusalem below is an arena of political competition over some interests that can be negotiated without great passion, and values of great intensity that do not lend themselves to compromise. Israelis expect more from Jerusalem than from other cities. Overseas Jews and Gentiles also expect more of Jerusalem. Some want it to be an ideal city. Others want to take the city from the Jews.

The emotions that surround Jerusalem leave their mark on policies pursued by the Israeli government with respect to the city, distinctive features of municipal finance, local politics, and the services received by city residents. At the same time, Jerusalem also shares certain traits with other cities of Israel. This chapter examines the traits which render Jerusalem a special place, and those which it shares with other municipalities.

The chapter opens with a brief historical background, and then describes Jerusalem's international and local distinctions. At focus are the international status and appeal of the city and its internal social divisions around ethnicity, religion, and other traits. Thereafter Jerusalem's blurred mix of private and public finance is analyzed. The in-

243

ternational status of the city and the entrepreneurship of the mayor
provide a strong base for private funding; the very base that strengthens Jerusalem's local autonomy. At the same time, as explained in the
discussion that follows, Jerusalem still operates within a national
framework that grants considerable powers to the bureaucrats of
central government ministries. All these international, local, private,
and public factors make Jerusalem a microcosm of Israel's social and
political tensions. Many of these tensions are around the clashing values and interests of the city's diversified social groups and neighborhoods. The final part of the chapter analyzes these tensions be
tween religious and secular Jews, Arabs and Jews, and Oriental Jews
and Ashkenazim.

HISTORICAL BACKGROUND

The position of Jerusalem in contemporary Israel cannot be understood without considering its role in Jewish tradition. From the time
of the King David (c. 1000 B.C.E.) Jews have viewed it as their Holy
City. It is Zion and the centerpiece of the Promised Land. In both ancient and modern times, it has been the focus of religious pilgrimage,
the site of Jewish communities, religious and national institutions.
Jews of all the world have attached their emotions and sent their donations to Jerusalem (Tcherikover 1959). Jerusalem is not only the
capital of modern Israel. It is the city of the Jewish people.

A period of development during Solomon's reign (965–927
B.C.E.) featured construction of the first Temple, which lasted for
more than 300 years until it was destroyed by the Babylonians.
Herod's reign (37–4 B.C.E.) saw another period of great building
which included the extensive refurbishing of the second Temple that
had been built by the Jews who returned from the Babylonian exile.
The Temples of Solomon and Herod were symbols of the glory that
was ancient Israel.

Teddy Kollek's tenure as mayor of Jerusalem that began in 1966
has been unusually long in the recent history of major cities, although
it has been only a moment in the long history of the city. Kollek along
with other Israelis in key positions have resisted proposals to construct
a Third Temple. Such a project would create yet another major problem with the Muslims, whose mosques have sat upon the Temple
Mount since the Middle Ages. However, other physical developments
in Kollek's period are comparable to those of Solomon and Herod.

Kollek is aware that his city is a place of contention among different peoples. He writes that during Jerusalem's 4,000 years it has been settled or ruled by Canaanites, Jebusites, Israelites, Babylonians, Assyrians, Persians, Romans, Byzantines, Arabs, Seljuks, Crusaders, Mamluks, Ottomans, British, Jordanians, and Israelis (Kollek 1980). Transitions have not been peaceful. By one accounting the city has been beseiged and conquered thirty-seven times (Benvenisti 1976, vii).

The historic importance of Jerusalem derived partly from its location in the center of the Jewish country. The site was attractive to David because it was midway between the large southern tribe of Judah and the northern tribes. It was an area that had resisted the Israelite tribes throughout the period of the judges. It has remained in foreign hands and contributed to a division of Israelites into northern and southern groups.

Once he took Jerusalem, David created a united kingdom of all the Israelite tribes. The Israelites had a permanent corps of administrators and an army for the first time. During most of its thousand years or so, however, the ancient Jewish country was a weak little place that suffered from being on the crossroads fought over by empires that were more powerful than it. The united kingdom of David and Solomon lasted for only eighty years until it gave way to internal division. Yet despite foreign conquest, exile, and emigration, Jerusalem has remained at the center of Jewish memories and faith since David's reign.

Jerusalem's location has proved important in modern times for a state that has depended on its military power. The city is built along mountain ridges, 2,500 feet above sea level, between the Mediterranean Sea to the west and the Jordan River to the east. It is about halfway along a north-south mountain ridge that links the Arab cities of Nablus, Ramallah, Bethlehem, and Hebron. Whoever controls Jerusalem has a strategic advantage over routes for commerce and defense.

During the War of Independence Jerusalem was cut off by Arab armies and local Arabs from villages alongside the road to the coast. The city's residents suffered through periods of severely rationed water and food. The hardships of the war and the constant threat of renewed hostility prompted many Jews to leave the city for the more secure and well-to-do cities of the coast. The population of less than 90,000 that was recorded in 1948 recalled what was a sleepy provincial town throughout the period of Ottoman rule.

Israel's government sought to develop the city by declaring it the national capital, and bringing immigrants to new neighborhoods and those left vacant by Arab refugees. Yet the city's Jewish population grew at a slower rate than the nation's between 1948 and 1967: 138 percent compared to 233 percent for all of Israel (Schmelz 1987; 49; Jerusalem Institute for Israel Studies 1983, 22).

Soon after the Israeli army occupied the city and its environs in the 1967 war, the government took steps to assure the city's security. It added substantially to the municipality's area by annexing land to the north, east, and south. It began to construct new neighborhoods for Jewish residents at several points chosen for their strategic importance, and built new roads down to the coast. In order to attract more Jews to Jerusalem, the government moved the headquarters of additional ministries to the city, and promoted other developments to increase jobs and housing. Since 1967 Jerusalem's Jewish population has grown more rapidly than the nation's: 170 percent between 1967 and 1986, compared to 149 percent for all of Israel (Central Bureau of Statistics 1987, 48–49; Jerusalem Institute for Israel Studies 1983, 22).

The Arab uprising that began in the West Bank and Gaza Strip in December 1987, the Intifada, has touched Jerusalem's neighborhoods and surrounding villages. Arab terrorists have killed Jews in the city's streets. Crowds of Jews have responded by destroying property in Arab neighborhoods and beating individual Arabs.

JERUSALEM'S DISTINCTIONS: INTERNATIONAL AND LOCAL

When the British controlled Jerusalem from World War I until 1948, they adopted regulations to assure a distinctive aura for the city. All new buildings would be faced in stone. Israel has continued that policy. As a result, Jerusalem is special in appearance as well as in spirit. Its buildings of yellow sandstone or white marble appear pink or gold, depending on the light. Housing is also more expensive than in other Israeli cities where precast concrete is the prevailing building material.

Israeli government planners put Jerusalem in its own category with respect to economic development. It is not a site for heavy industry. It is the seat of the capital, and a national center for religious, educational, and cultural institutions. When the air is especially clear, Jerusalem's mountain tops afford views across the Jordan Rift to the mountains of Moab in the east, and the coastal plain in the west.

Jerusalem's work force is more heavily concentrated in professional, managerial, clerical, and service categories than those of Tel Aviv or Haifa.[1]

The emotional appeal of Jerusalem has implications both for large issues of international politics and the daily lives of its residents. Jews of the Diaspora generally stand with those of Israel to support the declaration by Israel's government that Jerusalem will remain undivided and the national capital. The government of Israel allocates resources to make Jerusalem an attractive city, better than others in Israel, in order to legitimate Israel's rule. Jerusalem's hospitals, schools, museums, theaters, memorials, synagogues, sports facilities, and other institutions supplement their Israeli revenues by raising funds from overseas Jews and other friends of Jerusalem who contribute to this special place.

Jerusalem is made complicated by also being a holy city for Muslims and Christians, and being home to non-Jews who dispute Israel's control of their city. Non-Jewish organizations stake their claims in Jerusalem by supporting churches built on religious sites, hostels, schools, and hospitals. Some of them also insist that Israel withdraw from parts or all of Jerusalem. Their tactics range from reference to historic precedent or decisions of the United Nations (Colbi 1980), to acts of violence and proclamations in the most virulent of language. Not unusual is the following:

> Few other questions of our time have so deeply moved the world conscience and so gravely threatened world peace as the Zionist usurpation and continued occupation of Jerusalem and Palestine. It has perpetuated untold human misery and unleashed a seemingly unending reign of terror in a land held sacred by Muslims, Christians and Jews alike. As a result, more than a million men, women and children have been hounded out of their homes and forced to become refugees, while merciless Zionist persecution goes on throughout the length and breadth of their homeland (Islamic Council of Europe 1980, vii).

The writer of these words does not mention that the Jews of Palestine accepted the United Nations proposal of 1947 for dividing the disputed land into an Arab and a Jewish state. The Arabs rejected the plan, and invaded the new Israel as soon as it was declared. The full story of the Palestinian refugees, including the tendentious debate about their number, is too complex for this chapter. However, the

Arab rejection of compromise and the Arab invasion of Israel must be counted among the primary causes of this difficult issue.

The Jews have not been free of disputes among themselves about Jerusalem. Numerous groups have engaged in public denunciations of one another about who should do what, how, and when in the united city that emerged from the 1967 war. The principal actors include the municipality; central government ministries of Defense, Interior, Housing, Finance, and Religions; the rabbinate and individual rabbis; companies owned by the national government and the municipality; Knesset members and other prominent individuals from Israel and overseas (Benvenisti 1976, chapters 16, 18).

Jerusalem's disputes reflect its social divisions on ethnicity, religion, religiosity, and other traits. Soon after the War of Independence, the arrival of many immigrants from Yemen, Kurdistan, and North Africa produced a situation where the city had more illiterates than any other city of Israel. The presence of the Hebrew University, government ministries, and Hadassah Hospital also meant that the city had more college graduates than any other city. The unification of the city in 1967 gave it the highest percentage of Arabs among Israel's major cities. The attractions of the Holy City have brought many ultra-Orthodox Jews to Jerusalem. The high birth rates of religious Jews and their migration to Jerusalem assures chronic tensions over insufficient housing for religious families, the spread of religious neighborhoods, and the activities to be permitted in religious neighborhoods and elsewhere.

Teddy Kollek focuses on the different and contentious communities of Jerusalem when he says that the theme of the city is exclusivity rather than integration. He aspires to produce accommodation but does not expect brotherly love. At times the confrontations get to the mayor. His temper is legendary. In one reported incident, he responded with "Kiss my ass" to a constituent who threatened not to vote for him (Rabinovich 1988, 17).

Contentious claims make Jerusalem an interesting and tense residence. Jerusalem's friends compensate, in part, for the city's place at the focus of international politics, and the doubts raised about its residents' physical security. Outsiders who send donations to public facilities in Jerusalem make it a more attractive city than it would be if it had to rely on local or national funding.

Israel's government appreciates the international status of its capital, but does not want the world to define the city formally in those terms. Some decisions of the United Nations and proclamations of the Vatican would have Jerusalem separated from Israel and ruled as an international enclave. Israel asserts that it will protect the religious sites of non-Jews, but that Jerusalem must remain united under Jewish rule, as the capital of the Jewish state. It has contended with changing perspectives of (the United States, the White House, and State Department) as to whether East Jerusalem should be referred to as an occupied territory, and whether the city should be treated as a unit or as separate entities that are currently unified pending a formal solution (Slonim, 1984).

Most of the Arabs who were included within the city when Israel annexed a large area after the 1967 war have refused the offer of Israeli citizenships. By virtue of being city residents, these noncitizen Arabs can run for municipal office and vote in municipal elections. Yet Arab leaders have refused to stand for election. In some local elections, such as that of 1989, the large majority of Arabs has refused to vote as an expression of their opposition to Israeli rule.

Terminology is a political issue. It is common to use the labels New Jerusalem, West Jerusalem, or Jewish Jerusalem to refer to the western area of the city that was in Jewish hands after the 1948 war. East Jerusalem or Arab Jerusalem refers to that section of the city annexed in 1967. Some of these terms are only partly accurate. A section of the Arab neighborhood of Beit Safafa was in Jewish Jerusalem from 1948 until 1967. A number of Jewish neighborhoods have been built in East Jerusalem since 1967. Opponents of Israeli rule speak about "occupied Jerusalem." Some Jews object to the term "Arab Jerusalem." For many, "Palestinian" is the appropriate term for the Arabs of Jerusalem, while others object to its implications for the prospects of Palestinian statehood.

International pressures and Israeli sensitivities have led to bizarre behaviors. In order to deal with a population that does not recognize the legitimacy of the status quo, the Israeli government and the Jerusalem municipality have distorted or ignored their own rules. Arabs in East Jerusalem have been allowed to operate businesses and practice professions on the basis of their Jordanian licenses, without applying for Israeli licenses. Arabs in East Jerusalem also continue to use Jordanian currency despite regulations of the Bank of Israel that prohibit residents' use of foreign currency. Arab Jerusalemites travel to Jordan despite regulations that forbid contact with states that are formally enemies of Israel. Arab schoolchildren continue to study according to Jordanian curricula in schools that are financed by Israel.

Jordan participates in the charade. Its Aliya Airline has an office in East Jerusalem. The Arab Chamber of Commerce functions as a Jordanian consulate. It provides passports and other official documents to residents of Jerusalem who prefer to continue as Jordanians (Rubinstein 1980; Benziman 1980; Benvenisti 1976).

JERUSALEM'S FINANCES: INTERNATIONAL AND ISRAELI, PRIVATE AND PUBLIC

Because of its appeal to overseas donors, Jerusalem presents a thorough mix of governmental and nongovernmental bodies, which support themselves with a combination of public and private resources. All of this makes it difficult to deal with classic questions of political science, such as Who governs? How? and Who gets what? The international sources of funds and the international boards of directors that govern some of Jerusalem's most prominent institutions also dilute the government's insistence that Jerusalem remain under Israeli rule.

Foreign contributions to Jerusalem add to the residents' social services and cultural programs, and leave their mark on the character of the country's public finances and government administration. Jerusalem's public service organizations use their support from overseas as leverage to extract more money from municipal and national authorities. The ostensibly private Hebrew University and Hadassah Hospital have earned the label of quasi-governmental. They collect sizable resources overseas, but Israeli government grants routinely exceed 50 percent of their revenues. Along with the money, government officials demand a role in setting salaries for their staffs, the fees charged to students or patients, and decisions about new programs. After the privately funded Sha'are Zedek Hospital encountered financial difficulties, it was absorbed into the health system operated by the Histadrut (General Federation of Labor). This health system (Kupat Cholim Haclali) is a quasi-governmental entity that is subsidized heavily by the Israeli government and is often at the center of disputes between government ministries and the Histadrut concerning salaries, fees, and services.

The Jerusalem Foundation raises money from overseas donors. Its projects are formally independent of the Jerusalem municipality, but Teddy Kollek's status as city mayor and foundation president blurs the boundaries. More than other institutions, the Jerusalem Foundation confounds the issue of what is governmental and private, and what is controlled by Israel, Jerusalem, or overseas friends of Jerusalem (Sharkansky 1984).

The Foundation has supported more than 1,000 projects since it was created in 1966. Its playgrounds and flower gardens appear in every neighborhood. It built major facilities for museums and theaters, and subsidizes special attractions for schoolchildren. Community centers have gymnasiums, sports fields, and programs for dance, arts, and drama. Parks, walkways, and amphitheaters appear at ancient landmarks, gracefully restored for modern purposes. Churches, mosques, and synagogues have been built or refurbished. There are subsidized workshops for young artists, as well as apartments and studios for world-class artists, musicians, and intellectuals who visit the city. The Foundation supports archaeological excavations and restorations. It renovated buildings and streets in the Old City, repaired water, sewer, electric, and telephone lines, and provided cable television to replace unsightly antennas.

The Foundations' projects do not escape the barbs of Jerusalem's contentious groups. Arab sensitivities about Jewish incursions appear even when Foundation programs are directed at the physical or social problems of the Arab community, and staffed by Arabs. Religious Jews have blocked Foundation projects to construct sports or cultural facilities that are said to threaten the Sabbath or the sensitivities of religious neighborhoods.

The Foundation's financial outlays amounted to some $245 million from 1966 to 1991, and $20 million annually in recent years. Although many foundation outlays do not aid projects in conjunction with the municipality, per se, it is possible to gauge the magnitude of its activities by noting that Foundation outlays have approximated 10 to 16 percent of the municipality's operating budget.

The Jerusalem Development Authority was created in 1988 by a senior official of the municipality and a close confidant of Teddy Kollek. Its governing board includes representatives of the national government and the municipality. It is charged with encouraging, planning, and initiating activities concerned with the economic development of Jerusalem, and coordinating the city's development with government ministries, municipal officials, and other bodies.

The Moriah Company is wholly owned by the municipality, and serves as prime contractor for projects organized by the Jerusalem Development Authority. The company and authority have completed a large modern stadium and a zoo. They are developing several blocks of upper-income apartments and commercial buildings on a prized site between the Old City and the central business district. Elsewhere they are building a park for high-tech industry, shopping malls, a building for international conventions, several blocks of government offices, and tourist sites.

Quasi-governmental organizations such as the Foundation and the Authority have several advantages in Jerusalem. They can receive the money of foreign donors who wish to contribute to Jerusalem projects, in the context of laws that prohibit or discourage donations to government authorities, per se. Quasi-governmental organizations can borrow money in Israel and overseas, outside of restrictions of the Ministry of Finance that pertain to government authorities. The Jerusalem Development Authority can offer foreign investors the prospect of profit, and contract with architects and builders more freely and quickly than government ministries or municipal departments that are tied to detailed procedures that include competitive bidding. To date, major investors have been prominent overseas Jews who also contribute to projects of the Jerusalem Foundation. Some have coupled their investments in authority projects with sizable loans at modest rates of interest. The mayor's supporters assert that contributing to Jerusalem outweighs any expectation of commercial gain.

Quasi-governmental organizations raise some delicate problems. Kollek's dual role as mayor of the municipality and chairman of the Jerusalem Foundation provides him with the leverage of private resources over public resources, and vice versa. Kollek extracts money from the municipality and the national government to match the nongovernmental funds raised by the Foundation. He appeals to donors as a man who can use his status as mayor to push the Foundation's projects through to completion, and to supplement the private funds with public money. The intimate mixture of public and private roles provides extraordinary weight to the mayor in his negotiations with other government bodies. It also gives him unusual advantages when he approaches the voters for reelection as a man who can add to Jerusalem's amenities. Those who hold to conventional principles of accountability and a clear separation of private and public resources express some discomfort at the foundation's blurring the boundaries between private and public sectors.

JERUSALEM AND OTHER ISRAELI MUNICIPALITIES: CENTRALIZED AND BUREAUCRATIC

While Jerusalem is at the focus of the nation's aspirations and international interest, it also shares traits with Israel's other localities. Indeed, its uniqueness can be gauged best after a consideration of Israel's government structure and relations between government ministries and local authorities.

Israel is ruled from the center, with a large role for the professional staffs of national ministries and other government bodies. The International Monetary Fund ranks Israel among those democracies where the central government is most heavily involved in economic management. The combined budgets of governmental and quasi-governmental bodies sometime exceed gross national product (Sharkansky 1987).

Centralization is made easy because of small size and the country's history. Israel's 4.4 million people live in an area of 8,300 square miles. It is a bit larger than New Jersey, and a bit smaller than Massachusetts. Most Jewish families have been in the country for only a few generations. The country's people differ from long-established populations in identifying themselves more with the country than with its regions or localities. National politics reinforces centralization. It is based on proportional representation in a single electoral district. No member of the Knesset is formally a representative of a city or region.[2]

The dominant Zionist ideology helps to reinforce Israel's central government. The country's founders wanted to build a strong state in order to protect a people who had suffered from nearly 2,000 years of statelessness. The fact that most founders came from eastern and central Europe, where centralized states were the norm, also contributed to Israel's development.

Most citizens were poor when Israel became independent in 1948. Only the state could amass resources from taxes, loans, and overseas grants that were needed for developing agriculture, industry, housing, transportation, and social services. In these traits, Israel resembled many other new states that came on the scene after World War II. Like most new states, Israel provided a large role for the state in economic management.

Israel was pressed more than other new states by the animosity of its neighbors and by massive immigration. These unusual burdens added to the power of the central government. It had to finance and direct a large army, and to integrate immigrants who more than doubled the national population in less than ten years of independence.

Israel has no written constitution. The majority of the Knesset is unrestrained by anything beyond political will in enacting new laws about the municipalities, or in changing the laws which exist.[3]

Jerusalem and Israel's other local authorities experience the country's centralization in the regulations that govern physical planning, local revenues, and budgeting. The process of physical planning determines what structures may be built on which sites. Local authorities have a voice in this, but within a framework that is dominated by national and regional commissions, with a major role for the Interior Ministry. The national government's influence over physical planning is reinforced by land ownership. More than 90 percent of the country's land is held by the Israel Lands Authority. The Lands Authority leases its land for purposes that are consistent with its plans.

Local finances are defined by laws and regulations administered by national ministries of Finance and Interior. The taxes and fees of each locality, as well as details of its expenditures, must be approved by national government officials.

The formal rules of strict centralization are administered in a loose, somewhat chaotic fashion (Elazar and Kalchaim 1988). National ministries of Housing, Transportation, Education, Welfare, Health, Religions, and Defense make expenditures in the local communities and provide funds to local authorities in ways that are not fully coordinated by the ministries of Finance and Interior. Ministers seek to advance their own reputations by favoring projects that are not supported by their colleague-competitors in Finance or Interior. Teddy Kollek and other mayors offer national politicians the opportunity to be the patrons of local projects. Local welfare officers and educators take more discretion in administering their programs than the formal rules allow (Lazin 1986).

Much of what is special about Jerusalem gives it an advantage in the rough and tumble of Israeli politics. The municipality receives a special allocation from the central government for being the capital. The mayor and ranking administrators argue in the national ministries that extra budget allocations for roads, housing, and public facilities are necessary to improve the city's standing as the nation's showcase. They demand matching allocations from national ministries in order to complete projects that are supported by the Jerusalem Foundation or other overseas donors.

The city's special opportunities free it from having to skirt around the edges of some regulations that govern Israel's cities. One study found that Israel's mayors had borrowed substantial funds in violation of the rules established by the ministries of Finance and Interior. Jerusalem was distinctive among the large cities for the small size of its debt.[4]

Table 9.1. Percentage of Operating Budget Derived from Locally Raised Revenues

	1987–88	1970–71
Jerusalem	74	71
Tel Aviv	85	85
Haifa	82	77
Beer Sheva	64	71
All municipalities	76	78

Source: Central Bureau of Statistics. Various years. *Local Authorities in Israel: Financial Data.* Jerusalem: Central Bureau of Statistics and Ministry of Interior.

Aggregate data from Israel's major cities indicate that Jerusalem relies less than Tel Aviv and Haifa, but more than Beer Sheva, on revenues collected by itself from its own residents or businesses. When it is viewed over time, Jerusalem is treated more or less like other cities in issues of public finance. There have been periods of increased central government grants, and periods of increased reliance on local revenues. Table 9.1 indicates that the percentage of "independent" revenue in Jerusalem's operating budget (i.e., locally collected taxes and fees) in 1987–88 was not substantially different than it was in 1970–71.

OUTSIDE INVOLVEMENT IN JERUSALEM'S RELIGIOUS-SECULAR DISPUTE

At times the special status of Jerusalem works against local autonomy. Disputes involving religion seem especially prone to bring about the involvement of national and international figures.

Mayor Kollek was opposed in the early 1980s by leaders of the city's Orthodox Jewish communities when he sought to build a new soccer stadium on the city's northern outskirts with funding from the Jerusalem Foundation. Religious Jews opposed the project on account of its violation of the Sabbath, which is the occasion for most of the country's soccer games. The city's Orthodox neighborhoods were expanding to the north. Sooner or later the noise and traffic of the stadium would disturb their Sabbath rest and worship. Opponents of the stadium recruited allies from Jewish communities overseas. In a period when the religious parties held the balance of power in national politics, Prime Minister Menachem Begin and Minister of Interior Yosef Burg (a member of the National Religious Party) decided that Jerusalem could not build its soccer stadium.

Now there is a new soccer stadium in an area of the city far removed from religious neighborhoods. Religious leaders had opposed the construction of any soccer stadium in the Holy City, in a move that recalled the opposition of Jewish zealots to Greek athletic contests during the Hasmonean period (167 to 37 B.C.E.). In contrast to the situation during the Begin administration, the religious parties held no balance of power in the government that came to power after the elections of 1988.

One season of religious outbursts was directed against advertisements posted in bus stops. Religious Jews burned some bus stops on account of the immodest attire worn by women depicted in the advertisements. Liberal Jews from Israel and overseas decried the lack of free expression in Israel, while Orthodox Jews from Israel and abroad decried the lack of decency in the Holy City. While the police arrested some perpetrators, the advertising company negotiated with religious leaders in an effort to define the kinds of pictures that would be inoffensive. Such negotiations seemed futile when a bus stop that carried a picture of a mayonnaise jar, without any human forms, was burned.

The Jerusalem Center of Brigham Young University was at the center of another controversy during the mid-1980s. Religious Jews became alert to the Mormons' commitment to proselytizing some dozen years after the Mormons first opened a Jerusalem Center in temporary quarters, and after they had begun construction of their facility at a prized site on the Mount of Olives overlooking the Old City. Mass demonstrations blocked the continuation of construction. Member of Knesset Rabbi Meir Kahane proclaimed that the partly finished building should be completed as a rabbinical *yeshiva*. United States Senators from the Mormons' home state of Utah spoke about their support for Israel and expressed their concern about the rule of law in Israel. Jerusalem's mayor supported the project's continuation. An Israeli court ruled in favor of the university, and construction continued. A committee chaired by an official of the Justice Ministry was given responsibility for supervising the university's commitment not to proselytize.

These episodes appeared to be light comedy in comparison with a conflict that began in the middle of 1987. Secular Jews in Jerusalem

Project Renewal is another program meant to improve the quality of local decision-making. It was created by Prime Minister Menachem Begin in 1978 to accomplish several goals: facilitate fund raising among overseas Jewish communities; create a link between Diaspora Jews and specific locales in Israel; alleviate the social and economic problems of Israel's poorer urban neighborhoods and small towns, most of them heavily populated by Jews from Asia and North Africa; and involve residents of the sites to be aided. Project Renewal was to be different from typical Israeli social programs, where professional employees of national ministries and local authorities make decisions in behalf of the people to be served.

It is not easy to summarize the record of the neighborhood associations or Project Renewal. Several Jerusalem neighborhoods have benefited from Project Renewal. There have been impressive physical improvements of run-down housing, as well as new social programs. There have also been frustrating confrontations between local residents, representatives of overseas donors, and several bureaucracies that include the Ministry of Housing, housing companies owned by the government or the municipality, and departments of the municipality, as well as the professional administrators employed to manage each neighborhood's projects. Individuals involved with the neighborhood associations describe numerous local residents who feel more involved in public affairs as a result of the associations' activities, as well as municipal bureaucracies that resist allocating to the neighborhoods anything more than symbolic discretion about minor issues.

Local Elections

Jerusalem's diversity as well as Kollek's dominating personality figured prominently in the 1989 municipal elections. A coalition of secular parties campaigned to help the incumbent hold back the ultra-Orthodox. Religious parties ran counter campaigns against what they described as antireligious incitement. A small party campaigned on the promise to join Kollek's coalition with the slogan "Only Teddy Can."

Critics charged that the mayor exploited his status as the incumbent by including campaign material along with the salary slips of city employees. Activists in the Arab uprising called for a boycott of the elections by the residents of East Jerusalem. The success of this campaign hurt Kollek, who had done well among the Arabs in previous elections.

Jerusalem's municipal elections provided an opportunity for residents to select from among individual candidates for mayor, and to select a party list of candidates for the city council. Kollek's party (Jerusalem One) lost its absolute majority on the city council, even while he returned to the mayor's office.

Kollek polled 59 percent of the votes cast for mayor (down from his 64 percent in the elections of 1983), while the second-running candidate received only 16 percent. Kollek's party polled 36 percent of the vote for the city council; seven other parties each received between 4 and 12 percent. The loss of six seats on the council by Kollek's party was matched by the gain of four seats by an antireligious secular coalition, and again of two seats by Jewish religious parties.[7] Although slightly weakened, Kollek and his party colleagues remain the dominant figures in local politics. His age, now over 80, more than any details of municipal policy or administration, figures prominently in discussions of the city's political future.

CONCLUSIONS

Jerusalem is distinctive both in Israel and the world. Its status among Jews, their friends and enemies, assures the city special treatment by the Israeli government. Its private and quasi-governmental institutions benefit from resources that overseas friends contribute to improve the Holy City. Different kinds of Jews, as well as Muslims and Christians, have their own views about Jerusalem.

Israeli officials take pride in Jerusalem's role as an international city, and they appreciate the resources that it attracts from foreign contributors. Yet government officials are wary lest the world take Jerusalem's international status too literally. They continue to assert that Jerusalem is an Israeli city and the nation's capital, against existing declarations of the United Nations that it be turned formally into an international enclave.

The City of Peace has been generally free of overt division or communal violence since 1967, but there is tension. There have been Arab attacks against Jews, and Jewish attacks against Arabs. The Arab uprising that was centered in the West Bank and Gaza since December 1987 also reached Jerusalem and its outskirts. The Jews are not without their own internal conflicts. Disputes between religious and secular Jews, primarily around their different values and life-styles, are especially prone to bring about outside involvement of national or international figures. Oriental Jews are in tense relationships with Ashkenazim in some of the neighborhoods. In other neighborhoods, those of Project Renewal, they must confront the bureaucracies of both the central government and city hall.

Jerusalem is like other Israeli cities in being subject to the bureaucracies of the central government. Its mayor and other officials may do better than their counterparts in other cities in finding resources and local autonomy. At times they benefit from the view of national officials that Jerusalem must be treated generously. At other times, however, the city's status leads national officials to assert their own preferences about Jerusalem's management and to dominate its budget allocations and fiscal policies. The first effort to build a soccer stadium showed that Jerusalem's special status in Judaism can produce central government intervention in local issues. The experiences of neighborhood associations and Project Renewal show signs of community involvement, as well as the continuing assertiveness of central government and municipal bureaucrats.

Teddy Kollek is an international figure as well as mayor of Jerusalem. His Jerusalem Foundation collects substantial resources overseas, and helps him to pry additional funds from national ministries. He has also shown great concern for moderating the tensions that cut across the religious and ethnic communities of his city.

The city's long and contentious history requires a note of caution. What is described here is the current moment in a history of some 4,000 years that has included numerous changes in regime. Jerusalem is high on the agenda of Palestinians who want their own state, but not on the formal agenda that Israeli officials have been willing to negotiate. Perhaps outside the concern of most observers of international politics, but of importance to specialists in local administration, are the city's quasi-governmental organizations. They are still in their founding period when the entrepreneurial mayor who established them remains in office. Should they acquire a life of their own or become dormant with a change in the mayor's office, it will be appropriate to inquire again if local elected officials retain significant leverage on the city's economic development and its social programing.

Notes

1. The percentage of Jerusalem's Jewish work force employed in professional, managerial, and clerical occupations in 1983 was 63, compared to 54

in Tel Aviv and 57 in Haifa. Percentages employed in public and community services were Jerusalem—49; Tel Aviv—28; and Haifa—35 (Schmelz 1987, 103–5).

2. For a view that sees a growth of regionalism in Israel, see Gradus 1984.

3. A series of "Basic Laws" do require extraordinary majorities to change them. To date, however, no basic law has been enacted to provide a "bill of rights" for Israel's local governments.

4. The ratios of accumulated debt in relation to population at the beginning of the 1980s was Tel Aviv—.82; Haifa—.58; Beer Sheva—.38; and Jerusalem—.02. The source of the data is Central Bureau of Statistics, 1983. See Sharkansky 1987, especially chapter 5.

5. In violation of Sabbath prohibitions involving the use of electrical appliances.

6. The percentages of men from the following groups employed in professional, managerial, or clerical occupations during 1983 were: Jews of European and American origin—68–70; Jews of Israeli origin—53; Jews of Asian and North African origin—35–44; Christians—45; and Muslims—17. During 1981, the average number of persons in a Jewish household was 3.45, while the average number in a non-Jewish household was 5.40. Also during 1981, 54 percent of the Jewish families lived in a dwelling with one or fewer persons per room, while only 21 percent of the non-Jews lived in such conditions (Schmelz 1987, 105; Jerusalem Institute for Israel Studies 1983, 72–73).

7. *Jerusalem Post*, 1 and 2 March 1989.

References

Ashkenasi, Abraham. 1990. "Opinion Trends among Jerusalem Palestinians." Jerusalem: Hebrew University Leonard Davis Institute.

Benvenisti, Meron. 1976. *Jerusalem: The Torn City*. Minneapolis: University of Minnesota Press.

Benziman, Uzi. 1980. "Israeli Policy in East Jerusalem after Reunification." In *Jerusalem: Problems and Prospects*, ed. Joel L. Kraemer, 100–30. New York: Praeger.

Central Bureau of Statistics. 1983. *Local Authorities Financial Data, 1981/82*. Jerusalem: Central Bureau of Statistics and Ministry of Interior.

———. 1987. *Statistical Abstract of Israel 1987*. Jerusalem: Central Bureau of Statistics.

———. Various years. *Local Authorities in Israel: Financial Data*. Jerusalem: Central Bureau of Statistics and Ministry of Interior.

Colbi, S. P. 1980. "The Christian Establishment in Jerusalem." In *Jerusalem: Problems and Prospects*, ed. Joel L. Kramer, 153–177. New York: Praeger.

Elazar, Daniel, and Chaim Kalchaim, eds. 1988. *Local Government in Israel*. Lanham, Md.: University Press of America.

Goldberg, Giora, Gad Barzilai, and Efraim Inbar. 1991. "The Impact of Intercommunal Conflict: The Intifada and Israeli Public Opinion." Jerusalem: Hebrew University Leonard Davis Institute.

Gradus, Yehuda. 1984. "The Emergence of Regionalism in a Centralized System: The Case of Israel." *Environment and Planning D: Society and Space*, Vol. 2: 87–100.

Huppert, Uri. 1988. *Back to the Ghetto: Zionism in Retreat*. Buffalo, N.Y.: Prometheus Books.

Islamic Council of Europe. 1980 *Jerusalem: The Key to World Peace*. London: Islamic Council of Europe.

Jerusalem Institute for Israel Studies. 1983. *Jerusalem Statistical Data*. Jerusalem: Jerusalem Institute for Israel Studies.

Jerusalem Post. 1 and 2 March 1989.

Kollek, Teddy. 1980. "Introduction: Jerusalem—Today and Tomorrow." In *Jerusalem: Problems and Prospects*, ed. Joel L. Kramer, 1–16. New York: Praeger.

Lazin, Frederick A. 1986. *Policy Implementation and Social Welfare: Israel and the United States*. New Brunswick, N.J.: Transaction Books.

Rabinovich, Abraham. 1988. *Jerusalem on Earth: People, Passions and Politics in the Holy City*. New York: Free Press.

Rubinstein, Daniel. 1980. "The Jerusalem Municipality under the Ottomans, British, and Jordanians." In *Jerusalem: Problems and Prospects*, ed. Joel L. Kramer, 72–99. New York: Praeger.

Schmelz, U. O. 1987. *Modern Jerusalem's Demographic Evolution*. Jerusalem: Jerusalem Institute for Israel Studies.

Sharkansky, Ira. 1984. "Mayor Teddy Kollek and the Jerusalem Foundation: Governing the Holy City." *Public Administration Review*, Vol. 44 (July/August): 299–304.

———. 1987. *The Political Economy of Israel*. New Brunswick, N.J.: Transaction Books.

Slonim, Shlomo. 1984. "The United States and the Status of Jerusalem, 1947–1984." *Israel Law Review*, Vol. 19, No. 2 (Spring): 179–252.

Smooha, Sammy. 1989. *Arabs and Jews in Israel: Conflicting and Shared Attitudes in a Divided Society*. Boulder: Westview Press.

Tcherikover, Victor. 1959. *Hellenistic Civilization and the Jews*. New York. Athaneum.

GLOSSARY

ADP. *See* Arab Democratic Party.

AGUDAT ISRAEL. "Association of Israel" in Hebrew. Ultra-Orthodox religious political party.

ALIGNMENT. *See* Labor Alignment.

AMANA. "Covenant" in Hebrew. The settlement movement of Gush Emunim. Established in 1976.

AMIDAR. Large public construction and housing company. A subsidiary of the Ministry of Construction and Housing.

AMIGUR. Large public construction and housing company. A subsidiary of the Jewish Agency.

ARAB DEMOCRATIC PARTY (ADP). Arab political party formed before the 1988 Knesset elections.

ARAB IN ISRAEL. *See* Israeli Arab.

ASHKENAZI (pl. ASHKENAZIM). Hebrew word which means "German." A Jew of European or American Origin. Approximately 45 percent of Israel's Jewish population.

BLACK PANTHERS. Protest movement of the left working to improve the socioeconomic status of Oriental Jews. Attracted mostly Jewish Moroccan Youth. Began in the early 1970s in Jerusalem's poor neighborhoods.

BNEI AKIVA. "Sons of Akiva" in Hebrew. The youth movement of the National Religious Party.

BRITISH MANDATE. The British rule in Palestine from 1918 to 1948.

CAMP DAVID ACCORDS. Included two frameworks for peace, Egyptian-Israeli and for the Middle East, signed by Egypt, Israel, and the

267

United States at Camp David in September 1978. The Egyptian-Israeli framework resulted in the March 1979 peace treaty between the two states.

CIVIL RIGHTS MOVEMENT (CRM). Small left-wing political party. Founded before the 1973 elections.

DEGEL HaTORAH. Small ultra-Orthodox religious political party in the 1988 elections.

DEMOCRATIC FRONT FOR PEACE AND EQUALITY (DFPE). Arab-Jewish Communist election list established in 1977.

DEMOCRATIC MOVEMENT FOR CHANGE (DMC). Political party of the center. Headed by Yigael Yadin. Established seven months before the 1977 Knesset elections, ran only in 1977, and won 15 seats in the Knesset.

DEVELOPMENT TOWN. Government-sponsored new community established between 1948 and 1963. This status was conferred to 33 new communities at that time; 29 of them held this status in 1970 and 25 of them during the 1980s.

DFPE. See Democratic Front for Peace and Equality.

DMC. See Democratic Movement for Change.

DRUZE. Arabic religious sect (non-Moslem/Christian). Mostly Syrians and Lebanese. A small minority resides in northern Israel.

ERETZ ISRAEL (LAND OF ISRAEL). Denotes the biblical land promised to Abraham by God (Canaan). The current usage of the term also includes the West Bank and the Gaza Strip.

'ERUV. "Blending" in Hebrew. A symbolic act of blending several domains to make it lawful to carry objects from one domain to another on the Sabbath (the Sabbath perimeter).

FOUNDATION. See Jerusalem Foundation.

GAHAL. Hebrew acronym for "Bloc of Herut-Liberals." A Herut-Liberal party joint election list to the Knesset. Established in 1965 and expanded to Likud in 1973.

GALILEE. The northern region of Israel (mostly mountains).

GAZA STRIP. Narrow area of shoreline that extends some 20 miles along the Mediterranean coast to the Egyptian border. Captured by Israel from Egypt in the 1967 war.

GOLAN HEIGHTS. Region in northern Israel. Captured by Israel from Syria in the 1967 war.

GREEN LINE. The Israeli-Arab armistice lines from 1949 to 1967.

GUSH EMUNIM (also GUSH). "Block of the Faithful" in Hebrew. A fundamentalist-religious Jewish movement founded in 1974. Its main goal is to build Jewish settlements in the West Bank.

HAGANAH. "Defense" in Hebrew. The underground defense force of the Yishuv from 1920 to 1948. The military arm of the establishment headed by Mapai.

HALAKHA. Jewish religious code of laws and ordinances.

HAMULA. Arab word used to describe the extended family.

ḤAREDI (pl. ḤAREDIM). "Anxious" in Hebrew. A fundamentalist-religious Jew who strictly observes the *halakha* and does not accept Zionist ideology.

ḤASID (pl. ḤASIDIM). "Pious" in Hebrew. Denotes goodness. An adherent of a Jewish religious and social movement founded during the eighteenth century. The movement opposed the systematic logical learning of the Talmud and emphasized a spiritual and mystic approach.

HERUT. "Freedom" in Hebrew. Right-wing political party with a national ideology. A descendant of the Revisionists. Led by Menachem Begin. Founded in 1948. A major component of Gahal and Likud.

HISTADRUT (GENERAL FEDERATION OF LABOR). The largest trade union and a powerful force in the economy and politics of Israel. Founded in 1920. Dominated by Mapai and the Labor party.

IDF. *See* Israel Defense Forces.

INTIFADA. "Awakening" in Arabic. The Palestinian uprising and protest in the West Bank and Gaza Strip against the Israeli occupation of these territories. Began in December 1987.

ISLAMIC MOVEMENT. Extraparliamentary Arab organization. Participated in local elections in the Arab settlements in 1983 and 1989.

ISRAEL DEFENSE FORCES (IDF). The army of the State of Israel.

ISRAEL LANDS AUTHORITY (or ADMINISTRATION). Government agency that implements and administers the national land policy of the state of Israel according to 1960 law. Responsible for over 90 percent of all land in the state.

ISRAELI ARAB. Arab citizen of Israel who resides within the Green Line.

ISRAELI COMMUNIST PARTY. *See* Maki.

JERUSALEM FOUNDATION. Fund-raising organization for the city of Jerusalem. Formally independent from the city government yet headed by its mayor (Teddy Kollek). Set up in 1966.

JEWISH AGENCY (also JEWISH AGENCY FOR ISRAEL). Executive body of the World Zionist Organization (established by Theodore Herzl in 1897 to promote Jewish nationalism and Zionism). The representative body of the Yishuv. Currently active as a liaison between the state of Israel and world Jewry as well as in immigrant absorption, settlement, and Project Renewal.

JORDAN RIFT. Narrow strip west of the Jordan River. Natural geographic unit of the West Bank.

JUDEA. The southern area of the West Bank. The biblical name of the area.

KACH. "Thus" in Hebrew. Extreme nationalist religious list to the 1984 Knesset elections. Headed by Rabbi Meir Kahane. Outlawed by the Supreme Court before the 1988 elections.

KNESSET. "Assembly" in Hebrew. Israel's single chamber parliament with 120 members. Elected under proportional representation for a four-year term. Elects the government (cabinet) headed by the prime minister. The government is responsible to the Knesset.

KIBBUTZ (pl. KIBBUTZIM.). "Gathering" in Hebrew. A cooperative settlement which owns and manages all means of production and, to a high degree, also controls the consumption of its members.

LABOR. A generic term which describes all parties of the left with different levels of socialistic ideology. Currently includes the Labor party, Mapam, and other smaller parties (depending on the elections year). Used also as Labor bloc (camp).

LABOR ALIGNMENT (also ALIGNMENT). Election list of the left between 1969 and 1984 composed of the Labor party and Mapam. Also, an election list in 1965 composed of Mapai and one smaller party (Ahdut Haavoda).

LABOR PARTY. Ruling party of the left which led all coalition governments between 1969 and 1977 as well as the National Unity Government between 1984 and 1986. For its formation, see Mapai.

LABOR ZIONISM. A generic term which combines the socialistic ideology of Labor and the national ideology of Zionism. *See also* Labor *and* Zionism.

LAND OF ISRAEL. *See* Eretz Israel.

LIBERAL PARTY. Right-of-center party. A major component of Gahal and Likud.

LIKUD. "Unity" in Hebrew. A right-wing joint election list composed of Gahal and a few small parties. Founded in 1973. The ruling party between 1977 and 1992 (with the exception of 1984–86).

LITTLE TRIANGLE. Area in the central part of Israel. Heavily populated by Israeli Arabs.

LOCAL LIST. List for local elections. With no affiliation, formal or informal, to a political party.

LOCAL STEERING COMMITTEE (LSC). Local committee which prepares and operates the plan for the renewal of the neighborhood in Project Renewal.

LSC. *See* Local Steering Committee.

MAFDAL. Hebrew acronym for the National Religious Party.

MAKI (ISRAEL COMMUNIST PARTY). Small political party of the extreme left. Founded in 1919 as a non-Zionist party. Joined other groups in 1973 and 1977 to form a list of the extreme left.

MAPAI. Hebrew acronym for "Israel Workers' party." The dominant party in the Yishuv and the state of Israel since its formation in 1930 and until 1968. Leader of all government coalitions until 1968 when it merged with two other (smaller) parties of the left (Ahdut Haavoda and Rafi) to form the Labor party.

MAPAM. Hebrew acronym for "United Workers' Party." A left-wing party. A major component of Labor Alignment between 1969 and 1984. Ran independently in the 1988 elections.

MATZAD. Faction of the National Religious Party. Ran in the 1984 Knesset elections with Poalei Agudat Israel on the Morasha list.

MORASHA. "Heritage" in Hebrew. Religious election list in the 1984 elections. Comprised of Matzad and Poalei Agudat Israel.

MEMAD. "Dimension" in Hebrew. Moderate religious party. Founded before the 1988 elections.

MIMOUNA. A traditional festival; celebrated by Moroccan Jews.

MITNAGGEDIC (pl. MITNAGGDIM). "Opponent" in Hebrew. An opponent of the Ḥasidim and their teachings.

MOLEDET. Small political party of the extreme right in the 1988 elections.

MOSHAV (pl. MOSHAVIM). "Place of living" in Hebrew. A cooperative settlement which provides services to the production branch of each member's farm. Means of production and consumption are owned by each member. In some cases, production is communally owned.

MUKHTAR. Arab word used to describe a local community leader.

NATIONAL RELIGIOUS PARTY (NRP). The leading religious political party since its foundation in 1956. Suffered major loss of power since the 1981 elections. A constant junior partner in the coalition governments.

NATIONAL UNITY GOVERNMENT. Broad coalition government jointly led by the major party (election list) of the right and that of the left. Led by Likud and Labor party with the former ruling (senior partner) in 1986–88 and 1988–90, and the latter ruling in 1984–86. Also led by Gahal and Mapai (Labor party since 1969) with the latter ruling in 1967–70.

NEGEV. The southern region of Israel (mostly desert).

NIS. New Israeli Sheqel. The Israeli currency since 1985. In 1989, for example, one U.S. dollar was equal to 1.9182 NIS.

NRP. See National Religious Party.

OHALIM MOVEMENT. "Tents" in Hebrew. Protest movement working to improve the socioeconomic status of Oriental Jews. Active in the 1970s in Jerusalem's poor neighborhoods.

ORIENTAL JEW (also ORIENTAL). A Jew of Asian or African origin; more specifically, from Middle Eastern or North African origin. Approximately 55 percent of Israel's Jewish population.

OTTOMAN RULE (EMPIRE). The Turkish rule in Palestine until 1917.

PALESTINE LIBERATION ORGANIZATION (PLO). The national organization of the Palestinian Arabs. Includes also a military arm. Chaired by Yasser Arafat. Founded in May 1964.

PALMACH. Elite strike force of the Haganah from 1941 to 1948.

PLO. See Palestine Liberation Organization.

PLP. See Progressive List for Peace.

POALEI AGUDAT ISRAEL. "Association of Israel Workers" in Hebrew. Worker-oriented ultra-Orthodox religious political party. Founded in 1922. A component of Morasha in 1984.

PROGRESSIVE LIST FOR PEACE (PLP). A joint Arab-Jewish list to the 1984 and 1988 Knesset elections. Supported the creation of a Palestinian state alongside Israel.

PROJECT RENEWAL (also PROJECT). National urban renewal project to rehabilitate 160 poor neighborhoods. Initiated in 1977 by the Likud government and continued throughout the 1980s.

RATZ. Hebrew letters used for the Civil Rights Movement.

REVISIONIST. Nationalist movement of the right founded by Ze'ev Jabotinsky in 1923. The Palestine branch of the movement was later led by Menachem Begin and was absorbed into the Herut party after the establishment of the state of Israel.

SAMARIA. The northern area of the West Bank. The biblical name of the area.

SEPHARDI (pl. SEPHARDIM). "Spanish" in Hebrew. A Jew of Spanish/ Portugese origin or an Oriental Jew.

SE'ERANNA. A traditional festival celebrated by Kurdish Jews.

SHAS. Ultra-Orthodox religious political party. Aims to represent Oriental Jews. Split from Agudat Israel and founded in 1983.

SHINUI. "Change" in Hebrew. Small political party of the center. Founded as a protest movement after the 1973 war. A component of the Democratic Movement for Change in 1977.

SINAI PENINSULA. Region bordering with the Negev, Aqaba and Suez Gulfs, Suez Canal, and the Mediterranean Sea. Captured by Israel from Egypt in the 1967 war and returned under the 1979 peace treaty between the two states.

STATE OF ISRAEL. Established on 15 May 1948 in accordance with the United Nations General Assembly resolution of 29 November 1947.

TAMI. Hebrew acronym for "Tradition of Israel Movement." A religious political party. Aims to represent Oriental Jews. Split from the National Religious Party and founded in 1981.

TEHIYA. "Revival" in Hebrew. A nationalist party of the extreme right. Formed in 1980.

TENT CITY. Protest movement of Oriental Jews in 1990 composed mostly of residents of Project Renewal neighborhoods. Protested for the improvement of housing for Oriental Jews while emphasizing what it called "preferential treatment" given to Soviet Jewish immgrants in Israel.

TNUAT HAMOSHAVIM. "The Moshavim Movement" in Hebrew. The Labor-affiliated organization of the Moshavim in Israel. *See also* Moshav.

TZOMET. "Junction" in Hebrew. A small right-wing movement which merged into a joint list with the Tehiya towards the 1984 elections and ran independently in 1988.

ULTRA-ORTHODOX. The English term commonly used to describe Haredi.

WAR OF INDEPENDENCE. *See* War of 1948.

WAR, THE 1948 (ALSO WAR OF INDEPENDENCE). All-out war between Israel and five Arab states (Egypt, Jordan, Syria, Iraq, and Lebanon). As a result, Israel's territory was expanded beyond the original 1947 United Nations partition plan to the Green Line. From 15 May 1948 (the day the state of Israel was established) to 7 January 1949.

WAR, THE 1967 (ALSO SIX DAY WAR). All-out war between Israel and three Arab states. As a result, Israel's territory was expanded beyond the Green Line. Israel captured the Sinai Peninsula and Gaza Strip from Egypt, the West Bank from Jordan, and the Golan Heights from Syria. Between 5 and 10 June 1967.

WAR, THE 1973 (ALSO YOM KIPPUR WAR). All-out war between Israel and two Arab states. As a result, Israel captured territory from Egypt and Syria; Egypt captured territory from Israel in the Sinai Peninsula. From 6 October 1973 (Yom Kippur) to 23 October 1973.

WEST BANK. Region in east-central Israel. Encompasses two natural geographic units: the mountains of Judea (south) and Samaria (north), and the western narrow strip of the Jordan Rift. Captured by Israel from Jordan in the 1967 war.

YESHIVA (pl. YESHIVOT). "Sitting" or "meeting" in Hebrew. Talmudic and theological college of Jewish religious law and ritual.

YISHUV. "Settlement" in Hebrew. The Jewish community in Palestine before the establishment of the state of Israel.

ZIONISM. "Zion" in Hebrew is a synonym for Jerusalem. A national Jewish movement for the resettlement of the Jewish people in Palestine. Formed in the late nineteenth century.

LIST OF CONTRIBUTORS

Majid Al-Haj is Senior Lecturer of Sociology and Anthropology at the University of Haifa. His major areas of research are the family, migration and refugees, ethnic groups, and minorities in the Middle East. He has published numerous journal articles and book chapters in these areas. He is the author of several books including *Social Change and Family Processes: Arab Communities in Shefar-Am* (1987), and *Arab Local Government in Israel* (1990, with Henry Rosenfeld).

Efraim Ben-Zadok is Associate Professor of Public Administration at the College of Urban and Public Affairs, Florida Atlantic University. He was a faculty member at the State University of New York and Tel Aviv University. His fields of interest are urban and regional planning, urban politics and policy, ethnic groups, and housing integration. He has published journal articles and book chapters about local and regional issues in Israel.

Donna Robinson Divine is Professor of Government at Smith College. Her fields of interest are Zionism, Israeli politics and society, Egyptian politics and society, and Palestinian Arab politics and history. She has published extensively in these fields.

Giora Goldberg is Senior Lecturer of Political Science at Bar-Ilan University. He has written numerous journal articles and book chapters about Israeli politics, society, elections, and political parties. He is also the author of several books in Hebrew including *Political Parties in Israel—From Mass Parties to Electoral Parties* (1992).

Hana Ofek is a political scientist at Tel Aviv University specializing in public administration and policy. She is the author of several publications about renewal neighborhoods and public housing in Israel.

275

Ira Sharkansky is Professor of Political Science and Public Administration at the Hebrew University of Jerusalem. He is the author of numerous books, book chapters, and journal articles in political science, public administration, public policy, political economy, and urban politics. His recent books include *The Political Economy of Israel* (1987), and *Ancient and Modern Israel: An Exploration of Political Parallels* (1991). Several of his publications focus on urban policy in Jerusalem.

Neal Sherman is Senior Researcher at the Development Study Center, Rehovot, Israel. He also coordinates the collaborative MA program in regional development of the Center and Clark University. He has published and lectured widely on rural development policy and administration. His publications focus on rural settlements in Israel.

Yosseph Shilhav is Associate Professor of Geography at Bar-Ilan University and Research Associate at the Jerusalem Institute for Israel Studies. He has published extensively in his main field of interest—sociopolitical and cultural geography. Many of his publications cover the ultra-Orthodox neighborhoods in Israel. These include: *Growth and Segregation: The Ultra-Orthodox Community of Jerusalem* (1985, with Menachem Friedman), and *A 'Shtetle (Small Town) Within a Modern City* (1991), both in Hebrew.

INDEX

277